True Faith in the True God

True Faith in the True God

An Introduction to Luther's Life and Thought, Revised and
Expanded Edition

Hans Schwarz

Fortress Press
Minneapolis

TRUE FAITH IN THE TRUE GOD
An Introduction to Luther's Life and Thought, Revised and Expanded Edition

Cover image: Joe Reinke
Cover design: *Luther Posting the 95 Theses* (Detail) (also known as Luthers
Thesenanschlag), Ferdinand Pauwels – 1872, public domain.

Library of Congress Cataloging-in-Publication Data
Print ISBN: 978-1-4514-9008-4
eBook ISBN: 978-1-5064-0040-2

The paper used in this publication meets the minimum requirements of American
National Standard for Information Sciences — Permanence of Paper for Printed
Library Materials, ANSI Z329.48-1984.

Manufactured in the U.S.A.

This book was produced using PressBooks.com, and PDF rendering was done by
PrinceXML.

Contents

Preface

The figure of Martin Luther has not lost its fascination. This can be seen from the countless events that are being prepared for October 31, 2017, the five hundredth anniversary of Luther's posting of his 95 theses, which forever changed the landscape of Western Christendom. Our Institute of Protestant Theology at the University of Regensburg has a biennial seminar on Martin Luther and the Luther Sites, which will be held again over Reformation Day in 2017. We had to book our hotel rooms in Wittenberg four years in advance to be assured of accommodations.

The life of the great Reformer Martin Luther remains as fascinating as ever. There exists therefore no shortage of accounts and assessments of his life. However, it is somewhat different with his teaching. Though the index volumes on subjects are now completed on the more than one hundred volumes of Luther's writings in the authoritative German Weimar edition, it remains even today a difficult undertaking to give an account of Luther's teaching. One can always find the Luther one wants: the nationalistic anti-Semitic Luther, the anti–Roman Catholic Luther, Luther the liberator, or simply the pastoral Luther. Even the detailed bibliography of the *Luther-Jahrbuch* is of little help. It lists the hundreds of new articles on Luther that appear every year. But who can read all of this?

Even experts in the field of Luther research scarcely dare to write a comprehensive presentation of his thought. Yet there is the admirable book by the Bernhard Lohse (*Martin Luther's Theology: Its Historical and Systematic Development* [1995; Minneapolis: Fortress Press, 1999]), and the meticulous three-volume biography by Martin Brecht (*Martin Luther* [1981–87; Fortress Press, 1985–93]). I hope I have learned from them to avoid biases and to tell the Luther story how it unfolded itself.

The following study is an attempt neither to replace nor correct the life work of Lohse, Brecht, or of any other Luther scholars. Its purpose is rather to initiate interested novices into the life and thought of Martin Luther. That such a primer on the life and thought of Martin Luther is in demand I could see by having it already in a Russian, Slovak, and German edition. The study begins with a brief biography to familiarize the reader with the most important phases in the life of Luther. Then it leads directly to the center of his teaching. This is facilitated with ample quotations from Luther's own writings in order to provide insight into his own way of thinking. When one has understood the concerns that lay on Luther's heart, connecting lines can easily be drawn to other areas of Luther's thought that are not taken into consideration in the present study. In order to have covered completely the theology and ethics of Luther, I would have had to deal with many more such areas. Yet the concern here is with the center of Luther's theology. This core of his thought will allow us to perceive something of the fascination that Luther holds, as well as of that with which Luther himself was ultimately concerned: the recovery of a living and productive faith in God.

At this point I would like to express my heartfelt thanks to Will Bergkamp, who immediately welcomed my idea to update and modestly expand the first English edition of this book, which had come out in 1996. Dr. Mark Worthing, my former research assistant, translated the first English edition from German. Thanks to his superb job, I could rely on his translation for the second edition. Therefore my thanks go to him as well. I also must thank from the bottom of my heart my wife Hildegard for enduring with a husband who quickly escapes to his study to finish still another book.

Hans Schwarz
Regensburg, December 2014

Introduction

Martin Luther changed the face of Western Christianity more than anyone either before or after him. The reaction to his work led to a split in the West between the "traditional" believers and the adherents of the Reformation. Yet it would be a distortion of the facts to charge Luther with the greatest ecclesial schism of all time, for the exclusion of those favoring Reformation was instigated from the Roman side. Additionally, the framework of Western Christianity had already for some time been experiencing tremors. Since the work of John Wyclif (ca. 1320–1384) in England and John Huss (ca. 1368–1415) in Bohemia (present-day Czech Republic) frequent criticism had been voiced against the centralizing efforts of Rome. In the century of the Reformation the struggle for a regionalization of the church reached new heights. Yet a regional church had always been presupposed in Eastern Christendom. To this day there exists in the East only the titular primacy of the patriarch of Constantinople who exercises no binding authority over the other Orthodox patriarchs. One could nevertheless accuse Luther of destroying the doctrinal unity of the church. But even this unity between East and West had been irreparably destroyed through the edict of the Roman Pope Leo IX (1002–1054, pope: 1049–1054) against the Eastern church on July 16, 1054, which formalized the separate doctrinal development of the

Western church. One could even credit Luther with instigating a return to the doctrinal tradition of the early church and for rejecting the separate dogmatic and theological development of the West, at least to the extent that, according to his understanding, this development contradicted fundamental biblical teaching.

Much more important than this apologetic consideration, however, is the positive influence that Luther exerted. On the one side, he noticed the similarity of his teaching with that of John Huss, while on the other side he exchanged positional statements with King Henry VIII of England (1491–1547, king: 1509–1547), who aspired to create in England a church independent from Rome. Also not to be overlooked is Luther's considerable influence upon the Reformed wing of the Reformation in Switzerland led by Huldrych Zwingli (1484–1531) and John Calvin (1509–1564). Both of these Reformers made much effort to come as close as possible to his teaching, as can be seen, for instance, in their debates with Luther over the Lord's Supper. Even the left wing of the Reformation, from Caspar Schwenckfeld (1489–1561) to Balthasar Hubmaier (ca. 1485–1528), was not untouched by Lutheran ideas. Decisive for the Reformation in the West was also the fact that those loyal to the Roman Church, as was demonstrated at the Council of Trent (1545–1563), eliminated unnecessary ballast and returned to the center of the Christian faith even while rejecting that which they held to be ideas of the Reformation. It was no accident, therefore, that the Council of Trent devoted ample time to the doctrine of justification. Without the influence of the ideas of Luther such an emphasis would have been impossible.

Luther is of such central importance for Western Christianity that it is always profitable to recall the crucial data of his biography and the core of his thought. Of course, five hundred years separate us from Martin Luther, during which time the world and intellectual history have decisively changed. It is sometimes claimed that Luther stood at the beginning of the modern period. In this regard, however, one cannot overlook the fact that Luther lived before the Enlightenment and would have viewed our modern industrial society with wonder, if not indeed as something entirely incomprehensible. "How do I find a gracious God?"—the central question of Luther's life, which led him first into the monastery and pressed him next toward reformation—sounds strangely outdated for us. In Luther's day, however, it was an urgent question, since on account of the shorter life expectancy it was questionable whether one would even live to maturity. Luther had experienced this painfully in his own family. Two of his six children, born out of his marriage with Katharina von Bora, died before they reached adulthood. Luther himself was favored with more luck. Nevertheless, he was an old and frail man by the time he died at sixty-two years of age. His body was worn out and had been scarred from various ailments. It is no wonder then that for people of that period this earth offered little and they hoped at least for a better life eternal. Yet for this they needed first of all a gracious God who would not reject them, but would rather receive them into a better afterlife once their brief sojourn in this earthly valley of tears had ended.

When Luther inquired about a gracious God, he expressed a yearning common to nearly all of his contemporaries. For us in the privileged West, however, life presents almost limitless opportunities. Infant mortality has been reduced to a minute percentage. Thanks to modern medicine we can hope for a life free from prolonged pain and disease, and for senior citizens the possibility of an active and interesting life looms ahead. These prospects, however, touch only upon the surface data of our society. Not taken into account is the so-called two-thirds world, whose members stand closer to the conditions of Luther's time than does our affluent society.

Additionally, one must not forget what our own life is really like behind its glittering facade.

In a medieval family of seven children, one or two of them were expected to reach adulthood and have descendants of their own. In our small modern families, however, if even one child is severed from this life through an auto accident no one remains to carry on the tradition to the next generation. But yet what does "our tradition" mean when our communality is so meager that many cannot even find the courage to marry, or soon abandon their already consummated marriage? Stability and continuity are not characteristics of our modern society. Although we control much and believe ourselves to be able to do almost anything and to have most things well under control, we are haunted by naked fear: the fear of meaninglessness, the fear of losing our job, the fear of winding up life empty-handed. The effort to satisfy immediately every desire, to celebrate today rather than tomorrow, and to still gain some satisfaction out of life points to the fact that we are driven by angst.

Luther's Reformation discovery of a gracious God can still have a liberating effect upon us today. We need not be anxious, for we are not limited to our own selves and our own accomplishments. God himself is in command, the God who has always shown to be gracious and concerned for us.

Luther detested theological speculations since he was convinced that they led to doubt and uncertainty. But he also strongly rejected looking first to humans and their potential and then to God as a metaphysical scapegoat. In Luther's thought God occupied first place. Only when God is on our side, the God from whom and to whom we have our being and without whom we cannot accomplish anything, can we meet the future with confidence. The endeavor to accord the divinity of God first place runs through Luther's entire thought. Already in the battle hymn of the Reformation Luther stresses, "No strength of ours can match his might! We would be lost, rejected." (*Evangelical Lutheran Worship,* hymn #503, stanza 2). Luther was more than a seeker after God. He discovered in an existentially decisive manner that the God who created the whole universe is not an indifferent cosmic snob, nor a fatalistically threatening judge, but a God who desires only the best for us and opens for us a new and certain future. Luther arrived at this knowledge because he discovered in Jesus Christ the human face of God. In Jesus he recognized the gracious God. Through the living Christ Luther became aware that faith did not mean to assent to ecclesiastically stipulated propositions, but rather to trust and to rely upon the God who leads us to new shores.

1

Luther's Life and Work

Most likely Martin Luther was born on November 10, 1483. Luther's colleague Philip Melanchthon (1497–1560) was among those who late made efforts to date his birth to 1484, since it was believed that a conjunction of planets in that year pointed to the beginning of an important new religious development. It is certain, however, that Luther was born in Eisleben, a small village on the edge of the Harz Mountains, near the geographic center of present-day Germany. It is also certain that the day after his birth he was baptized in the parish church of St. Peter and Paul and given the name of the patron of that day, Martin of Tours (316–397). He remained only a few months in Eisleben, where his family had moved from the village of Möhra, before they finally settled in nearby Mansfeld.

Childhood and Education

Luther always stressed that he had humble origins: "I am the son of peasants. My great grandfather, grandfather and father were all simple farmers."[1] But this was far from being true. The family from which his father, Hans Luder, came was one of the well-to-do rural families in Möhra.[2] In the area around Möhra there was some copper mining in which the Luder family was involved. But the grade of the ore was rather poor, so Hans Luder moved to Eisenach where he continued to mine, and then to Mansfeld. In Eisenach Hans Luder married Margarethe Lindemann. This marriage of a peasant with the daughter of a prosperous citizen was not a violation of the social stratification that prevailed in the late Middle Ages, but was quite intentional, since some members of the Lüdemann family were also miners It was most likely on suggestion of the Lüdemann family that Hans Luder moved to the county of Mansfeld in 1483. When he arrived there he was not without means, and became overseer and a co-owner of a copper mine, and after some years of several more. In 1491 Martin Luther's father was numbered among the "four lords" of Mansfeld who represented the citizens and worked with the city council. In contrast to his ancestors, therefore, he had achieved a considerable level of success. Hence one should not conclude that Luther grew up in poverty when he said of his parents in 1533, "In his youth my father was a poor miner. My mother carried all her wood on her back. It was in this way that they brought us up."[3] This was far from the truth. Prior to 1500 Martin established a lifelong friendship with two sons of the most prosperous overseers of smelters.[4] They were members of the same social group.

However, his parents were naturally very frugal. Only in this way were they able to achieve such prosperity. Their upbringing of their children, which Luther experienced as oldest or perhaps second

1. Luther, "Tischrede," no. 6250 (undated), in *WA TR* 5:558.13–14.
2. Cf. for the following "Die Familie Luder in Möhra und Mansfeld," in *Fundsache Luther. Archäologen auf den Spuren des Reformators*, ed. Harald Meller (Stuttgart: Konrad Theiss, 2008), 78–85.
3. Luther, "Table Talk," no. 2888a (1533), in *LW* 54:178.
4. So Andreas Stahl, "Neue Erkenntnisse zur Biographie Martin Luthers," in Meller, *Fundsache Luther,* 91.

oldest son, was equally strict. For the father it was clear that the son should achieve an even higher standard of living than the parents. And to achieve this he needed a good education. Therefore between 1491 and 1501 Luther attended consecutively the Latin schools in Mansfeld, Magdeburg, and Eisenach. He had no good memories of the school in Mansfeld, which he compared to a "prison" and "hell" and where he learned very little, despite the many whippings and his fear of the teachers.[5] The school in Magdeburg, on the other hand, appears not to have been as bad. One learned there the Latin of the medieval period and Christian hymns. If the students were caught speaking German while school was in session they were beaten. Shortly before Easter 1497, Luther's father decided to send his son along with a friend to Magdeburg, since a school was run there by the Brothers of the Common Life, which enjoyed a good reputation. However, this school did not particularly impress Luther, either.

After only a year Martin was brought back to Mansfeld and from there was sent to Eisenach, where several relatives of the family lived. Martin was enrolled there in the community school of St. George. Additionally, he sang in the boys' choir and collected contributions for it from the residents of the town, as did the other boys. It was through this activity that he came into contact with the Schalbe family and their active religious life. This family had given significant bequests to the small Franciscan monastery at the foot of the Wartburg castle. Luther had the opportunity to eat regularly with the family. In this connection, one must also mention the Cotta family, who were related to the Schalbes. Both families were well off and were represented in the city council. Through the Cotta family Luther learned to appreciate good music and was exposed to a good family life, which he still spoke of years later. Another significant

---

5. Cf. Walther von Loewenich, *Martin Luther: Der Mann und das Werk* (Munich: List, 1982), 42; and Luther, *In epistolam S. Pauli ad Galatas Commentarius* (1535), in *WA* 40 I:531.24–25.

influence on Luther during this period was the vicar at St. Mary's, Johannes Braun, who was to become a fatherly friend to him long beyond his stay in Eisenach. The years he spent in Eisenach were the happiest of his youth and in 1530 he still referred to it as his "dear city."[6] It was here that the shy boy was transformed into a happy young man. After three years, that is, at age eighteen, it was time for him to begin university studies. Only two cities were considered: Leipzig, which was geographically closer, and Erfurt, which was more progressive. Luther's father decided upon Erfurt, since he did not want to save money by sending his son to the wrong place.

Erfurt was at the time one of the three or four largest cities in Germany. It lay at the intersection of major transportation routes and its economy was booming. In 1483 the cathedral in Erfurt received a new organ, which was one of the most famous in Germany and was comparable to that of St. Peter's Cathedral in Rome. Twelve different religious orders influenced the life of the church in Erfurt, and there was a great veneration of relics to be found there. Erfurt therefore proudly called itself "little Rome." It had well over ten thousand residents and was the largest city that Luther ever lived in for any length of time.

In the summer semester of 1501, Luther began his basic studies in the arts at the University of Erfurt. The program consisted of the so-called trivium of grammar, dialectic, and rhetoric, required for the bachelor's degree, and the quadrivium of arithmetic, astronomy, geometry, and music, required for the master of arts degree. The core of the trivium was dialectic, that is, logic, while the quadrivium focused mostly on mathematics. This study normally lasted four years and was characterized by rigorous memorization and recitation,

---

6. Luther, *Eine Predigt, wie man Kinder zu Schulen halten solle*, in *WA* 30 II:576.13.

which means that today's "academic freedom" did not exist at that time.

Luther lived in a student dormitory that enjoyed a good reputation despite the fact that it was known commonly at the *Biertasche* ("beer bag"). Residents were required to rise at 4 a.m. and to be in bed by 8 p.m. The clothing was uniform and the meals prescribed. Within the academic program itself one had to complete a certain plan of studies, at the end of which the master's examination was taken. Even regular attendance of worship services was required. Nevertheless, Luther, like the other students, managed to enjoy himself and did not neglect his social life. One of his fellow students, the humanist Crotus Rubeanus (ca. 1480–ca. 1545), later said of Luther, "You were once the musician and learned philosopher of our company."[7] Luther, however, did not waste his time and completed the trivium with his bachelor's examinations in the autumn of 1502. Afterward he devoted himself to the scientific, metaphysical, and ethical writings of Aristotle and studied the disciplines of the quadrivium. On January 7, 1505, the earliest possible date, he took the master's examinations and was second best of seventeen successful candidates. Luther recalled later with pleasure the graduation festivities with all the accompanying academic ceremonies. Luther's father was of course greatly pleased with the good performance of his son and addressed him thereafter with the respectful and formal German *Ihr* rather than the informal *Du*. Although Luther later distanced himself somewhat from the value of a university education, he continued to take pleasure in the Latin classics.

After the completion of his master's degree Luther was required to teach for two years in the faculty of arts. He was also allowed to use this time to study in one of the three higher faculties of medicine,

---

7. Cited in Otto Scheel, *Martin Luther: Vom Katholizismus zur Reformation,* vol. 1 (Tübingen: J.C.B. Mohr [Paul Siebeck], 1917), 296, n. 66, from a letter written in Bamberg in April 1520.

theology, or law. Erfurt was not at all known for medicine, and theology didn't fit into the plans of Luther's father. Hence only law remained—an option that also held the promise of a successful career either at a princely court or in the mining industry. Luther's father had even already found a bride for his son from an affluent family and had bought his legal books for him. Thus Luther began lecturing on April 24, 1505 and started his study of law on May 20. A month later he returned to Mansfeld and remained there for a week with his parents.

During his return journey on July 2nd, a very severe thunderstorm surprised him a few hours outside of Erfurt, near the small town of Stotternheim. A bolt of lightning struck very near to him and the jolt threw him to the ground. In panic and fear of death he cried out, "Help me Saint Anne! I will become a monk!"[8] For Luther the study of law was thereby over. Luther was well familiar with St. Anne, the "grandmother" of Jesus, who was one of the most venerated saints of the late Middle Ages and the patron saint of miners. Just why Luther made good on his vow we may never precisely understand. One has here only hints, such as the fact that from the very beginning he was never particularly enthusiastic about the study of law, that he was very shaken by the sudden death of a close friend in 1505, or that he had already had positive experiences with the theological writings of Thomas Aquinas (1225–1274) and William Occam (ca. 1285–1349). The theory that the psychological confrontation with his father played a role is likely unfounded since this conflict arose in earnest only after Luther's decision to become a monk. Still there might be some truth to the idea that a disagreement with his father contributed to his decision. Luther was twenty-two years old and therefore old enough to get married. His father, who planned the

---

8. Luther, "Tischrede," no. 4707 (1539), in *WA TR* 4:440.9–10.

career of his son, had perhaps summoned him to Mansfeld to inform him that a suitable bride had been found. Years later he remembered in a letter to his father, "Your intention was even to tie me down through an honorable and rich marriage."[9] But all of this is conjecture.

Speaking in 1539, Luther said,

> Afterward I regretted having made the vow and many tried to dissuade me from it. I remained by my vow, however, and invited many good friends on the day of Alexius (July 16) to a farewell party since on the next day they would bring me to the monastery. As they sought to prevent me, however, I said: "Today you see me but never again!" Then they accompanied me with tears in their eyes. My father was very angry because of the vow but I remained firm in my decision and never considered leaving the monastery.[10]

A serious conflict arose between Luther and his father, who had an entirely different life in mind for his son. He wrote him an angry letter in which he once again addressed him with the informal *Du*. In some ways Hans Luder was more "modern" in his thinking than his son. He was the modern success-oriented person for whom the family's upward movement in society was more important than the greatest religious sacrifice that one could bring to God. Although he gladly welcomed priests and members of religious orders into his home, he did not feel obligated to them. Once, as a priest sought to convince him to give a special donation to the church, he answered, "I have many children. I will leave it to them since they need it more."[11] The son, on the other hand, saw the religious life as a goal worthy of striving for, even though monasticism had already lost

9. Martin Luther, in his dedicatory letter to his father (Nov. 21, 1521) of his writing on monastic vows, in *WA* 8:573.24.
10. Martin Luther, *WA TR* 4:440.11–17.
11. According to Martin Luther, commenting on Matt. 21:12, *Matth. 18–24 in Predigten ausgelegt (1537–40)*, in *WA* 47:379.9–10.

much of its former prestige and had become increasingly the object of disdain and ridicule.

Luther went against all reason and the warnings of his friends and father and, choosing the way out of the world, entered the monastery. In Erfurt alone he had the choice between six different monasteries. From among these Luther decided to enter the monastery of the Augustinian Eremites. The monastery operated a theological school and belonged to the reform-minded branch of this order of mendicants. This means that the rules of monastic life were taken there especially seriously and were strictly observed. Of all his books, Luther took with him into the monastery only the works of the Latin poets Plautus and Virgil.

After about six weeks Luther began his novitiate. He was assigned a cell, clothed in the monastic garb, had his head tonsured so that only a small circle of hair remained, and had to apply himself to physical labor. This included not only the cleaning of the monastery but also begging for donations from the residents of the city, which was customary at that time. The life of the Augustinian Eremite was strictly regulated. Luther, for instance, had to walk with his head bowed and his eyes directed toward the ground and was only allowed to drink something during meal times. Of course he was also given a Latin Bible, the text of which he soon learned so well that he could find immediately any reference.

Luther fulfilled the requirements of his novitiate to the full satisfaction of his superiors. After the first year it was unanimously decided that he be allowed to make his profession. Shortly thereafter he was informed that he was to become a priest. In preparation for this office he had to learn the detailed explanations of the canon of the Mass by the Tübingen theology professor Gabriel Biel (1410–1495). Biel, the last important representative of Occamism, influenced him greatly.[12] On April 4, 1507 Luther was consecrated a priest in the cathedral of Erfurt. On May 2nd he celebrated his first Mass in the monastery church, to which he invited his father at the suggestion of his superiors. Surprisingly, Hans Luder accepted the invitation and appeared in Erfurt in the company of twenty friends on horseback, most likely with the intention of impressing the monks. He also donated twenty gulden to the monastery kitchen to pay for the guests. This was quite a large amount, since a university professor at Wittenberg only received eighty gulden a year as salary.[13] At the reception following the Mass a conversation took place between Luther and his father that revealed that the older Luther still disagreed with his son's decision. He reminded him of the honor that a son owes his parents and argued in regard to the "appearance" at Stotternheim, "Just so it wasn't a phantom you saw!"[14]

Martin, however, remained firm in his commitment. He studied next the general curriculum of his order and then theology at the University of Erfurt. In autumn of 1508 he was suddenly sent to Wittenberg to teach moral philosophy on the faculty of arts there. The University of Wittenberg was founded in 1502 by the elector Frederick the Wise (1463–1525). The town itself, as Luther commented in 1532, lay on the edge of civilization: if one would go only a short step farther, one would be in the midst of barbarism. Luther was not especially happy about his new assignment and was glad that after a short year there he was allowed to return to Erfurt. In the fall of 1509 he had completed his theological studies, earning him the rank of a *sententiarius*, which meant that he was now qualified to interpret the *Sentences* of Peter Lombard (ca. 1100–1160), the most important theological textbook of the Middle Ages. Before he could

12. William Occam maintained that God's will is the cause of all things and its own rule. He also claimed that universal ideas have no foundation in reality but only individual things exist.
13. According to Helmar Junghans, "Neue Erkenntnisse und neue Fragen zu Martin Luthers Leben und Umwelt," in Meller, *Fundsache Luther,* 144.
14. Luther, "Table Talk," no. 3556a (1537), in *LW* 54:234.

hold his first lecture, however, he was called back to Wittenberg. It was therefore in Wittenberg that he lectured on the *Sentences* until 1510.

In the meantime a conflict had developed within his order between the rigorists and those advocating a more conventional praxis. On account of this conflict, the superior of the German rigorist Augustinian community, Johann von Staupitz (ca. 1465–1524), sent Luther to Rome together with an Augustinian monk from Nuremberg in order to have the problem settled there. This was the longest journey that Luther had ever undertaken or would ever undertake and the only one that would take him into a foreign country. The journey in general left a great impression upon him, especially what he saw in Italy. He did not see Rome through the eyes of a tourist but came with the intention of taking full advantage of the city's treasure of relics and storehouse of grace. It was only later that the worldliness of the priests and the opulence of the cardinals' palaces left a negative impression on him. In 1510, however, he was very much impressed by the treasures of relics and the many holy sites. He took his assignment seriously and celebrated Mass in all the important churches of the city.

Shortly after his return from Rome Luther was transferred once again to Wittenberg, probably in September 1511. Von Staupitz had so much to do with the administration of the Augustinian Order that he needed to give up his position as professor of biblical interpretation. In order that the order would not lose this position, he wanted Luther to study toward a theological doctorate, which Luther very much opposed with many different arguments, among them his ill health and his inadequacy. But the will of von Staupitz, his superior, prevailed. Luther started his studies leading to a doctor of theology, and his graduation ceremony soon took place on October 18 and 19, 1512. In his doctoral oath Luther not only committed himself to obedience to the church but also to theological truth, which latter commitment he often referred to in the following years. Frederick the Wise was so interested in seeing his new university expand that on instigation of von Staupitz he paid the academic fees of fifty gulden, required for the doctoral degree, for the theologian of the mendicant order.

From Augustinian Professor to Reformer of the Church

After the completion of his doctorate Luther was appointed professor of biblical exegesis on the theological faculty of the University of Wittenberg, a position that he held until his death. Despite his academic career Luther found no rest in his spiritual life. He sensed the wrath of God more keenly than most others of his time. Even the study of the Bible did not help him in this regard, for there he read only of the righteousness of God. How could he, however, as a person turned in upon himself, stand up before divine righteousness? The church answered that this was done in that one obtained the grace of God through the sacraments. But the most important sacrament, the Holy Eucharist, was of no help to him here since the preconditions of its worthy reception were humility and repentance. Luther was never certain whether he was repentant enough and whether he had confessed everything that he ought, regardless of how frequently he confessed—and he often went to confession several times a day. Hence he was unable to experience the peace that the sacraments were supposed to bring. Even good works were of no help to him. He recognized clearly the egoism that was concealed within the performance of good works. One did not perform such works freely or out of gratitude toward God, but rather in order to win God's favor. Even the figure of Christ brought no peace to him, since he had learned to know him as judge but not as savior. This is no surprise. When one enters today the sacristy of St. Mary's in Wittenberg, the parish church in which Luther usually preached, one sees a stone plaque worn by the elements hanging on the wall and depicting Christ with "a sharp, two-edged sword" issuing from his mouth (Rev. 1:16). The faithful encountered Christ as the stern judge.

Luther, however, was not left alone in his doubt and spiritual turmoil. Von Staupitz took Luther under his arm. In Luther's struggles von Staupitz saw something useful, for without them he surmised Luther would probably have become a proud and perhaps even arrogant academician. As Luther continually brought the problem of his sinfulness before his confessor, however, von Staupitz admonished him that he had never committed any "real" sins and that he should not bother Christ with trivia. He also helped him positively with his problems by explaining that genuine repentance begins with the love of righteousness and of God, and that that which scholastic theology views as the last stage of repentance, namely God's love, is really its beginning. Repentance does not lead to a righteous and loving God but rather proceeds from this God. Similarly, von Staupitz sought to explain to him how he should think of the question of predestination. One must begin by contemplating the wounds of Christ, inflicted upon him for our sake, and not with the question of whether one has been elected or rejected. With this starting point the debate about predestination can be positively settled. In 1520, von Staupitz gave up his office as superior general of the Augustinian order and went to Salzburg to become the abbot of the Benedictine monastery of St. Peter. In later years Luther continued to express his gratefulness to von Staupitz, but also regretted that this man who had been so influential upon him remained with his pre-Reformation faith and labeled Luther's followers as heretics.

The decisive breakthrough that lead to Luther's Reformation-oriented thought came in the so-called tower experience, in which it became clear to Luther through his reading of Rom. 1:17 that the righteousness of God is not that righteousness with which God judges us, but that which he attributes to us and that carries weight before him. Luther often stressed, however, that he did not receive his theology through some moment of enlightenment but had to work on it throughout his life. The real turning point for the Reformation, however, is without doubt to be attributed to the year 1518, for it was then that Luther came to the conclusion that the word of God alone is the only means of grace and that it can only be accepted through faith. The related fourfold *alone*, namely, "Scripture alone," "grace alone," "faith alone," and "Christ alone" (*sola scriptura, sola gratia, sola fide*, and *solus Christus*) is essentially the key insight behind the Reformation. In 1518, therefore, the Reformation had reached a point of no turning back.

In 1513 Luther held his first lectures in biblical exegesis over the Psalms. He sought to make them comprehensible by relating them to Christ. After he completed his lectures on the Psalms in 1515 he came to his second major lecture series in 1515–1516, over Paul's Epistle to the Romans. Already here his Reformation insight can be seen when, for example, he says, "For the righteousness of God is the cause of salvation. And here again, by the righteousness of God we must not understand the righteousness by which He is righteous in Himself but the righteousness by which we are made righteous by God. This happens through faith in the Gospel."[15] Following his lectures on the Epistle to the Romans, Luther held lectures on the Epistles to the Galatians and to the Hebrews.

15. Luther in his *Lectures on Romans*, in *LW* 25:151, in his comments on Rom. 1:17.

Theologically Luther was influenced during this period by the mysticism of the Middle Ages, for instance by Bernard of Clairvaux (1090–1153), who was highly respected within his order, or by the *Theologia Deutsch* (German theology), an anonymous mystical writing of the fifteenth century that Luther edited twice for publication and for which he wrote a foreword in 1518. He also valued the insights of Johannes Tauler, the fourteenth-century Dominican mystic.

Within his order Luther gained increasing recognition. In the autumn of 1511 he was made preacher of his monastery and in 1514 was additionally called to be preacher at St. Mary's, the parish church of Wittenberg. In 1512 he was made vice prior of his monastery and dean of its general program of studies. Finally, in 1515 he was named district supervisor of the ten or eleven monasteries of his order in Saxony.

Luther took all these various responsibilities very seriously. The reform of the universities was also important to him. Thus, he wrote in the spring of 1517 to Johann Lang in Erfurt, his fellow Augustinian and friend,

> Our theology and St. Augustine are progressing well, and with God's help rule at our University. Aristotle is gradually falling from his throne, and his final doom is only a matter of time. It is amazing how the lectures on the Sentences are disdained. Indeed no one can expect to have any students if he does not want to teach this theology, that is, lecture on the Bible or on St. Augustine or another teacher of ecclesiastical eminence.[16]

In the matter of university reform Luther was supported by the private secretary and court preacher of Elector Frederick the Wise, George Burkhardt (1484–1545), who, because he came from the town of Spalt near Nuremberg, named himself *Spalatin*. Especially

---

16. Luther, "Letter to John Lang. Wittenberg, May 18, 1517" in *LW* 48:41–42.

significant is the fact that Spalatin won the elector over to Luther's side. Through his efforts toward university reform and through Spalatin, Luther also came into contact with humanism, which he especially valued because of its emphasis upon the biblical languages of Greek and Hebrew.

In his September 1517 disputation "On Scholastic Theology," Luther parted ways decisively with Aristotle. Of greater historical importance, however, is October 31, 1517, the day before All Saints, on which Luther tacked his famous 95 theses to the north door of the castle church in Wittenberg. This church door was, so to speak, the bulletin board of the university on which notices were normally placed. Luther, who likely wrote out his theses by hand, challenged learned persons from Wittenberg and other locations to an academic debate over the value of indulgences. Those who could not come were asked to respond in writing.

On the same day Luther sent a letter to Archbishop Albrecht of Mainz, in which he asked him to admonish Tetzel to stop preaching indulgences and to revoke his own instructions concerning indulgences. Along with the letter, Luther included a copy of his 95 theses so that Albrecht could see how dubious was his belief in indulgences, which traditionally belonged to the sacrament of penance. Since the eleventh century the so-called works of penance were initiated immediately following the spoken absolution and were understood as a means to reduce temporal punishment, including the punishments of purgatory. Theologically, indulgences were explained to be efficacious on the basis of the excess good works of Christ and the saints who had done more than was necessary for their own salvation. The church, as the administrator of this treasure, understood itself as being able to distribute these excess merits among the penitent faithful.

The income from the sale of letters of indulgence, that is, the certificates that verified that a specific number of years of penance in purgatory had been canceled, was increasingly applied to cultural and social projects. Hence the elector Frederick made use of indulgence money to support his university and to build a bridge over the River Elbe. What Albrecht of Mainz had in mind, however, was particularly questionable from a moral point of view. He was not only archbishop of Magdeburg and administrator of the bishopric of Halberstadt, but he had also become the archbishop of Mainz, thereby gaining the title and status of an elector and a cardinal. Such amassing of multiple offices, however, was forbidden by ecclesiastical law. For this reason Albrecht had to acquire the appropriate dispensation from Pope Leo X (1475–1521, pope: 1513–21) and pay the normal fees required to hold these additional positions. Since he was not able to raise from his own resources the enormous sum of money required for the deal—in today's money it would be one million US dollars—he borrowed the money from the rich merchant family of the Fuggers in Augsburg. In order to be able to pay back this money the pope allowed him to sell indulgences in his own territories. Half of the money raised was to be used for the building of St. Peter's in Rome; however, because Pope Leo X was himself continuously in financial difficulty, a portion of this money came to him personally. The other half was immediately collected, as it came in, by a representative of the Fuggers and went toward paying off the debt of the Archbishop.

Albrecht was able to acquire the services of Johann Tetzel (ca. 1465–1519), an experienced indulgence preacher, for this work. Tetzel, a Dominican friar, had already been active in such work for more than a decade. Tetzel was not modest with his promises and boasted that he has already brought salvation to more souls with his indulgences than had St. Peter with his preaching. Frederick the Wise forbid Tetzel from setting a foot on his territory because he didn't want the money of his subjects to flow into other lands. Tetzel, however, set up his tent precisely on the border of electoral Saxony so that many residents of Wittenberg were able to purchase indulgences from him. With their letters of indulgence in hand, they then came to Luther asking him for absolution on the basis of their certificates, without it being obvious that there was any real repentance of sins. Luther did not protest against the indulgences until he saw Albrecht's letter that promised the full forgiveness of all sins through the purchase of the indulgences. It was not necessary to show remorse or to confess any article of faith; one could even purchase indulgences for the dead.

As a responsible teacher of the church Luther felt obligated to intervene. This was then the occasion for the formulation of the 95 theses. In his first thesis, he explained what repentance actually ought to be, namely, not a onetime act but a life-long attitude toward God. Luther additionally contended that penance cannot be limited to that of a sacramental kind. Also, the pope is not able to forgive sins, but rather only to declare that they have been forgiven by God. Of course, it was the furthest thing from Luther's mind to attack the pope, since he believed at the time that the pope would do the right thing if he were just aware of what was actually taking place, a belief he continued to hold for some time. Because the anticipated disputation never took place and Archbishop Albrecht didn't show any sign of response, Luther sent copies of the theses to several influential persons. To his great surprise the theses immediately appeared in printed form and were spread rapidly over all of Germany, "as if the angels themselves were the messengers," as Friedrich Myconius, a contemporary of Luther, wrote.[17] In gratitude

---

17. Friedrich Myconius, *Geschichte der Reformation [1517–1542]*, ed. Otto Clemen (Leipzig: Voigtländer's Quellenbücher, 1914), 22.

for the theses, the great artist Albrecht Dürer (1471–1528) even sent Luther a collection of wood engravings and copper etchings.

Tetzel, however, was convinced that the heretic Luther would be burnt within three weeks and his ashes sent to heaven in a bathing cap. To Luther's disappointment, a professor of theology from the University of Ingolstadt, Johann Eck (1486–1543), attacked him and characterized Luther as a heretic and a Hussite. In order to produce something more useful on the topic for the German people than his Latin theses, in 1518 Luther wrote his "Sermon on Indulgences and Grace." Within only a few months, more than twenty thousand copies of the sermon were printed in twenty editions—an amount unheard of at that time.

From the Heidelberg Disputation to the Diet of Worms

In the same year of 1518, a disputation was held at the general assembly of the Augustinians in Heidelberg that Luther, as a district supervisor, was obligated to attend. In the meantime Albrecht had already informed the Roman Curia—the administrative apparatus of the Holy See and the central governing body through which the Roman pontiff conducts the business of the Church—of Luther's activity, and the Dominicans had also denounced him in Rome. The journey to Heidelberg was therefore not without danger. The Augustinians, however, stood by their fellow member and gave him the honor of presiding over the disputation. He used this opportunity to portray his theology of the cross as opposed to a theology of glory.

In Rome the desire was to quiet this "monastic squabble" with Luther as quickly and discretely as possible by summoning him to Rome. Even Tetzel had been brought forward against Luther and laid out his position in 106 theses on the occasion of his licentiate examination. Here he defended his jingle: "As soon as the coin in the offering box rings the soul out of purgatory springs."[18] Although the Dominicans promoted Tetzel to a doctorate in Rome, the Roman authorities recognized that he went too far. The papal diplomat Karl von Miltitz (ca. 1490–1529) gave Tetzel a dressing down by threatening to bring charges against him in Rome because of his immoral lifestyle and his questionable financial practices. For Tetzel this was such a severe blow that he retreated to his cell in the Dominican monastery in Leipzig, where he died a broken man in 1519. Luther nevertheless felt sympathy for Tetzel, and wrote him a consoling letter before the latter's death in which he encouraged him "to be of good cheer and not to fear my memory . . . [and not to become] a victim of his conscience and of the pope's indignation."[19] We see here, as in other instances, that Luther was always at heart a pastor, even to people with whom he seriously disagreed with theologically.

The elector Frederick arranged that Luther not have to travel to Rome but that he receive a hearing at the conclusion of the Diet of Augsburg in 1518 before the papal legate Cardinal Cajetan (1469–1534). As a Dominican it was clear to Cajetan what his decision would be. He was nevertheless friendly to Luther but could not persuade him to back down from his position. Upon the advice of friends Luther finally fled Augsburg by night through a small gate in the city wall and made his way by horseback to Coburg, the southernmost point of electoral Saxony. In the meantime, Rome sought to find other means by which the matter could be laid to rest. Karl von Miltitz was to convince the elector to exert his influence upon Luther. If he was successful Elector Frederick was to receive the golden rose of the pope and his two illegitimate children would be declared legitimate. When he was unable to achieve anything, Miltitz sought to negotiate with Luther. It was even relayed to the elector

---

18. Cited in Nikolaus Paulus, *Johann Tetzel, der Ablaßprediger* (Mainz: Franz Kirchheim, 1899), 139.
19. Luther, "Preface to the Complete Edition of Luther's Latin Writings" (1545), in *LW* 34:335–36.

that someone from his inner circle, with the hint that Luther was intended, would be named to cardinal. Luther, however, would not budge. He would only promise not to write anything further, on the condition that his opponents also remain quiet. The silence on the side of Luther's opponents, however, did not last long, and so Luther also once again took up the pen. In 1519 he authored no less than forty-two writings, ranging from sermons to an exposition of the Lord's Prayer and the first volume of his commentary on the Psalms.

In the same year the well-known disputation with Johann Eck took place in Leipzig, in which Luther's collaborator Andreas Carlstadt (1486–1541) initially argued Luther's position. Eck saw himself as the victor inasmuch as he was able to bring Luther to concede that even councils could err. Afterward it was felt that other universities should decide who was right. The Sorbonne University in Paris demanded so much money for such a verdict that even Duke George of Saxony (1471–1539), in whose territory Leipzig was located, could not consider to pay it, and Erfurt did not wish to venture an opinion. Many humanists came to the aid of Luther, but the theologians of the Universities of Cologne and Louvain declared Luther a heretic. This, however, did not particularly trouble Luther, since these same faculties has already condemned the humanist Johannes Reuchlin (1455–1522) for seeking to rescue the Hebrew language and its literature from being completely forgotten.

In 1520 Luther's most significant Reformation writings appeared: *Of Good Works, To the Christian Nobility of the German Nation, The Babylonian Captivity of the Church*, and *On the Freedom of a Christian*. Even Duke George of Saxony, an outspoken opponent of the Reformation, wrote to Rome concerning Luther's *To the Christian Nobility* that "although not everything in this book is wrong it is not necessary that it come to the light of day since it is not necessary that a scandal arises. . . . If everyone remains quiet then eventually even the stones will speak."[20] In this writing Luther characterized the so-called Donation of Constantine as a forgery. This document, which presumably dates back to around 800, claims that the emperor Constantine, upon his conversion to the Christian faith, ceded the Western half of his empire to Pope Sylvester I (pope: 314–335) and thereafter took up residence in Constantinople, present-day Istanbul. Luther contended that the pope could never be the successor of the Roman emperor. The pope should not exercise secular authority, but rather be the most learned among Bible scholars and should concern himself with such things that have to do with faith and the holy life of the Christian. Luther went on to say that the entire church, however, was in need of reform. This must begin with the mendicant monks and extend to the priests and holders of ecclesiastical offices, many of whom, for instance, had a bad conscience because of their failure to observe celibacy. The priesthood of all believers was also stressed, as was the need for every Christian to be able to affirm and defend the faith. As one saw from the Council of Nicea, councils were not called by the pope but by the emperor. This should once more become the case. In regard to the Mass Luther held it to be necessary that the laity once again have access to the cup and that the idea of transubstantiation, the view that bread and wine are physically changed into the body and blood of Christ, could not be an object of faith since the sacrament of the Eucharist is itself a mystery. Finally, the Mass could not be a good work or a sacrifice since the Last Supper of Jesus was not a sacrifice.

In the meantime Rome continued to actively seek ways of silencing Luther. Von Miltitz sought to persuade the elector Frederick to extradite Luther. He was even threatened with the

---

20. Duke George in a letter of October 1520 to "Dr. Johannes Hennigh, dean of Meißen, currently in Rome," (No. 175), in *Akten und Briefe zur Religionspolitik Herzog Georgs von Sachsen*, vol. 1: 1517–1524, ed. Felician Geß (Leipzig: B.G. Teubner, 1905), 139.

Interdict, which meant that it would be forbidden to hold any worship services within his territory. Frederick, however, responded evasively that as a politician he didn't understand anything of religious matters. He could not be blamed for not allowing Luther to stand trial before the archbishop of Trier since he himself couldn't determine anything criminal concerning Luther or his activity. In Rome patience wore thin and in 1520 Luther was placed under the ban in the bull *Exsurge Domine*. This meant that Luther had lost all rights and anyone could kill him without any legal consequences. Eck had the thankless job of proclaiming the bull in Saxony and had permission to add other names to that of Luther. In many places, however, he was merely ridiculed.

At the advice of von Miltitz, Luther wrote to Pope Leo X, in whose integrity he continued sincerely and naively to believe. He included with the letter a copy of his writing *On the Freedom of a Christian*, in which he put forward the famous paradox that a Christian is a free master over all things and is subject to no one, but at the same time is a servant to all and is subject to all. The Christian has, therefore, a twofold nature, namely a spiritual and a worldly nature. In spiritual things the Christian is subject to no one but in worldly things to everyone.

When Luther first saw the papal bull in October 1520 he thought initially that it was a forgery. Finally, even Frederick the Wise began to have doubts and consulted the famous humanistic scholar Erasmus of Rotterdam (1466–1536) as to what he ought to think of Luther. Erasmus responded that "he has done much wrong who attacks the monks in their bellies and the pope in his crown."[21] In Cologne and Louvain there occurred the first public burnings of Luther's books. In Cologne, however, the enterprise was not particularly successful,

---

21. Luther, "Table Talk," no. 131 (November/December 1531), in *LW* 54:19.

since the students there supplied lists containing the works of Luther's opponents to those charged with gathering the books to be burned. As Luther heard of the book burnings, there appeared a notice on December 9 on the door of the parish church in Wittenberg asking people to assemble at 9 a.m. the following day at the Elster gate, where, in good apostolic fashion, they were to help with the burning of the godless books of papal laws and scholastic theology. After several works concerning canon law and writings by Eck and the polemical theologian Hieronymus Emser (1478–1527) had been committed to the flames, Luther stepped forward nervously and threw a small volume into the fire. Only few noticed at the time that it was the papal bull banning him. On the next day Luther began to hold his lectures in German, instead of Latin as he had previously done. Luther was ready, at this point, to break with an entire tradition.

Finally his case was to come before the emperor. The elector Frederick was able once again, as was the case at Luther's hearing at the conclusion of the Diet of Augsburg in 1518, to obtain the assurance from the young Emperor Charles V (1500–58; emperor: 1519–58) that Luther receive safe passage to and from the Diet of Worms, where he was to appear before the emperor. Although the papal legate protested, Charles V held to his promise. The monk was to be allowed safe passage to Worms, was to receive his hearing, and was to be allowed to return to Saxony. Luther's journey to Worms resembled a triumphal procession, with the town of Wittenberg supplying a coach for his journey. After various papal intrigues failed to produce any results, Luther finally arrived at his hearing in Worms, appearing for the first time before the emperor and the other officials on April 17, 1521. He was officially questioned by Dr. Johann von der Ecken of Trier, representing the emperor, who asked whether a stack of approximately twenty books placed before Luther were indeed his own writings and whether he was prepared to recant all or any part of these writings. Someone requested that the titles be read aloud, upon the completion of which reading Luther admitted to being their author. As to the second question, however, he asked for time to think the matter over. This was granted to him and he was summoned to appear once again before the Diet on the afternoon of the following day.

Luther had prepared carefully beforehand, since he was not allowed to read any prepared statement at his hearing. He began by apologizing in case he addressed anyone with the wrong title, since he had spent most of his life in his monastic cell and not at royal courts. He then divided his books into three categories. In the first category were works of a devotional nature in which even his opponents could find nothing to fault. One could not, therefore, expect that he recant these writings. The second category of writings contained books against the pope. To recant these books would only strengthen the papal tyranny and would open not only a window but a gate to further unchristian conduct. The third category consisted of publications directed against private individuals who defended the tyranny of Rome and condemned godly teaching. In these writings he admitted to often expressing himself more harshly than was appropriate. Since it was not entirely clear from his speech whether his answer was yes or no, Johann von der Ecken demanded from him a straightforward and unqualified answer to the question whether he wished to retract anything. Luther responded in Latin,

> Unless I am convinced by the testimony of the Scriptures or by clear reason (for I do not trust either in the pope or in councils alone, since it is well known that they have often erred and contradicted themselves), I am bound by the Scriptures I have quoted and my conscience is captive to the Word of God. I cannot and I will not retract anything, since it is neither safe nor right to go against conscience. I cannot do otherwise, here I stand, may God help me, Amen.[22]

With this statement someone had for the first time openly bound himself before the world and the church to the principle of conscience. Everything could be demanded of a person except one's faith, for this was a matter of conscience. Nevertheless, it was often forgotten by those who later cited Luther that he stressed that his conscience was itself bound to the word of God. Luther did not advocate a freedom of conscience in the sense of personal autonomy, but rather for the person as he or she is understood to be ultimately responsible only to God. Even his electoral prince Frederick admitted later privately to his secretary Spalatin that Father Martin had spoken very well. He then added, however, as an afterthought and half in admiration of Luther, "In my opinion he is much too audacious."[23] The emperor, on the other hand, commented already upon his first encounter with Luther, "He will never make a heretic out of me."[24] The day after Luther's second appearance before the Diet, the emperor wrote what was at the same time both a personal and official declaration in which he placed all things under the protection of the Catholic faith and the Roman Church. He viewed Luther as a heretic and did not wish to have to listen to him any longer. Nevertheless he kept his promise and guaranteed him safe passage home under the condition that he not preach or cause unrest along the way.

From the Wartburg to the Diet of Augsburg

On his return journey Luther was "abducted" on May 4 near the castle Altenstein and ended up finally in Wartburg castle near Eisenach. His elector had sent a message beforehand to Luther

22. "Luther at the Diet of Worms," in *LW* 32:112–13.
23. Cited by Irmgard Höß, *Georg Spalatin, 1484–1545: Ein Leben in der Zeit des Humanismus und der Reformation* (Weimar: Hermann Böhlaus Nachfolger, 1956), 197.
24. So the dispatch of Aleander "to the Vice Chancellor Medici" on April 29, 1521, printed in Theodor Brieger, *Quellen und Forschungen zur Geschichte der Reformation*, vol. 1 (Gotha: Friedrich Andreas Perthes, 1884), 170.

informing him of the planned abduction, but did not himself wish to know where Luther would be taken so that when asked he could answer with good conscience that he did not know where Luther was. Luther spent the time following his abduction as Junker Jörg (Knight George) in the Wartburg. He let his hair and beard grow long and carried a sword on his side and wore a golden chain around his neck. For his own safety he was accompanied by a servant whenever he rode out of the castle. The life of a knight and the loneliness of the Wartburg did not particularly agree with Luther. Yet he wasted no time getting to work within his Patmos, as he called the castle in allusion to the place of John's banishment (Rev. 1:9).

In September 1522 the New Testament appeared translated into German and became known as the September Bible. For his translation Luther selected the language of the Saxon court, which was used by every prince and king in Germany. He thus made use of a German dialect that was easily accessible to everyone. The rapid and broad popularity of this translation was therefore only natural. Luther wrote introductions to the individual parts of the New Testament, in which he also attributed varying degrees of weight to the different New Testament writings.

Luther considered Wittenberg to be in good hands during his stay at the Wartburg since Philip Melanchthon, the great nephew of the humanist Reuchlin, had been active there as professor of Greek since 1518. Luther was very much impressed by the language skills of Melanchthon, who went from being a follower of the learned humanist Erasmus to a close coworker of Luther. Luther had an almost childlike trust in Melanchthon, even when the latter went increasingly in his own, often compromise-oriented direction. Luther in fact praised Melanchthon's 1521 work *Loci communes*, which can be rightly viewed as the first Protestant dogmatics text, so much that he saw it almost as a canonical book.

Yet unrest soon developed in Wittenberg, especially spawned by Andreas Carlstadt, who felt that Luther's reforms were taking too long and did not go far enough. When Luther visited Wittenberg incognito in December 1521, he was satisfied by what he saw there, for the situation had quieted down in the meantime. He had barely returned to the Wartburg, however, when the unrest began again, aggravated especially by the so-called Zwickau prophets, who claimed to have received personal revelations from God. In the Augustinian monastery the religious images were burned and the side altars removed. People even wanted to overturn the whole social order and to kill all the priests and religious officials. Although the city council introduced reforms such as a new church constitution and social changes, the unrest continued among the townspeople as well as among the students and monks. It affected even the university. Finally the city requested help and, against the wishes of the elector, Luther returned to Wittenberg in order to restore peace and order through the so-called Invocavit sermons. Beginning on March 9, on Invocavit Sunday, Luther preached on eight consecutive days in the Wittenberg parish church. He was not afraid and let the elector know that he stood under "a far higher protection than the Elector's."[25] God alone would protect him.

Many reforms that were demanded by the enthusiasts Luther placed in the category of optional matters, that is, adiaphora. Thus paintings and other religious works of art could either remain in the church or be removed. Only if one worshiped such things, however, must they be removed and destroyed, and even in such a case this was only to be done by those bearing proper authority to do so. In this series of sermons Luther laid out the fundamental principles of his approach to churchly reform: patience toward those still hesitating

---

25. Martin Luther, "Letter to the Elector Frederick, Borna, March 5, 1522," in *LW* 48:391.

and freedom in regard to external ceremonies. Luther also preached in other places on the matter of reform, even when this sometimes involved personal risk, since he had to leave the territory of the elector on occasion for this work.

In 1523 Luther once again took up his lecturing duties at the university and toward the end of the year produced an evangelical order of worship in which, among other things, he called for the introduction of Communion with bread and wine and for the pastor to read the words of institution loudly and clearly while facing the congregation. In that same year Luther also wrote *On Temporal Authority: To What Extent It Should Be Obeyed*, a writing in which he encouraged Christians to actively participate in political life. He also put forward here his well-known thesis of God's two forms of government within the world: the government to the left is concerned with external order and maintained with force, and the government to the right is maintained without force through the gospel. In the following year (1524) Luther once again had to deal with the enthusiasts led by Carlstadt, as well as with the theologian and social utopian Thomas Müntzer (ca. 1489–1525), who had turned the peasants toward rebellion for the sake of his utopian plans. In this same year Luther laid down his monk's habit.

The year 1525 was decisive for Luther in three ways. First, he distanced himself from Erasmus of Rotterdam. Second, he married Katharina von Bora. Third, he turned sharply against the peasant rebellion. This revolt reached its peak with the publication in 1525 of *The Twelve Articles* (12 Artikeln aller Bauernschaft), a manifesto of the Swabian peasants in what is today the Swabian district in the state of Bavaria. This revolt was an especially delicate problem for Luther, for his opponents among the princes could very easily attribute the revolt to his reforms. If, however, he spoke out against the demands of the peasants, many of which were just (for instance that congregations be allowed to elect their own pastors and force the resignation of those who do not preach the gospel, or that the tenth portion of too many products was being demanded by those in authority), then he risked turning the majority of the generally poor and exploited peasants against him.

Luther viewed the unrest not as a politician but rather as a pastor. Hence he spoke out in the first place against the princes, who oppressed the peasants to such an extent that they could not hold up any longer under such conditions. He challenged the princes to deal in a reasonable manner with the peasants. Luther admonished both sides to peace over *The Twelve Articles.* He consistently rejected the option of armed rebellion, and contended that one should not be misled into rising against a government even when it is evil and suppresses the gospel. The law should not be taken into one's own hands.

In the meantime, however, the rebellions in Southwestern Germany, Franconia (present-day northern Bavaria), Austria, Saxony, and Thuringia continued to escalate. On both sides, atrocities were committed. When Thomas Müntzer forced the council of the town of Mühlhausen in Thuringia to resign and established a dictatorship of the elect, Luther felt that things had gone too far. Villages, castles, and monasteries were stormed by fanatical masses, plundered, and burned. All order seemed to be transformed into chaos. Hence Luther added a new chapter to the second printing of his *Admonition to Peace: A Reply to the Twelve Articles of the Peasants in Swabia* and extended the title to read, "[Also] Against the Robbing and Murdering Hordes of Peasants." He now admonished the princes that it was their duty to restore order. If the peasants behave as wild dogs they must be treated as such.

In the midst of the unrest that was now being put down with cruel force, which led to the killing of Thomas Müntzer, Elector Frederick of Saxony died. On his deathbed Frederick wrote, "Perhaps the poor have been given just cause for such rebellion, especially through withholding from them the Word of God. The poor have thus been weighted down by us secular and ecclesial authorities in many ways. May God turn his wrath from us. If it be God's will, then it will come about that the common people shall rule. If it is not his divine will . . . then things will soon change."[26] Indeed things soon did change, and peace again returned. Yet the price was high. Estimates have it that one hundred thousand peasants had died, many of them having been innocent.

Luther acted in this affair according to his conscience and without regard to his popularity. He did not recognize, however, that there might be situations in which a social class must rise up against oppression. His explanation of the distinction between the two forms of God's government could also have taken this possibility into account. Through the suppression of the peasants' revolt, the wildfire growth of the Reformation came to an end, and from this time on the Reformation proceeded in a more regulated manner.

In September 1524 Erasmus's book *Diatribe de libero arbitrio* (Exposition on free will) appeared. Erasmus originally had a positive impression of Luther, for he saw him as a legitimate critic of the dominant morality of the day, as well as a supporter of classical studies. Luther likewise held Erasmus's edition of the Greek New Testament in high esteem and used it in the Wartburg as the basis for his translation of the New Testament. He soon noticed, however, that Erasmus was unwilling to break with the Roman Church, in which he found so many advantages. On his part Erasmus came to see a catastrophe in the making in Luther's harshly worded reform

---

26. From a letter of Elector Frederick of Saxony to Duke Johann of Saxony (April 14, 1525), printed in Carl Eduard Fürstemann, *Neues Urkundenbuch zur Geschichte der evangelischen Kirchen-Reformation* (Hamburg: Friedrich Andreas Perthes, 1842; reprint: New York, 1976), 259.

writings, and he did not wish to be drawn into this tragedy. His main concern was that academic studies continued to advance peacefully. Thus several of Erasmus's friends were able to convince him to write something against Luther. In his writing on free will, he stressed the salvific effectualness of the human free will. This, of course, struck a deeply negative chord with Luther.

Luther took his time with his response. Finally he wrote *De servo arbitrio* (On the bondage of the will), one of the broadest and most thoroughly thought-out treatments of a theological problem ever composed by Luther. He began by complimenting Erasmus for being the only one to recognize the real difference between the Reformation position and the old faith. All the other questions of conflict over the pope, purgatory, and indulgences were secondary. Luther then came to the core of his treatment, and rejected in the strongest terms the teaching that we have a free will that is capable of accomplishing anything toward our salvation. The human will is like a beast of burden standing between God and the devil. When God sits upon it, it goes in the direction that God desires, and when Satan rides it, it goes where Satan wishes. Thus it does not depend upon us to go to one rider or the other, but both fight over possession of us. A free will in regard to spiritual things exists only in our dreams. In this way Luther drew the battle lines. Although Luther showed himself to be open to humanism and owed much to it, he did not represent a synthesis between the thought of classical antiquity and the biblical gospel. The word of God alone was important for Luther, which spoke, as he understood it, of the unmerited acceptance of sinners.

In the middle of the year 1525, which was at the same time the year of crisis and of decision for the Reformation, there took place another important event that left many contemporaries shaking their heads. On July 13, 1525, Luther was married in a private and unannounced ceremony in his home, the black cloister in Wittenberg, to the former nun Katharina von Bora (1499–1552). The ceremony was performed by the pastor of the Wittenberg parish church, Johannes Bugenhagen (1485–1558). Two weeks later, as was the custom at the time, a larger celebration was held to which guests were invited, including Luther's parents. This celebration was seen as the public and legal confirmation of a marriage and included a procession to the church. Even Luther's friends were not certain what to make of his marriage. For his enemies the marriage of this former monk to a runaway nun was a welcome scandal. Already the year before he had laid aside his monastic habit and begun to preach in his academic gown. Now he had also entered into the covenant of marriage, thereby turning visibly away from the monastic way of life.

Luther did not take this step because he was passionately in love; his conception of marriage was very realistic. To the best of our knowledge Luther yearned after the security of marriage and became increasingly unhappy with his bachelorhood in the black cloister, where he was practically the only monk left. He had already previously written positively about marriage, and for years had contended that the celibacy of the priesthood and the monastic rejection of marriage, especially when these were forcibly imposed, go against the will of God. Being banned as a heretic, Luther expected an early death by the political authorities. Yet he wanted to make a statement on this matter through his own example before it was too late. He had even challenged Cardinal Albrecht of Mainz in the same year to marry and to transform his territories into secular estates.

Luther's wife, the twenty-six-year-old Katharina von Bora, came from an impoverished Saxon noble family. She had lived in the cloister Nimbschen since she was nine years old. But some of the nuns wanted to leave the monastery. In the night before Easter 1523 the councilman of the city of Torgau, Leonhard Koppe, arrived with a wagon at the monastery and twelve nuns including Katharina escaped into the world. Three could return to their families and for the others Luther was looking for suitable husbands. On several occasions Luther was encouraged to take a wife himself, a suggestion, however, which he had consistently rejected. For Katharina he had in mind the son of a patrician family from Nuremberg. She was willing to marry him, but his parents did not want to have anything to do with an impoverished former nun. Finally Luther stopped looking for a husband, since rumors had it that Katharina would want as a possible spouse either Luther's friend Nicholas von Amsdorf (1483–1565), or Dr. Martinus himself. Thus Luther wrote in a letter of 1525, "Before I die I will still marry my Katie."[27] An interesting side story involving Luther's marriage was that Albrecht of Mainz sent Luther a gift of twenty gulden, which Luther wanted to refuse. His wife, however, was more practically oriented and accepted the money gladly.[28] With his marriage Luther also fulfilled a long-standing wish of his father.

The marriage was blessed with six children. Hans, who was born a year after Luther's marriage to Katharina, later studied law and became a legal official in the court of Duke Johann Frederick in Weimar. The second child, Elisabeth, lived only eight months. Magdalena, their third child, died at thirteen years of age. Martin, the fourth child, studied theology but never became a pastor. He died at age thirty-four in Wittenberg. The fifth and most gifted child was Paul who, although he was sickly as a child, went on to study medicine and was court physician in Gotha and later held a similar position in the court of Elector August in Dresden. After the

---

27. Luther, "Letter to John Rühel. Seeburg, May 4, 1525," in *LW* 49:111.
28. According to Martin Brecht, *Martin Luther: Shaping and Defining the Reformation 1521–1532*, trans. James Schaaf (Minneapolis: Fortress Press, 1990), 2:201.

death of Luther, the sixth child, Margarethe, married the East Prussian nobleman George von Kunheim.

Despite all the work Luther had to do he enjoyed his children and family, a fact that can especially be seen in the letters he wrote to his son Hans during his stay in the castle of Coburg. He also composed the Christmas song "From Heaven Above" (*ELW* 268) for his children. Concerning his marriage he wrote, "God has willed and brought about this step. For I feel neither passionate love nor burning for my spouse, but I cherish her."[29] Luther always appreciated his wife, even if it was not always easy for her to live with him, especially since he was especially generous in financial matters and often brought home more guests than she was expecting. Katharina was a good manager of the household. Upon his marriage, the elector gave Luther a salary of two hundred gulden a year, which was equivalent to that which Melanchthon earned. Though not especially high, this was the largest salary paid to Wittenberg professors. Later Luther's salary was raised to three hundred gulden a year. Katharina was also able to acquire a small farm, the money for which again came mostly from the elector. She raised many animals, including cows, pigs, goats, chickens, geese, ducks, and doves, as well as a small dog. She also brewed her own beer and had a fish pond. She kept exact records of income and expenses. Although Luther was a very strict father, the family found much enjoyment together. Music was especially appreciated and after the evening meal, Luther often took up the lute and the family sang together, with Luther contributing his strong singing voice. Playing games with the family and with guests was also a frequent occurrence with Luther, who was a good chess player. Katharina outlived her husband by six and a half years.

---

29. Luther, "Letter to Nicholas von Amsdorf. Wittenberg, June 21, 1525," in *LW* 49:117.

In the years following his marriage Luther especially devoted himself to the "visitation" of the various churches and other ecclesiastical institutions in Saxony, which means that he evaluated the economic and spiritual situation of the individual congregations and pastors, and improved it where possible. In order to raise the level of knowledge among pastors and laypersons alike, Luther wrote his *Small* and *Large Catechisms*, which were published in 1529. To administer the affairs of the church one also needed a supervisor. But none of the bishops had joined the Reformation. Luther then thought of the elector as the transitional head of the church. The elector was, so to speak, to serve as emergency bishop in his land and to direct the supervision of the churches. This move, which was consistent with the political tendency of the late Middle Ages in which the secular rulers took on increasing ecclesiastical authority, developed from a stopgap measure into a permanent arrangement. The oversight of the churches in Lutheran lands thus became primarily the responsibility of the secular rulers. The regional Protestant churches of modern Germany trace their origin back to this arrangement, and their borders still largely follow the old political borders of the territories of the sixteenth-century German princes.

In 1529 the Marburg Colloquy took place at the instigation of the Landgrave Philipp I of Hesse (1504–67). The attempt was made here to reconcile the Reformed position of the Southern Germans with that of the Lutherans. Behind this effort lay the hope that if the theologians could speak with one voice then the princes also would be able to come together and form a common front against the Roman Catholics who threatened the Reformation with extinction. The Colloquy concluded with a common confession of faith, the Marburg Articles, written by Luther and signed by all the participants. Huldrych Zwingli, the Swiss Reformer of Zurich, and Martin Luther showed an amazing degree of agreement in their theological positions. Some time afterward Luther recalled how Zwingli, with tears in his eyes, had said at Marburg, "God knows that I have no greater desire to consider anyone my friends than those from Wittenberg."[30] In fourteen points the parties were completely agreed. Only in article 15, which dealt with the presence of Christ in the Eucharist, were the two sides unable to agree, since the Zwinglians understood the presence of the body of Christ only in a spiritual sense while the Lutherans stressed Christ's real, bodily presence. Yet it was still hoped that the two sides might be able at some point to overcome their differences on this issue. Luther, however, was right when he said of Zwingli that he was of a different mind. Zwingli was more rationalistic in his thinking than Luther and was not able to comprehend how Christ, who is seated at the right hand of God, could also be understood to be really present in the eucharistic meal. He was also much more influenced by humanism and therefore viewed Luther's biblicism with skepticism.

In the following year the Diet of Augsburg was held. Clemens VII (1478–1534, pope: 1523–1534), a cousin of Leo X and an illegitimately born Medici (the wealthy Florentine merchant family), was pope at the time. Although his personal conduct was above reproach, he was interested primarily in Italy and had little interest in Germany. Additionally, the Turks had laid siege to Vienna in the autumn of 1529, which meant that the emperor could not afford to risk any religious conflict in his own empire and was dependent upon the support of all the princes. This situation proved advantageous for the Reformation and the emperor promised to hear the judgments and opinions of all sides at the upcoming Diet. Because Luther was still under the papal ban, he could not travel to Augsburg but had to remain in the castle of Coburg, the southernmost point of electoral

---

30. Luther, "Tischrede," no. 129 (November/December 1531), in *WA TR* 1:53.27–28.

Saxony. The other theologians, including Melanchthon, traveled to Augsburg with the elector John the Steadfast (1468–1532), who had succeeded his brother Frederick the Wise, and Saxony's electoral chancellor Gregory Brück. Luther participated actively in the events of Augsburg from the Coburg through the reports of messengers.

Melanchthon, relying upon previous confessions, composed the *Confessio Augustana*, or the Augsburg Confession, for the Lutheran princes. Luther was in agreement with the content of the document but admitted in a letter to his elector that "I cannot step so softly and quietly."[31] Against the wish of the Emperor Charles V, this confession was read on June 25, 1530 before the emperor, the electors, and the other representatives by the other Saxon electoral chancellor, Dr. Christian Beyer. The reading lasted approximately two hours. The emperor listened attentively. Even the bishop of Augsburg admitted afterward in private conversation with friends that what was read could not be repudiated, for it was the truth. The Diet concluded, however, with a new confrontation: the emperor gave the Protestants, as he put it, a final six-month extension of peace before he would begin to punish violations of the Edict of Worms (which forbid any prince to give safe haven to Luther and ordered that his books be burned) as breaches of the peace. This act brought the Lutherans to overcome their disagreements and to found the Schmalcald League in 1531, the evangelical alliance forged in Schmalkalden, a small town south of Eisenach in Thuringia. Luther was forced through this move to view the right to oppose the emperor in a more nuanced manner. "Is it allowed to offer resistance to the emperor?" he asked. He answered, "I for my part as a theologian advise against this. If the lawyers, however, are able to

---

31. Luther, "Letter to Elector John. Coburg, May 15, 1530," in *LW* 49:297–98.

show that according to their laws it is permissible, then I am willing to concede that their laws are applicable."[32]

From Schmalkalden to the Death of Luther

Shortly before the Diet of Augsburg Luther's father died, followed a year later by the death of his mother. Both Luther's father and mother received letters from their son shortly before their death that reveal Luther to be a faithful son and pastor.

In 1537 an opportunity once again arose for a possible reconciliation with the Roman Church, when the churches of the Reformation were invited to attend a papal council in Mantua. Since it was not an imperial council but rather a papal one, however, the members of the Schmalcald League declined to participate. Nevertheless, in anticipation that a council might be called, Luther composed the so-called *Schmalcald Articles*, named after the town of Schmalkalden where the articles were agreed upon by leading theologians and pastors of Lutheran territories. The articles were divided into three parts, with the first consisting of those points upon which both sides agreed, followed by those points that were open to discussion, and finally, those nonnegotiable issues upon which all discussion was futile. Luther, however, was not able to participate in the discussions in Schmalkalden because he was suffering so severely from kidney and gallstones that many awaited his impending death. The stones, however, were passed and Luther slowly recovered, although he never regained his former strength.

He was frequently plagued by sickness during the remaining decade of his life, especially from pain caused by stones but also by severe headaches and depression. When he suffered a fainting spell during a worship service in spring of 1537, he realized that

32. Luther, "Letter to Wenzeslaus Link in Nuremberg" (January 15, 1531, no. 1772), in *WA BR* 6:16.14–16.

everything could quickly come to an end for him. Yet he did not fear death, because he had long since committed his life into God's hands. It also became increasingly clear that the Reformation was not leading to a renewal of the entire church but to the formation of a new (evangelical) church. There is no proof, however, that Luther became melancholy and abrasive toward the end of his life, as his opponents claimed. Indeed, the events of the last years of his life themselves speak against this.

The counts of Mansfeld increasingly were in conflict with one another because Count Albrecht III, the lord of the region where Luther was born, was involved in repeated strife with his brother Gebhard over the possession of the copper mines. Luther had already written to his "dear lord" twice, and in 1545 Albrecht announced himself ready to accept Luther's mediation. Thus Luther, Melanchthon, and the theologian and lawyer Justus Jonas (1493–1555) traveled to Mansfeld, but the negotiations, due to other circumstances, did not lead to a resolution. A second attempt also had to be broken off early because Melanchthon became ill. Finally, a new journey was planned for January 1546, in which Luther was accompanied, among others, by his three sons. It was very cold, and shortly before arriving in Eisleben Luther suffered a fainting spell, which he held to be of little significance. On February 1 he was in good enough spirits to write his wife a humorous letter addressed "to my dearly beloved mistress of the house, Katharina Luther, a doctor, the lady of Zölsdorf [and] of the pig market, and whatever else she is capable of being." He signed the letter, "Your loving Martin Luther, who has grown old."[33]

On February 14 he announced his return to Wittenberg, since the negotiations were nearly completed. On the 15th he had to cut short

---

33. Luther, "Letter to Mrs. Martin Luther. Eisleben, February 1, 1546," in *LW* 50:290–92.

his sermon because of a dizzy spell. The negotiations finally came to an end. One document was prepared by Luther on February 16 and also signed by Justus Jonas. But there was a lengthier one of February 17. Though Luther was unable to attend the closing session because of his weakness, his name was listed with the other participants. Later he ate supper with his colleagues, and about eight o'clock he went to his room as usual to pray. Shortly thereafter he complained of chest pains, but finally he went to bed and fell asleep. At 1 a.m. he once again complained of chest pains and then lay down on a couch. He expected that he would die in the city where he had been born and baptized and committed his soul to God. At this point the town clerk, two physicians, Count Albrecht and his wife Anna, and several other persons joined him. Luther noticed that the end was near. He thanked God that he had revealed his Son to him and commended his soul into God's hands. Then he prayed three times: "Into your hands I commend my spirit. You have redeemed me, true God. Indeed God has loved the world."[34] Afterward he was quiet. Then Justus Jonas and Michael Zoelius, the Mansfeld court preacher, called out to him, "Doctor Martinus, honored father, do you die in the faith in Christ and in the teachings that you have preached in his name?" This question was necessary so that his opponents would not be able to say that Luther recanted on his deathbed. Luther answered clearly so that he could be heard with a yes. That was his last word. At about a quarter to three he took his last breath. The great reformer had died.

On February 22, 1546 his funeral service was held in the castle church in Wittenberg by Johannes Bugenhagen. Melanchthon, representing the university, held a speech in Latin at the conclusion of the service eulogizing Luther. Luther died almost as he had predicted: He had said just two days before his death, "As soon as I

---

34. For this and the following quote, cf. the report of Justus Jonas from February 18, 1546, printed in Christof Schubart, *Die Berichte über Luthers Tod und Begräbnis* (Weimar: Böhlau, 1917), 5, 9.

return home to Wittenberg I will lay down in a coffin and give the maggots a fat doctor to eat."[35]

Although Luther, by no fault of his own, did not always contribute to worldly peace, the last work of his life was dedicated to political peace. He led a great many persons out of the anxiety and uncertainty of their religious beliefs into the freedom of the gospel. Even the reformation of the Roman Catholic Church, which was begun at the Council of Trent (1545–63), would not have taken place had it not been for Luther.

When we compare the brevity of our lives with the incomprehensible duration of the history of the world, and when we consider the endangerment of our lives through the increasing destruction of the environment, then Luther's question, "How do I find a gracious God?" becomes comprehensible. When one only has the privilege of being a guest upon this earth, the wish to know whether anything positive can be expected beyond this earthly life is only natural. The Reformation theology of Martin Luther provided an answer to this question that is still convincing today. Clearly and simply the answer is this: through our efforts we can neither guarantee our earthly life nor can we come to enjoy eternal life. Only the almighty God, as Creator, Sustainer, and Redeemer of this world, can lift us out of the finitude of our existence. There can be no talk here if we ourselves having earned something. Through the life and message of Jesus Christ God made known that he not only preserves us in his grace in this life, but that he also desires to provide us the fulfillment of eternal life. The appropriate reaction to this undeserved grace is our turning positively to God in active thankfulness.

With these short sentences the essentials of Luther's whole theology are summarized. His thought and words had to do with

---

35. Luther, "Table Talk," no. 6975 (February 16, 1546), in *WA TR* 6:303.12–14.

the priority of God. God must, so to speak, always take the first step in order that we can take the next steps. There is no cooperation of equals between humans and God, but only on the basis of God's preceding grace can humans become partners in God's worldly and salvific activity. Luther's emphasis upon the priority of God did not arise out of some strange medieval conception of authority; instead, he was concerned that making our salvation depend upon any cooperation between us and God could have fatal consequences, because of the uncertainty owing to our human finiteness. Luther's concern was not for rational security for our earthly lives, which is at any rate not possible, but rather for a certainty of faith that is able to serve as the foundation for coping with the difficulties of our present and future. In this regard Luther put his trust realistically in God and not in human ability, which proves all too often to be insufficient. This insistence upon the priority of God confronts us immediately with this question: How one can know God?

2

True Knowledge of God

Right up to the beginning of the modern era it was self-evident for most people that God does indeed exist, for nature and human reason testified in a multitude of ways to the work and being of God. With the Enlightenment of the seventeenth and eighteenth centuries, and the blossoming of scientific and technological knowledge and the "conquest" of the world in the last two centuries, this situation changed dramatically. Humans have come to believe that all that exists has come about through natural processes. When the French mathematician and astronomer Pierre Simon Laplace (1749–1827) presented Napoleon with a copy of his five-volume work on the mechanics of heavenly bodies, Napoleon asked him curiously what place God had in his system. Laplace, full of pride, is reported to have answered, "Sir, I have no need of that hypothesis." God had become, so to speak, homeless, and theologians increasingly avoided making any connection between God and nature. The great twentieth-century theologian Karl Barth (1886–1968) contended that faith in God must be entirely grounded in Christ if it is not to deteriorate into superstition. Interestingly, however, an increasing number of natural scientists are now asking questions about the relationship between God and the natural order. Even in our age, which is so ruled by reason, the conviction remains strong that not everything can be attributed to accident. Hence the mathematician and physicist of Tulane University, Frank J. Tipler (b. 1947), for instance, has written a substantial volume titled *The Physics of Immortality* (1994), in which he contends that all of our knowledge cannot simply disappear within the vastness of the universe. There must be a final integrating figure, called God, in which everything finds its connectedness and meaning.

Luther would, of course, have agreed with such a natural theology, for he was convinced that all people have some knowledge of God. Christ, in contrast, brought us a special knowledge of God. Hence Luther wrote, "There is a twofold knowledge of God: the general and the particular" (*Duplex est cognitio Dei, generalis et propria*).[1] That Luther attributed a natural knowledge of God to all persons is first of all grounded in his comprehensive understanding of God. Hence he wrote in his explanation of the first commandment in his *Large Catechism*,

> A "god" is the term for that to which we look for all good and in which we are to find refuge in all need. Therefore, to have a god is nothing else than to trust and believe in that one with our whole heart. As I have often said, it is the trust and faith of the heart alone that make both God and an idol. If your faith and trust are right, then your God is the true one. Conversely, where your trust is false and wrong, there you not have the true God. For these two belong together, faith and God. Anything on which your heart relies and depends, I say, that is really your God.[2]

1. Luther, *Lectures on Galatians* (1535), in *LW* 26:399.
2. Luther, *The Large Catechism*, in *The Book of Concord: The Confessions of the Evangelical Lutheran Church*, ed. Robert Kolb and Timothy J. Wengert (Minneapolis: Fortress Press, 2000), 386.

All of us have something in which we trust and to which our heart clings and what therefore serves as our "god," be it reason, career, or family. Yet there is no direct path from this general dependence on some sort of ultimate concern to a knowledge of the one who really is God. Thus, Luther wavers in his judgment of this natural knowledge of God, for on the one hand he criticizes it as a projection, but on the other hand he counts it as genuine knowledge.

Natural Knowledge of God

In a sermon from 1529 Luther spoke of the ambiguity of the natural knowledge of God:

> The whole world names as God that in which humans put their trust in times of distress and trial, that in which they take comfort and depend upon, and that from which one desires to receive all good things and that can provide help. So the pagans have done when they first of all made Jupiter a helper and a god. . . . Afterward they created many false gods based upon their reason. The Romans established any number of gods which were necessary to help them with their various concerns, so that one helped people in war, one was given this power and another that power; one was to make the corn to grow, and another to help at sea in case of shipwreck. As many needs, good things, and uses as there were upon the earth, so many gods were chosen until they also made plants and garlic into gods. . . . Thus does reason describe God: He is that which helps a person, is useful, and beneficial. One detects here that reason only knows as much about God as Paul attributes to it in Rom. 1:19–21 when he says that one knows that God is.[3]

Because God has inscribed this knowledge indelibly in the human heart, it cannot arise from human reason. The Epicureans and other atheists indeed sought to deny this awareness of God, "but they do it by force and want to quench this light in their hearts. They are like people who purposely stop their ears or pinch their eyes shut to

3. Luther on Deut. 5:6, *Predigten über das 5. Buch Mose* (1529), in *WA* 28:609.29–610.19.

close out sound and sight. However, they do not succeed in this; their conscience tells them otherwise."[4] Hence Luther emphasized in his exposition of Jonah, "Such a light and such a perception is innate in the hearts of all men; and this cannot be subdued or extinguished."[5] If pagans, for instance, called upon their gods, whom they really believed to possess a divine nature, then "this demonstrates that there was in their hearts a knowledge of a divine sovereign Being."[6] All religions, therefore, testify to the existence of a divine being who is invisible, eternal, and powerful. So it is that human beings are naturally aware of the ultimate contingency and dependence of their existence. We are neither responsible for our own existence nor do we fully control it. "Because of a natural instinct the heathen also have this understanding; they know that there is a supreme deity."[7] Luther makes frequent reference to Rom. 1:19ff. when here and elsewhere he contends that "they have a natural knowledge of God." The natural perception of God and general knowledge about God did not originate from human beings, for nature as his creation already testifies "that humans shall call upon God."[8] In order to rightly honor God, the Jews received the law from him on Mount Sinai, while the gentiles were given the law in their hearts. No one is excluded from the natural knowledge of God, for "there has never been a nation so wicked that it did not establish and maintain some sort of worship."[9] In light of the fact of the universal veneration of God Luther always stressed that all people "have a general knowledge of God."[10] But by

4. Luther, in his exposition of Jon. 1:5, *Lectures on Jonah* (1526), in *LW* 19:54. The Epicureans, named after the Greek philosopher Epicurus (ca. 341–ca. 270 B.C.) were known for their fearlessness before the gods and their pursuit of happiness.
5. Luther, in his exposition of Jon. 1:5, *LW* 19:53.
6. Luther, commenting on Rom. 1:19, *Commentary on the Epistle to the Romans*, trans. J. T. Mueller (Grand Rapids: Kregel, 1976), 43.
7. Luther, on Gen. 17:7, *Lectures on Genesis* (1535–45), in *LW* 3:117, for this quote and the following.
8. Luther, *Über das 1. Buch Mose. Predigten* (1527), in *WA* 24:9.20–21.
9. Luther, expounding upon the first commandment in *The Large Catechism*, 388.

what means do people obtain this the natural knowledge? Here we encounter first the law, then reason, and finally philosophy.

Knowledge of God through the Law

According to Luther the knowledge of God that is gained from the ethically obligatory law, as, for example, the Ten Commandments, is a common possession of all persons. "The knowledge contained in the law is known to reason," explained Luther.[11] "For to have a God is not alone a Mosaic law, but also a natural law, as St. Paul says (Rom. 1:20), that the heathen know of the deity, that there is a God. This is also evidenced by the fact that they have set up gods and arranged forms of divine service, which would have been impossible if they had neither known nor thought about God. For God has shown it to them."[12] Hence the Ten Commandments, according to Luther, belong to the category of general or natural knowledge of God, and indeed blend together with natural knowledge in many ways. The natural law, which is found in its purest form in the Ten Commandments, demands the honoring of God in the first table (Commandments 1–3) and requires the love of one's neighbor in the second table (4–10). Since God has engraved the natural law equally in the hearts of all people, we are therefore able to know him. In the twentieth century, comparative ethology has discovered that Decalogue-like prescriptions are present in many cultures and even in the animal kingdom. These prescriptions further social contacts and survival in general.[13]

---

10. Luther, *Lectures on Galatians*, 399.
11. Luther, on John 1:18, *Auslegungen des ersten und zweiten Kapitels Johannes in Predigten* (1517/38), in *WA* 46:667.10–11.
12. Luther, *Against the Heavenly Prophets in the Matter of Images and Sacraments* (1525), in *LW* 40:96–97.
13. Cf. Ernest Thompson Seton, *The Ten Commandments in the Animal World* (Garden City, NY: Doubleday, 1925), and Wolfgang Wickler, *The Biology of the Ten Commandments*, trans. D. Smith (New York: McGraw-Hill, 1972).

Knowledge of God through Reason

Luther was very skeptical of the human use of reason and philosophical reflection. He knew that humans can quickly find a "reasonable" argument that allows them to do what they wish to do and to avoid doing what God wants. Likewise, he held philosophy to be too speculative, for it produced many claims about God that Luther felt clearly contradicted Scripture. Yet despite these limitations he viewed reason and philosophy as originally being good gifts from God through which one is able to know much about God. Especially in *On the Bondage of the Will* (1525), Luther stressed that reason is able to say some things about God, for there is no reason that does not recognize him. This reasoned knowledge of God is gained from his work, particularly creation, and from God's rule, that is to say, divine working in history. This knowledge, therefore, did not originate with human beings, but from God, who gave us reason in order that we might know God.

"God has planted such light and understanding in human nature so as to give us an indication and a picture of his divine rule and shows us that he alone is Lord and creator of all creatures."[14] Reason, for example, opens up the possibility of ascertaining a Creator and Sustainer on the basis of teleology and order in nature in the so-called proofs for the existence of God. Even the knowledge of God from those laws recognized by humans can be categorized epistemologically under reason, for it understands his commandment and with it the distinction between right and wrong. Nevertheless, knowledge of God based on reason does not stand on firm ground because, as Luther well knew, people do not want to believe that God punishes sin and therefore they prefer to follow their own thinking.

14. Luther, "Epistel am Sonntag Trinitatis. Röm 11:33–36," *Crucigers Sommerpostille* (1537), in *WA* 21:510.39–511.1.

They tend to compromise this knowledge and turn to speculating about God through their own rational reflections. Natural reason can indeed know "that this Godhead is something superior to all other things," so that all people can call on a divinity.[15] Yet this God-given knowledge is often perverted through human high-handedness and leads to idolatry, that is, to the following of other gods rather than the true God.

Knowledge of God through Philosophy

Philosophy, which Luther uses almost interchangeably with reason, also turns its attention to the created order and deduces from it who rules the world. It knows that there is a first mover (*primum movens*) and a highest being (*summum ens*), as Plato (B.C. 428/27–348/47) had already shown. Yet the will of the Creator remains hidden from reason, for humans are blinded by their sinful self-centeredness and cannot see the world as it really is. Of course, the Platonists came to the conclusion, through their speculations, that God is spirit and rules the world and is the ground of all that is good in the natural order. But they were so blinded by the sovereignty and majesty of God in his works that in their search for God they did not recognize him. Why God made things the way God did and why God rules in the way God does are questions for which the philosophers have no answers.

The speculative knowledge of God produced by philosophy also fails in the end because it focuses on the naked majesty of God (*nuda majestas dei*), which is beyond human comprehension. According to Luther, speculative philosophy seeks to reach the beyond from the here and now. As the German philosopher Immanuel Kant (1724–1804) later demonstrated, this is impossible because God

---

15. Luther, on Jon. 1:5, *Lectures on Jonah* (1526), in *LW* 19:53.

cannot be reached from a human starting point. Luther admits that speculative philosophy is able to discern some things about God. Yet it often becomes lost in abstract speculation.

Intuitive Knowledge of God through God's works

Finite human beings are unable to obtain an unambiguous knowledge of God. At the same time, however, Luther firmly believed that God could be intuitively known by humans.

> One cannot comprehend God, yet one senses his presence, for he lets himself be seen and known by one and all and he reveals himself as a good creator who acts for our good and gives us all good things. This is attested by the sun and moon, heaven and earth, and all the fruits which grow from the earth. But the fault does not lie with the creator that in such works and in his innumerable good acts we do not recognize God, as if he desired that he should be hidden from our eyes. No, the fault lies not with God but with us, for human nature is so corrupted and poisoned through original sin that we are not able to notice, let alone know and understand God.[16]

It is not God's fault but our own that the experiential and intuitive knowledge of God from his works is so ambiguous. Human beings want to comprehend God from a human starting point and from the natural order. But because of our sinful turning away from God we are no longer able to clearly perceive him. Nevertheless, the natural order allows us to perceive something of God and reflects something of the deity, for it teaches "that there is a God, who gives us all things good and helps us against all evil."[17] This intuitive sensing of God's working in nature and history is one of the roots of human religiosity and of the worship of God in the world religions. Luther agreed with

---

16. Luther, "Tischrede," no. 6530 (undated), in *WA TR* 6:20.19–29.
17. Luther, *Eine kurze Form der zehn Gebote, des Glaubens und des Vaterunsers* (1520), in *WA* 7:205.17.

the tradition of the Middle Ages that one could detect the footprints of God in nature. But to what extent is this a true knowledge of God?

Speculative reason was able to come to the conclusion that God can do all things. But this fact does not yet tell us anything about the direction and intention of God's working. Through reason one can determine the attributes of God: God is almighty, eternal, all-knowing, and so on. But we cannot thereby know his will. The recognition of the power and greatness of God is a fundamental moment of all religion, for it is written in the heart of every person that God is all-powerful and all-knowing. Further, we are able to recognize the justice of God. We do not worship God as an impersonal highest being, but rather seek to enter into a dialogue with him that involves calling upon him and receiving something from him. "Therefore all men know that God is our Refuge, and they implore his help and protection."[18] In the hearts of all people, therefore, the knowledge is planted that God helps and upholds those in distress and in crisis. Nevertheless, this God-given knowledge, according to Luther, has been wrongly interpreted, for these deeds are not attributed to the true God but rather to false objects, namely idols. People can indeed be monotheists, that is, believe rightly that there is but one God, but this too can be twisted into the worship of a false god. The knowledge that there is a deity who is just, helps in time of need, and guides and rules all things is not accorded to the one God but is transferred to a pseudo-god or an idol.

We encounter here, according to Luther, a threefold limitation of the general knowledge of God. First, without the self-revelation of God in Jesus Christ the knowledge of God is subjective, for it lacks the corrective of the revelatory Christ event. Second, the knowledge of God is threatened by the sinful efforts of human beings to change

18. Luther, on Gen. 43:23, *Lectures on Genesis* (1535–45): *LW* 7:336.

the true knowledge of God through their own wishes or conceptions. Finally, the general knowledge of God is only a preliminary stage on our way to God, in view of his revelation in Jesus Christ, which is a better alternative that replaces it. Those who continue to follow a general knowledge search for a God of their own wishes and desires, and not the true God who reveals himself finally in Jesus Christ.

Subjectivity of the General Knowledge of God

According to Luther the most severe problem of the natural knowledge of God is its subjective character. Because everyone pictures God as they see fit, the result is the diverse human forms of God's veneration, because "as each one shapes a god for himself, so he also worships."[19]

Similarly, the natural law, which is supposed to be binding for our ethical behavior, is interpreted in different and often contradicting ways. Some consider good what others despise as bad and vice versa, for the orders established by God can be understood in very different ways. In Luther's view, God always encounters us just as we imagine God to be. If we think, for example, that God is angry, then so he is for us. "The God you believe in is the God that you have. If you believe that God is gracious and merciful, you will such a God."[20] The general knowledge of God, therefore, adapts itself to our own subjective conceptions, so that God becomes what we trust in and what brings us happiness. With this we find ourselves standing before a subjective projection of God. That does not mean, however, that God adapts to suit our wishes; it means only that our conceptions of him are changeable. Instead of trusting in God we believe in a deity of our own wishful thinking. Hence it is, according to Luther,

---

19. Luther, on Jon. 1:4, *Lectures on Jonah*, Latin text (1525), in *LW* 19:11.
20. Luther, in a sermon from September 10, 1525 on Luke 17:11–13, in *WA* 17 I:412.19–20.

of utmost importance to have "a correct and proper feeling about God."[21]

The fact that we believe in God is not decisive, but rather that we believe rightly in God, or, what for Luther was the same thing, that we believe in the right God. The danger of projection in a general divine knowledge consists in the fact that this knowledge is not allowed to be guided by God but that he is made to adapt to our own wishes. For Luther, an example of this is to be found in pagans, who "did not worship this divinity untouched [that is, the deity as manifested to them] but changed and adjusted it to their desires and needs."[22] Because the general knowledge of God has no corrective outside of the created order, it usually proclaims a projection of human desires as divine.

Limits of a General Knowledge of God

As Luther continually emphasized, all of us have some inkling of God. But we usually develop it in such a way that it results in a caricature of him. Our sense and understanding transform our knowledge about God into a fantasized picture. The idolatry that follows from this is a distortion of the true religion and led Luther to comment sarcastically that "religion, however, is the greatest of all human achievements" (*Religio autem est optima omnium humanorum operum*).[23] In this way Luther would agree with the German nineteenth-century philosopher Ludwig Feuerbach (1804–72) that religion is a projection of the human mind. Because human reason does not let itself be led by God, its knowledge of him is consequently false and inappropriate. In this way religion degenerates into pseudo-religion and the worship of God becomes nothing more than the

---

21. Luther, on Jon. 1:4, *Lectures on Jonah*, Latin text (1525), in *LW* 19:11.
22. Luther, on Rom. 1:19, *Lectures on Romans* (1515–16), in *LW* 25:157.
23. Luther, on Isa. 65:1, *Vorlesung über Jesaia* (1527–29), in *WA* 25:383.10–11.

veneration of idols. Luther would agree with the claim of the Austrian ethnologist Wilhelm Schmidt (1868–1954) of an original monotheism, meaning that all peoples originally had one religion. Yet through human sinfulness this religion fragmented and degenerated into various individual religions. In regard to a genuine knowledge of God in today's religions, one can speak only of general fundamental conceptions but not of concrete and correct details.

Insufficiency of a Natural Knowledge of God

Due to our alienation from God we cannot correctly interpret his work in the world. We tend to confuse cause and effect and to see ourselves as the author of that which is actually God's work, while at the same time we view our own work as coming from God. The work of God, however, should not be difficult to recognize, for it always aims at the preservation and salvation of both us and the world. Since God uses the cooperation of his creatures as his instruments in sustaining and working in the world, humans are often led to the false assumption that they themselves are the agents of this work. Also, in observing the natural order, humans often conclude that everything takes place by natural means and that nature is grounded in itself. The sinful alienation of human beings from God has already progressed so far that they dispute the efficacy of God and put the causes of all occurrences down to immanent effects. God, in the process, becomes superfluous. Because the natural knowledge of God is prone to so many misunderstandings, it cannot serve as the starting point of faith for Luther.

Special Knowledge of God

According to Luther there is only one appropriate knowledge of God, namely God's Word that took on human form in Jesus Christ.

Hence Luther writes that Christ is like God: "He does not desire that you wander all over looking for him, but where the Word is, there you should go; and so you grasp him correctly. Otherwise you tempt God and fall prey to idolatry. For this reason God has given us a particular manner as to how and where we would seek and find God, namely through the Word."[24] Luther rejects the natural knowledge of God for Christians when he says, "It is extremely dumb to want to endeavor to know God. Therefore one should remain with the Word." (*Stultissimum, ut darnach trachten eum cogoscere. Idea haerendum in verbo*).[25] Seen from the perspective of Christian faith the natural knowledge of God is able to tell us very little. "If God had wished to be known to us through reason, then God would not have come to us in the flesh."[26] Through the revelation in Christ the knowledge of God has taken on a new and deeper dimension because, as Luther writes in his exposition of the book of Jonah, a great advantage is to be seen is this manner of revelation: "So there is a vast difference between knowing that there is a God and knowing who or what God is. Nature knows the former—it is inscribed in everybody's heart; the latter is taught only by the Holy Spirit."[27]

The knowledge of God through the revelatory Christ event takes place through God alone. God becomes human and thereby is able to be known by us, yet as the object of our knowledge God remains always God. God manifests God's self to us in his self-revelation in a concrete human form. For Luther, revelation in this context implies first of all the self-manifestation and self-objectification of God. The logical epistemological premise that something can only be known by that which is similar to it remains valid here. Hence God takes

---

24. Luther, *Sermon von dem Sakrament* (1526), in *WA* 19:492.22–26.
25. Luther, *Predigten über das 5. Buch Mose* (1529), in *WA* 28:608.8–9.
26. Luther, in a scholia of 1534 on Isaiah 4, *Vorlesungen über Jesaia* (1527–29), in *WA* 25:106.43–44.
27. Luther, commenting on Jon. 1:5, *Lectures on Jonah* (1526), in *LW* 19:55.

the initiative in the act of revelation and in its acknowledgement. Revelation is not a lesson about God that relates to us certain facts about him, but rather a self-disclosure in which God makes his own self known. God reveals himself either in human hearts or in an external word. According to Luther, the revelation in the human heart is not a mystical indwelling of God but is comparable to the knowledge that God has taken on human form. God does not, however, reveal God's self in such a way that God is fully absorbed into this revelation, for despite becoming human, "God does not leave heaven."[28] This self-disclosure does not only tell us that God is and what God's attributes are, but discloses to us God's internal and otherwise unfathomable being. Hence in contrast to the general knowledge of God, this knowledge does not remain a surface knowledge but leads to God's innermost intentions.

In God's self-disclosure that which is without limits takes on a bodily form—the person of Jesus Christ. God is not comprehensible, unless God allows his own self to be comprehended. In analogy to the real presence of Christ in the Eucharist, in which the living Christ is present in bread and wine, the omnipresent God becomes visible to us in the revelatory Christ event in a specific place and time. That which is finite is enabled to take up the infinite into itself. Humans find God, therefore, in visible form in the historical revelation of the Christ event. When God discloses God's self, God must at the same time enter into the created order, into the categories of space and time, to encounter us beneath the mere "outward appearance" of that work.

---

28. Luther, in a sermon on Genesis 11, *Predigten über das erste Buch Mose* (1523–24), in *WA* 14:213.13.

Incarnation as God's Entry Point into History

The almighty, infinite God came in the incarnation of Jesus Christ into our finite world. For this reason Luther calls the incarnation God's greatest work, which contradicts all the rules of human logic. The life of Jesus is the center point of God's self-disclosure, for in a unique, historical event in the fate of a concrete, historical person, the Eternal One has entered into history. The place we can comprehend God is not in nature, as pantheism claims, but in the life of a single, historical person. The humanity of Jesus becomes our point of access to the unknowable transcendence of God. God becomes knowable for us by entering into creation in space and time, that is, in the categories in which God works in the natural order and in which we are able to know God.

When God becomes a part of human history, he also comes into contact with our sinful alienation from him. Yet he does not himself become sinful, but deals instead with our sin. Jesus Christ, as the Wholly Other, stands completely on our side in order to bring God to us. God's order has been distorted through the antigodly powers of destruction, but he lives within it so that through him God can come close enough to us that we are able to recognize him. Because God takes on human form in his self-disclosure, anthropomorphic characteristics of this revelation are unavoidable.

Anthropomorphic Characteristics of God's Self-Disclosure

God has not changed in this self-revelation. As accommodation to our finite nature, which is alienated from God and which the infinite God cannot accept, God has disclosed his own self in the incarnation in a way that is appropriate to human beings. Since God came to us in a human being, we make use of anthropomorphic concepts to describe God's activity. For instance, we say that God speaks to us in a friendly manner, is happy, sad, or suffers, as can be seen especially in the Old Testament, which Luther interprets in a christocentric manner. We must necessarily speak of God's works using human concepts, or else remain silent. This does not mean that God becomes a new being in this self-disclosure, but rather that God shows to us what God really is and always has been as a hidden, transcendent being.

But this self-disclosure is not a depiction of God in which God still remains secluded. True, God does not exhaust his own self in this self-revelation, but remains God (*deus ipse*). Yet now God meets us in two ways: first, almighty and sovereign as the mysterious God, the *deus absconditus,* the hidden God who makes us tremble. This kind of God image is especially pronounced in the wrath of God. Then there is the revealed God (*deus revelatus*) in Jesus Christ, who desires our communion. This is the one to whom we should turn, and not to the unfathomable and hidden God who causes in many persons not only confusion, but also fear and despair. The distinction between God as he is (*deus ipse*) and the revealed God (*deus revelatus*) guards Luther against the radical personification of the idea of God, which would mean that God is nothing other than a fully perfected human, as the philosopher Ludwig Feuerbach contended. God cannot be fully grasped in the personal categories we use to describe him. Rather, it is the other way around. We cannot make any concrete statements about the very being of God, God's very self, but only about the Word of God. God is revealed and manifests his loving will in God's Word and in his Son. What God is like in and of God's own self is neither of interest to us nor necessary for our salvation. Only God's self-disclosure, God's Word, and the gospel are decisive for us. Luther had no interest in a speculative theology, but only in a theology spawned by the practical life issues of human beings. This is to be seen in the fact that for Luther all knowledge of God proceeds from God's revelation in Jesus Christ.

Knowledge of God through Christ

In a table talk from 1531–32 Luther declared, "True theology is practical, and its foundation is Christ, whose death is appropriated through faith." (*Vera theologia est practica, et fundamentum eius est Christus, cuius mors fide apprehenditur*).[29] Three aspects of this statement are important:

1. The foundation of theology is Christ.
2. The work of Christ is only understood through faith.
3. True theology is practically oriented, that is, it is directed toward the redemption of human beings.

Luther, in an anti-speculative way, centers his theology in Christ and the redemption that he has wrought. Only through the person of Jesus can one rightly draw near to God, for "the humanity [of Christ] is that holy ladder of ours . . . by which we ascend to the knowledge of God."[30] The unique position of Jesus consists in the fact that it is through the imprint of his words and actions that we come to the knowledge that God loves us. Jesus is the loving connection and the comforting glimpse to God. Only when we begin with Christ are we able to make appropriate statements about God and God's work, because through the unity of Father's and the Son's will God relates to us just as the Son relates to us. In Jesus Christ, the human face of God, God has disclosed to us his heart. True knowledge of God is not speculation about God, but rather the knowledge of the Father's will, which is made known in the sending of the Son.

29. Luther, "Table Talk," no. 153, in *LW* 54:22.
30. Luther, commenting on Heb. 1:2, *Lectures on Hebrews* (1517), in *LW* 29:111.

Luther can even make the excessive claim that "the visible God was fully hidden to humanity before the advent of Christ."[31] It is only through Christ that we are able to move from an outside view of God to an inside view. From the actions of God in Christ we learn that God loves and accepts his creation. Christ, therefore, is not primarily significant as preacher, miracle worker, or moral teacher, but as mediator of the divine redemptive will. Christ points to the goal of God's work that moves unalterably toward its completion, toward the triumph of God's loving will in a new, purified creation. Yet in Luther's view it is not sufficient to simply look to Christ, because others do that as well and then interpret him according to their own preferences. We must rather look correctly to Christ.

Theology of the Cross as Guiding Principle

In his commentary on the Psalms Luther contended, "The cross alone is our theology" (CRUX sola est nostra Theologia).[32] He separated himself thereby from a mystical or speculative theology and centered all his thinking on the revelation of God in Christ. The cross of Christ becomes the center from which one views all theological statements. In adopting this approach, Luther does not follow the popular medieval theology of the imitation of Christ, but stresses instead the nearly incomprehensible outrageousness of the Christ event, because this Christ has suffered in our place. The theology of the cross, which focuses on the historical figure of Jesus and his death on the cross, stands in contrast to every speculative theology that consciously and in light of concrete human history seeks to make understandable God's saving activity. Luther never tires of emphasizing that Jesus and his death on the cross contradict all human ideas about what God must do to achieve our salvation. Hence we

---

31. Luther, in his explanation of Psalm 25, *Dictata super Psalterium* (1513–16), in *WA* 3:143.9–10.
32. Luther, in his explanation of Ps. 5:12, *Operationes in Psalmos* (1519–21), in *WA* 5:176.32–33.

dare not begin with how God (according to our own ideas) must act, but we must instead hold firm in our thinking to how he actually did act.

For Luther the theology of the cross has the same significance as our reflection on the incarnation of God. Hence he contends in the *Heidelberg Disputation* of 1518 that "true theology and recognition of God are in the crucified Christ." (*Ergo in Christ crucifixo est vera Theologia et cognitio Dei*).[33] If one wishes to know God, according to Luther, one must not attempt to force one's way directly to the majesty of God through reason but must rather focus on the incarnation of God. The sign under which God's self-disclosure in Christ must occur is the cross, for this is the work of God that destroys and condemns our "reasonable" deliberations. If we would have thought out God's salvation, we would have thought of something great and impressive and not of a shameful cross. Therefore salvation on the cross cannot be a human invention. God wills to be known in the weakness of the figure of the crucified Christ so that he might annihilate our wisdom, which imagines God's revelation to be very different. The cross as the sign of the revelation of God also guards against deceitful imitations. While the majesty of God can easily be counterfeited into a fantasized image of our own ideas, the cross will not be imitated or distorted by any religion, philosophical speculation, or by our own fantasy. "One cannot love the cross," remarked Jürgen Moltmann (b. 1926), a Reformed theologian following Luther on this point; what is not loved will also not be imitated. Therefore it cannot be a human invention that God let his Son die on the cross in order that we might be redeemed. Apart from this, the cross of Christ also means that Christ, as a sign of his solidarity with humans, intentionally wishes to

33. Luther, in his explanation of thesis 20 of the *Heidelberg Disputation*, in *LW* 31:53.

be weak in order to place himself on the same level as humans and to suffer along with us on earth.

For Luther it is an outrageous thing that God would be born as a child and die on a cross. One cannot understand this event through human speculation. Instead, God must lead our understanding if we are to recognize the meaning of this event. But whoever bypasses Christ does not recognize in him the hidden God. Such persons are called "enemies of the cross" by Luther because they discard the value system of God. They label as bad the good of the cross, that is, the incarnation of God; and they call good all that is bad in their own thoughts, that is, their abstract, philosophical reasoning.[34] Although the cross looks bad and unappealing on the outside, it is not something bad, but rather something good, because Christ and thereby God has made it his own and has destroyed the bad works of the exalted. Bad works are those through which one hopes to stand before God, including speculative theology, through which one seeks of his or her own power to fathom God.

The theology of the cross, however, points not only to the cross, and the humbling and incarnation of God; it is also for Luther an indication that God always works under the appearance of the opposite. Luther is clear when he contends that in Christ God brought to perfection when he destroyed, that he made alive when he crucified, that he saved when he judged, indeed, that he revealed himself when he veiled himself. Hence Luther can name the cross the true negative theology.[35] God works, according to Luther, like a dental surgeon who makes dangerous, difficult, and disfiguring incisions but nevertheless does good work.[36] Even if one is at first afraid that things are only going to get worse, nonetheless the

---

34. Luther, on thesis 21, ibid.
35. Cf. Luther in his exposition of Ps. 90:7, *Enarratio Psalmi XC* (1534–35), in *WA* 40 III:543.1–2.
36. So Luther in his explanation of thesis 6 of the *Heidelberg Disputation*, in *LW* 31:45.

surprising healing process comes in the end and the pain is replaced by a feeling of well-being.

Two aspects of this work of God under the appearance of the opposite need special emphasis:

1. Every self-achieved knowledge of God is shattered on the cross of Christ. Luther once said that there is no religion in which reason is made to seem so absurd and stupid as in the Christian religion, yet he nevertheless believes in Jesus Christ. Through the hiddenness of God in his saving work on the cross all the wisdom of the world is refuted. God wishes to be recognized only in suffering and to condemn all wisdom that seeks to comprehend things unseen with the help of those things that are seen. God must open our eyes so that we can rightly recognize his miraculous work, the cross of Christ, and its true meaning.

2. An ascending knowledge of God that seeks to work its way up from us to God or one that, in contrast, begins with the mysteries of God is destined to fail. God can only be known when we allow ourselves to be taken by God into God's astounding work on the cross.

Why does Luther so strongly emphasize the hiddenness of God's work under the appearance of the opposite? He intends thereby not just to say that God does not wish to be sought where God has not revealed his own self; it is also decisive for Luther that God alone, in the revelatory event, is the one who works. God chose the way of the cross that he might remain the sovereign Lord of all saving work and of the entire revelatory event. No one expected this event to occur as it actually did. Even the so-called astrologers inquired first in Jerusalem about the newborn king of the Jews, not in unimportant Bethlehem (Matt. 2:2). Yet God does not allow his own self or the divine self-disclosure to be grasped by any rational principle. Only on the basis of that which has taken place can we describe it, and then only in approximation. But are we then completely dependent on faith, that is, to the repetition of that which God first tells us, so that there remains no place from reason?

3

Faith and Reason

It has often been concluded that reason is of little value to Luther since justification is through faith alone. Moreover he described reason as a "whore," joining the person who adduces the most persuasive arguments. Luther, however, neither despised reason nor spoke of a simplistic, unquestioning belief in the word of God. As a university graduate, who had a BA, a MA, and a PhD behind his name, he was well-schooled in the use of reason, that is, in logical thinking. He also possessed a healthy measure of natural curiosity. He wanted very much to determine, for instance, exactly what took place when one fell asleep. Yet he was never successful in this. He would lay awake in bed and suddenly he was asleep. He was of the opinion that death must be a very similar experience: "For just as we do not known what happens to us when we fall asleep and all of a sudden it is morning when we awake, so will we suddenly arise on judgment day, not knowing how we died and how we came through death."[1]

---

1. Luther, in a sermon on Judica Sunday on John 8:46–59, *Fastenpostille* (1525), in *WA* 17/2:235.17–20.

He makes use here of his powerful gift of observation in order to illustrate a theological point. As Luther's criticism of the Epistle of James shows, he also used reason for the expression of theological critique for, since this epistle nowhere mentions Christ, he did not believe it could have much theological value. In Luther's opinion this epistle is on the fringe of the New Testament, a fact that many New Testament experts have since then confirmed. When Luther speaks of *ratio* (reason) or faith one must also carefully note the connection in which he uses these terms. Reason is, for Luther, first of all a gift of God meant to serve the fulfillment of earthly tasks. Because reason can be led us astray by our sinful arrogance, it can only arrive at the right conclusion in matters pertaining to God when it is led by the Holy Spirit.

Significance and Limitations of Reason

If we use reason in our sinful inclinations, for instance to cheat a person, this shows at once that reason is no impartial means. It is subject to our intentions. Yet it does not simply belong to us. It is foremost a gift of God to be used and treasured as such a gift.

Reason as a Gift of God

In his explanation of the first article of the Apostles' Creed in the *Small Catechism*, Luther writes, "I believe that God has created me together with all that exists. God has given me and still preserves my body and soul: eyes, ears, and all my limbs and senses, reason and all mental faculties."[2] Humans have received reason as a part of their very nature from God. Hence reason is a good gift of God. It distinguishes humans from other creatures, and because of this we are

---

2. Luther, *The Small Catechism*, in *Book of Concord: The Confessions of the Evangelical Lutheran Church*, ed. Robert Kolb and Timothy J. Wengert (Minneapolis: Fortress Press, 2000), 345.

called to have dominion over creation. Human reason is the source and conduit of all human culture; it is the foundation of legislation, the arts, and human inventiveness. Luther can therefore say, "It is certainly true that reason is the most important and the highest in rank among all things and, in comparison with other things of this life, the best and something divine."[3] Luther also welcomed the efforts of the humanists to bring the sciences to bloom through the study of ancient texts and languages.

It is the regal duty of reason to serve this earthly life. It is the highest court of appeal in the world and has the task of judging norms and putting forward decisions concerning the correct order and administration of worldly things. Even theology may not hinder reason in these tasks, for theology does not question the structures of public life, nor does it discover any new arts. Theology must acknowledge the validity of reason in these areas and recognize it as a creation of God. Yet it must always be made clear that reason serves only to this end: that we might live in the world in an orderly fashion.

Reason as an Instrument of World Order

Luther stresses that "reason, as beautiful and wonderful as it is, belongs exclusively in the worldly realm where it has its dominion and its kingdom. But in the kingdom of Christ the Word of God alone has the say."[4] Reason is related to the world; but the word of God, that is, the gospel, has to do with the kingdom of Christ. We find ourselves, therefore, in two different realms of being: in the kingdom of the world, which is ordered through reason, and in the kingdom of Christ, or of faith. Luther makes a similar distinction elsewhere when he writes,

---

3. Luther, *The Disputation concerning Man* (1536), in *LW* 34:137.
4. Luther, on Exod. 13:11–13, *Predigten über das 2. Buch Mose* (1524–27), in *WA* 16:261.29–32.

In temporal things and in those things which concern human beings the person has enough reason and needs no other light apart from reason. Thus God does not teach in the Scriptures how one is to build houses, make clothing, marry, go to war, sail ships, or other similar things, for in these matters the natural light of reason is sufficient. But in divine things, that is, in those things which concern God—for instance that humans do what is pleasing to God and thereby become holy—in these matters human nature is so stone stiff and completely blind that it cannot even to the extent of a hair's breadth show us what these things are. It is presumptuous enough to tackle such matters and to stumble into them like a blind horse, but everything which it discusses and determines is as surely false and in error as God lives.[5]

This distinction also demonstrates that the Bible as God's word cannot be used as a textbook for biology or history. Knowledge in these fields is gained through reason alone, indeed, through the natural and historical sciences.

On the other hand, reason cannot dispute the fact that God created human beings and the world or that history ultimately depends upon the will of God. If reason seeks to make statements about whether humans are a creation of God or whether history corresponds to God's will, then reason, according to Luther, is overstepping its area of competence. Reason must restrict itself to that which it has access to, namely the knowledge of the world. Reason must leave open the question whether there are other areas that impact upon our existence over and above its own area of competence as a knowing and valuating capacity. Hence, when we speak of an ultimate meaning or final cause of human existence, reason can only examine the internal, formal logic of such statements; it is not able to take a position as to their legitimacy. We are confronted here with a distinction between the physical world that we can see and touch, and the noumenal world, the world in itself, as Immanuel Kant later

5. Luther, in a sermon on Isa. 60:1–6, *Kirchenpostille* (1522), in *WA* 10/I/1:531.6–16.

described it. Our understanding and reason, in Luther's view, are much too limited to comprehend the world in itself and the majesty of God hidden behind it.

Reason that concerns itself with the world, however, presents its own problems for humanity. We no longer live in an original unity with God, but rather in opposition to him. The self-glorifying sinfulness of human beings now impairs even the use of reason to uphold order in the world. For Luther it is indeed clear that the logical, technical, and cultural abilities of reason have not been destroyed through our alienation from God. Even for sinners 2+2=4. Yet the danger remains that the person as sinner will use reason to further his or her own sinful self-glorification and, for example, in drawing up a bill will egoistically pervert reason such that 2+2=5. Indeed, Luther concedes that a sinful and godless person can be a good and upright ruler, parent, or business person. Atheists cannot be morally disqualified from the very beginning. Yet fallen humans are faced with the temptation to misuse reason. This can occur in a twofold way. They can be untrue to their duty to live as God would have them to live. Or they can conceal and ignore the one who gave them reason and made possible their achievements in the first place. They boast of their own accomplishments and insist that they themselves have brought all them about rather than to thankfully acknowledge that it was God who gave them reason. Reason is then misused for one's own glory, instead of serving to honor and glorify God. Even Christians are not immune to this, and therefore they require daily contrition and repentance. With non-Christians the danger is even greater, for they consider the misuse of reason to be natural and are therefore often not aware of their false path.

In matters of faith, too, natural reason comes to totally erroneous conclusions. "Natural reason produces heresy and error; faith teaches and holds to the truth, for it clings to the Scriptures which neither deceive nor lie."[6] That means that reason, as a substitute for faith, misses God and creates for itself a false god. Luther characterizes reason as a whore or a fool, for it lets itself be influenced by human intentions, instead of unalterably leading humans to do that which is right. Because reason is restricted to this world and earthly reality serves as its final standard, it stands immovable in its contrast to faith. The reality of which faith speaks is not real for reason. Hence it often seeks to oppose faith. This very possible dissonance shows itself even today, for example, in the frequent discord between the natural sciences and Christian faith. But scientific results as pure knowledge of the world cannot stand in opposition to faith because the logical structure of the creation cannot oppose its Creator. Only certain interpretations of this structure that are viewed in isolation can stand in contrast to faith in God the Creator. The world that is fathomed by reason must not, according to Luther, be seen for its own sake but must always ultimately be connected to God as the source and goal of all that is. Only in this way can the question of meaning that arises out of the world be resolved.

In Luther's view the essential correspondence of reason with natural law likewise leads human beings to forget God and to seek a this-worldly explanation for everything. According to natural law, which is directed toward reasonable behavior, there exists a strict causal connection between cause and effect. Popular wisdom has expressed this with the proverb: "He who makes his bed must lie in it." If this causal connection were also to be applied to human salvation, one could conclude that salvation could be obtained through right behavior. Yet such a work's righteousness contradicts the preceding grace of God through which God offers us communion with him. We ourselves can never work our way to

---

6. Luther, in a sermon on John 1:1–14, *Kirchenpostille* (1522), in *WA* 10/I/1:191.14–16.

God. Save for the "wonderful" reign of God, through which he gives us his grace, reason is closed off, blind, and deaf.[7] If reason wishes to address matters of the gospel, it must first be renewed through the Holy Spirit.

Of course, the laws of logic are valid as applied to the *structure* of statements of faith even without the work of the Holy Spirit. But without faith and the knowledge of God reason stumbles about in the dark in regard to the content of faith because it is limited to purely this-worldly relationships and analogies. Yet through the acknowledgment of the work of God reason becomes a highly effective instrument for the faithful. Purified reason that recognizes its boundaries serves the faithful as an instrument for reflection, proclamation, and convincing of the truthfulness of the gospel. It becomes theological reason and helps to rightly understand and expound the Scriptures. In this way reason serves faith, but does not abolish it by setting itself and its own constructions in the place of faith. In this connection reason must not be seen as standing in opposition to faith, but reason has instead in its explication of faith a meaningful and important assignment. Faith, however, is not grounded through reason but through God. Both reason and faith are God's gifts. They must not be viewed as mutually independent of one another, but as being dependent upon God so that they are able to serve us in a complementary fashion. But what precisely does Luther mean by "faith"?

Content and Structure of Faith

One is often tempted to portray Martin Luther as a pure subjectivist when speaking of his understanding of faith. This is supported by

7. Cf. Luther in his sermon from December 21, 1536 in Lichtenberg, *Predigten des Jahres 1536*, in *WA* 41:736.23–737.9, where he clearly speaks about how limited reason is in its knowledge of God's work.

statements such as, "We have as much as we believe and hope," or "You have as much as you believe."[8] Faith seems to be nothing more than a projection of one's own wishes, as Ludwig Feuerbach claimed in the nineteenth century, believing he was following Luther in this point. This assumption, however, has been and still is wrong. Luther did not understand faith as agreement with particular articles of belief, but rather as total, fundamental trust in God. Faith for Luther is personal trust, just as I have faith in someone, meaning I trust him or her. We have a much better personal relationship with someone when we totally trust this person than when we trust the other person only half-heartedly. Trust also sheds light on the relationship between believing and having. If we completely trust someone we become totally involved with that person so that we rely upon that person.

Faith as Personal Trust

With Luther one must first of all distinguish between two forms of faith: so-called historical faith and existential faith. Luther once distinguished between them in the following manner:

> I have often spoken of two types of faith. You believe that Christ is such a man as described here and preached in the entire gospel; but you do not believe that he is such a man for you. You question whether you have and will have such from him and you think: yes, he is such a man for others like Peter, Paul, and the pious saints; but who knows how he stands to me and whether I should rely on him and put my trust in him just as these saints do? Behold, this kind of faith is nothing, it neither receives nor tastes Christ [in the Eucharist] and can also not feel any desire or love for him. It is a faith about and not a faith in Christ, it is a faith held even by the devils and all evil persons.[9]

---

8. Luther, commenting on Psalm 33, *Dictata super Psalterium* (1513–16), in *WA* 3:180.26; and in *The Sacrament of Penance* (1519), in *LW* 35:16.

9. Luther, in a sermon on Matt. 21:1–9, *Adventpostille* (1525), in *WA* 10/I/2:24.2–13.

Luther can speak very drastically to say that even the devil has faith. Even the devil admits that Christ lived on the earth as a human being, died, and rose again. Yet the devil does not connect this with an existential faith that Christ came upon the earth, died, and rose again for him. Because this existential faith is missing in him, he must remain alienated from God and cannot acknowledge Christ as his Lord. In another context Luther says that historical faith does not save. Historical faith is intimately connected with reason, since it either focuses on items that can be known (by reason) or on items one simply holds to be true. But we can believe very much, hold it to be true, and nevertheless have no existential relationship to God.

Faith, for Luther, is a deeply existential matter. Luther is not irrational, so that faith would be another form of being gullible, nor does he oppose reason. For Luther faith emphasizes the connection of something or someone with our own existence above the purely factual. It points to another dimension beyond that which can be empirically discerned. This becomes clear in Luther's exposition of the Apostles' Creed. In explaining the first article, which reads, "I believe in God, the Father almighty, Creator of heaven and earth," Luther says,

> I believe that God has created me together with all that exists. God has given me and still preserves my body and soul; eyes, ears, and all limbs and senses; reason and mental faculties." Likewise, in regard to the second article, he writes: ".I believe that Jesus Christ, true God, begotten of the Father in eternity, and also a true human being, born of the Virgin Mary, is my Lord. He has redeemed me.[10]

Concerning the third article, Luther writes similarly about faith in the Holy Spirit and in the holy Christian church: "I believe that by my own understanding or strength I cannot believe in Jesus

---

10. Luther, *The Small Catechism*, in *The Book of Concord*, 354–55.

Christ my Lord or come to him, but instead the Holy Spirit has called me."[11] Faith does not consist simply in the listing of data but establishes the existential relationship to particular facts. This presupposes the personal Other that is the object of faith and through whom faith is made possible, strengthened, and guided. But because God and Christ are not immediately and physically present, our faith is oriented in the first instance toward the word.

Word of God and Faith

One cannot comprehend Luther's understanding of faith when the word of God is not taken into consideration, for both belong inseparably together. God calls us to faith through the word, and God works faith through it, while at the same time faith is directed by this same word. God can only be rightly known through his word. According to Luther true faith can only be directed toward God, for it is God alone whom we can trust absolutely. Faith is trust in God. When we present ourselves unconditionally to God, then God will really be treated as God, namely as the One to whom an unlimited relationship of trust is possible. If we reserve a certain area for ourselves and shut God out of it, then we are like the persons in the story of the temptation. In the form of the serpent, the tempter insinuated to Eve that she didn't necessarily have to take God so seriously and could decide something without God's knowledge of it. With this she fell from faith and from her relationship of trust in God. When we grasp hold of the word in which God makes known to us that he is gracious, then God becomes real for us. God becomes for us a living God and does not remain an abstract idea.

In the relationship between faith and the word it is decisive that God's word always precedes faith. It is not I who seek my God,

---

11. Luther, ibid., 355.

but the Christian message first addresses me. Hence my faith is not grounded upon my decision or my searching, but rather upon the prior word of God. True faith is not the result of human effort and is therefore not a human work, but instead is a gift of God. God speaks to us in and through faith. Of course human beings, when they hear the gospel, are intellectually able to respond to God with a yes and can willingly do this. But for Luther faith is more that an affirmative confirmation, such as one might give to a weather report when one agrees with the forecast. Faith is directed toward the God who encounters us in revelation and consequently encompasses our entire existence. In 1522, in the preface of his translation of Paul's Epistle to the Romans, Luther wrote,

> Faith is not the human notion and dream that some people call faith. . . . When they hear the gospel, they get busy, and by their own powers create an idea in their hearts, which says, "I believe"; they take this then to be a true faith. But, as it is a human figment and idea that never reaches the depths of the heart, nothing comes of it either and no improvement follows.[12]

Faith as one's own decision for God is a preposterous presumption. It would entail believing that we are able by our own power to turn again to God and to undo all the past things that separate us from God. Faith, however, is much more the invitation of God, through which, without our deserving it, he gives us again that Other whom we seek but cannot find on our own. Everything, therefore, depends upon the word that God surprisingly and undeservingly gives us and that lifts us to a level on which we come into contact with the living source of our life. The word of God meets us in our existence that is estranged from God and makes possible and demands the answer of faith.

12. Luther, *Preface to the Epistle of St. Paul to the Romans* (1522), in *LW* 35:370.

Since faith is a personal and existential affair, Luther continually stressed that no one can believe for another. Everyone must be responsible for their own faith. Yet faith is not an individual matter, even if Protestantism after Luther often gave this impression. The believer is never alone but is always part of a community of believers. This community is bound together by their common relationship to God. Hence not only do faith and God belong together, but also faith and community.

Luther often identifies the Word of God with the Scriptures and does not always make a distinction between the Word and the words. This is especially clear in the disputes over the Lord's Supper and Jesus' words, "This is my body." Against all efforts at a spiritualization of the meaning of the word *is* in the biblical text, Luther insists that this bread *is* Christ's body. Luther can therefore also demand a humble submission to the written word. His frank criticism of certain biblical writers or texts demonstrates, however, that this does not lead him to any kind of literalism regarding the Scriptures. Because Luther distinguishes between the center and the periphery of Scripture, he can take the Bible literally on one hand, and on the other hand can interpret it symbolically, according to the context of each particular text of Scripture. It was only the later Orthodoxy and Pietism that again "flattened" this contextual understanding of Scripture. Nonetheless, Luther has been often accused of having replaced the living pope with a paper one, that is, with the word of God. This accusation is, however, unfounded. Luther did not hold faith to be grounded in any external authority but rather in one's own experience of the trustworthiness of the divine Other. The danger of a subjectivism of faith is here ruled out inasmuch as Luther never relied on experience alone, but always had to verify this over against the word of Scripture. Hence he also fought decisively against the "Spiritualists," who despised the "external Word."

Assurance and Risk of Faith

Luther writes, "When you wish to say on your deathbed: the pope has said this, the councils have decided that, the holy fathers . . . have determined this, the devil will immediately bore a hole and break in asking, 'What if it is not true? Could it not be that they have erred?' So you are pushed right back down. Thus you must know without doubt that you can say, 'This is the Word of God and there I stand.'"[13] Faith is not interchangeable; one cannot replace one's faith with that of another. Everyone must believe for his or her own self. The community of faith can only provide help and direction. It cannot substitute for the risk and engagement of one's own faith. Of course Luther himself had many models for faith, such as the church fathers and the saints. Yet one's own existential decision of faith to trust in God wholly and without exception cannot be relieved by such models.

At the same time faith does not exist in isolation, for the word and the content of faith protect Christians in their hearts and consciences. God's word speaks to individuals and testifies to them in such a way that through this action every other mediating authority is eliminated. It comes down to, then, a direct encounter between one's own self and God's word. In regard to Luther many have spoken of a loneliness of faith in which the person as an individual stands before the almighty God without any protection or help. Luther himself had experienced something like this when, in 1521, he stood before the emperor at Worms without any protection and openly confessed his faith. Luther, to be sure, stresses that everyone must confess his or her own faith and must bear the consequences for decisions of faith. But he also recognized the necessity for mutual strengthening and encouraging in faith. Hence he mentions that the weaker our own

13. Luther, in a sermon on Matt. 7:15ff., *Predigten des Jahres 1522*, in *WA* 10/III:259.13–18.

faith is, the more we need the faith and prayers of others so that our faith will again become strong. While no one can make the ultimate decision of faith for another, it is nonetheless important for Christians that they do not stand alone in faith but are kept, encouraged, and supported through the community of faith.

Luther also does not understand faith as assent to that which one is otherwise able to verify. Faith stands directly in contrast to seeing and knowing. God's hiddenness and faith are mutually dependent. Luther can even say that God conceals himself and his saving work in order to make room for the faith to which he calls us. Faith is not a substitute for seeing or for scientific knowing but has rather to do with another dimension concerned with personal trust. So it is that all one's life faith remains subject to temptation, for it is beset by that which is visible, by the empirical, and by evidences. In this world faith is not able to take refuge in any "island of saints" and create a life of faith without threat and temptation. Faith, in the tradition of Luther, also stands in opposition to the methodological atheism of the natural sciences that systematically exclude faith from their view of reality. Over against such methodological atheism faith stands firm in protest, holding securely to belief in God as the ultimate source and goal of all that is.

Faith under Assault

The source of the threat to faith follows from the manner and way that God works in our world. In the first place, it is not empirically obvious that God is the source that stands behind all things, because God rarely intervenes directly in the events of the world. Additionally, God always works under the appearance of the opposite, that is, in a way that we would not expect God to work. Such divine activity is ambiguous because it stands in contradiction to what one might expect. It is therefore important for Luther that faith doesn't fall victim to temptation and let loose of God. Temptation and struggle are much more a school of faith that should teach us not to take the path of least resistance but rather to put our trust completely in God and to cling to his word. Even when God's word contradicts what seems to be obvious we must not give up, but should rather hold on trustingly to the previously demonstrated power of God's word to keep God's promises. God's word has proven itself and will continue to do so.

The experience of struggle and temptation (*Anfechtung*) also arises, according to Luther, from the law and gospel, the double form of God's word. While the law is often identical with the visible order, the gospel brings that which is surprising, unexpected, and often in opposition to the empirical. If we want to believe the gospel, we must at the same time believe in God against the law—that is to say, against reason and the empirical. One must flee directly from the word of the law to the word of the gospel, according to Luther, for "a Christian is the kind of hero, . . . who deals with all kinds of impossible matters."[14] But such heroism must constantly be practiced, as Luther says in his explanation of *The Small Catechism*, so that the old (timid and sinful) person within us daily is put to death and a new person arises who lives in purity and righteousness before God eternally. While faith must assert itself over against empirical experiences, it would be wrong to think that for Luther faith and experience are always at odds and stand opposed to one another. The Christian does not believe *despite* knowing better. Luther also knew the experience that produces and strengthens faith.

---

14. Luther, in a sermon on Mark 8:1–3. *Predigten des Jahres 1528*, in *WA* 27:276.8–9.

Faith and Experience

Experience makes faith what it is. The act of faith is indeed a pure risk, a complete reliance upon the word. One can compare the act of faith with learning to swim. If we are placed in deep water we no longer reflect on learning to swim. We are no longer able to live from the theory of swimming but take a risk and learn that we do not sink, and so our risk is justified in the act of swimming. Faith bears up, therefore, despite all the risks. Luther is even able to suggest that someone who thinks that his or her faith is certain perhaps doesn't have faith at all. This person is living much more from reflecting on faith than from the act of faith. At the same time, another person who seems to be bogged down in doubt in reality has a stronger faith because he or she does not go into deep water with calculations but with fear and trembling. Faith means to be certain of the word of God, but not certain of oneself as a believer. But still faith and experience belong together, for I experience the fact that the word of God is powerful over me, that it carries me and does not let me go.

Seen from a neutral distance, it is not possible to distinguish true faith from false faith. Only when faith actually takes place is this possible. False faith originates from human beings and focuses on the individual. True faith, however, originates from the Holy Spirit who is at work in the word. We experience true faith when we are touched by it existentially. It is as if we are taken hold of and led by God, and do not fall away from God as the true and powerful One even when we have doubts. We see an example of this in Luther at the Diet of Worms, where he confessed that his conscience is held prisoner by God's word. The person of faith, therefore, is not autonomous, but *theonomous*, subject to God's authority; such a person lives for God and from God.

The experience of faith for which God and not some fiction is both object and subject of faith does not remain unclouded. The risk of faith often seems to be irrational and against all reason. In this struggle, which Luther strongly emphasized and experienced himself, he doesn't present any ideological slogans of perseverance, but points instead to the empirical and historical anchoring of faith. In this regard his own baptism was especially important. With it he wished to show that he could not be abandoned by God when God had already said yes to him in baptism. In his dispute with the Anabaptists regarding the validity of infant baptism, he comforted himself with the fact that God would never have let something that was contrary to Scripture stand for so long. Yet he admitted that such a historical argument was not unambiguous. He ultimately found an argument that overcame his doubts about infant baptism in the invitation of Jesus: "Let the little children come to me" (Luke 18:16).

Even one's own history can become a faith experience. Luther writes, "At this point experience must enter in and enable a Christian to say: 'Hitherto I have heard that Christ is my Savior, who conquered sin and death; and I believed it. Now my experience bears this out. For I was often in the agony of death and in the bonds of the devil, but He rescued me and manifested Himself. Now I see and know that He loves me and that what I believe is true."[15] From the perspective of faith, one's own life history can be seen as a part of God's journey with us and as an evidence of God's grace. The person of faith experiences in his or her own life that in the word of God Christ is present with his power and overcomes sin, the devil, and deathly fear.

Faith is not grounded upon an experience that precedes it but rather, as a work of God, faith comes before the experience. First we

15. Luther, *Sermons on the Gospel of St. John* (1537), in *LW* 24:151.

believe the word, which means we trust God, and then it will be seen that this trust is not misplaced. What we believe even becomes the object of our experience. In the beginning there is the hearing of the word of God and faith in Jesus Christ. Then comes for Christians the experience of the reality of Christ in their hearts.

Nevertheless, the experience will not be an unlimited verification of faith and will not guarantee that the risk of trust was worthwhile. In the case of the love between two people, one's own subjective feelings repeatedly interfere with the reality of the common bond. These questions make us doubt whether we still have faith and whether this faith is in a living Other or in some fiction. The tension between faith and experience remains throughout our life. But it is not always of the same strength. Although there are ups and downs in the life of faith and in the certainty of faith, faith continually wins ground so that our own experience increasingly confirms our faith. The tension between faith and experience will only be broken when faith, at the eschatological completion of all things, itself becomes visible. "Only then will we be absolutely certain of what we have believed, namely, that death and all misfortune have been overcome."[16]

Following Luther, we must distinguish between certainty and security. Ultimate security is impossible for the venture of faith. Nevertheless the certainty increases so that the venture of faith is rewarding, because it opens a new dimension to God. Moreover, faith offers the only possibility of the encounter with this new dimension, in which our life is guided by God.

16. Luther, in a sermon on Mark 16:1–8, *Sommerpostille* (1526), in *WA* 10/I/2:223.6–8.

4

The Divinity of God

At the center of Martin Luther's theology stands the divinity of God. This could also be said for the Swiss Reformers Zwingli and Calvin. But for them the world is the stage on which God's sovereignty should and will be executed. Though Luther was interested in worldly affairs and God's workings in them, his emphasis was on the absolute human inability to domesticate God, to use God for our purposes. God is God and nevertheless this sovereign and almighty God cares for us, as shown in Jesus Christ, God's human face.

With his emphasis on God's sovereignty, Luther starkly contrasts with our modern view of life, influenced by the Enlightenment, that puts us humans in the center. We desire to have an important say in all matters that concern us, from the question of whether God treats us justly all the way to who will finally be included in God's saving will. Luther, however, has his own very different experience regarding human ability and insights. Medieval piety, out of which Luther came, was characterized by a fear of God's punishments and by the attempt to prove oneself to be well-pleasing to this God through indulgences, monastic asceticism, pilgrimages, and frequent attendance of worship services. Luther recognized, however, the immense difference between God and humans and between our finite abilities and God's omnipotence. Without God we cannot transcend our human limitations. Even with the best of intentions we are only able to partially realize our plans for our lives. Therefore God is not able to build upon anything we might contribute, but creates where there is practically nothing. God is from first to last the deciding force in the matter of our salvation. This emphasis upon the unconditional work of God within Luther's theology is based upon his realistic assessment of humanity. If human beings participate in a decisive way in salvation and in the governance of the world, then their finite power and limited insight make it uncertain until the very end whether or not the intended goal will be reached.

Efficacy of the Divine Will

It is characteristic of Luther's conception of God that God is not understood statically from the perspective of God's being but rather dynamically from the perspective of God's will. Luther sees in God the supreme will that can have no equal. God himself sets the standard by which his own will is measured. It is through his emphasis on God's will that Luther recovers a dynamic understanding of God, because the divine will is first and foremost action oriented.

God Is Continually at Work

God is the supreme will who is continually at work. God is not an inactive spectator of world history who in deistic fashion set the machinery of the world in motion and then retreated from the scene. Rather, God participates actively, decisively, and creatively in the events of this world. Luther does not understand this activity to be periodic or selective, for God does not take breaks and cease working, but is a continuously active power. God is also active everywhere; Christians need not fear anyone, since they are constantly under the protection of God's will.

God Is Almighty

God would not be God without the power to carry out his will. If God wanted to, according to Luther, he could transform a stone into water, the desert into food, nakedness into beautiful clothing, poverty into wealth, death into life, shame into glory, bad into good, and enemies into friends. There is nothing that God cannot do and no thing or condition that he cannot change. God's activity needs nothing and presupposes nothing, not even matter. Neither is God bound by the laws of nature, since they were the result of God's own creation, even though he works primarily within their limits. In *The Bondage of the Will* (1525), he writes, "The will of God is effectual and cannot be hindered."[1] God accomplishes everything through his will; God's counsel cannot be impeded and his will cannot be resisted. God created heaven and earth and is thus more powerful than these, even if many people do not believe it. No one can evade God's omnipotence, regardless of how ingeniously one might attempt to do so.

Luther's statements about the omnipotence of God could be derived from a theology of glory that seeks to shed light upon the omnipotence of God through logical deductions and speculation. Already in the Old Testament and in pagan writings Luther discovers such approaches, most of them arising out of a general knowledge of God. In the spirit of Luther one might even say that the knowledge of the omnipotence of God is not only to be gained from God's

1. Luther, *The Bondage of the Will* (1525), in *LW* 33:38.

self-disclosure in Jesus Christ, but that it is also testified to in other religions and in philosophy.

But why does Luther emphasize the omnipotence of God so strongly? First, it is affirmed by the testimony of Scripture. From the Scriptures Luther learns that God is Lord of lords. For Luther this is also attested to by the Hebrew word *adonai* (lord), a term often used in the Old Testament to speak of God. Through the miraculous signs in Egypt God demonstrated that "the gods" obey him and that he is more powerful than they are (cf. the Egyptian plagues in Exodus 7–10). And when the New Testament speaks of Christ sitting at the right hand of God, this provides an additional graphic expression of God's almighty power. Furthermore, Luther recognizes that the assertions of God's omnipotence are a central theological and christological concern. The credibility of the First Commandment and its promise depend upon these assertions, for if God were not almighty, God would merely be one god alongside of other gods. Even Christology is dependent upon the doctrine of God's omnipotence. How could Christ be our Lord and the Lord of all if God were not almighty? Hence the assertion of God's omnipotence is not only an attribute of God, but characterizes his very essence.

God Works Everything

The knowledge of God's influence is closely bound with that God's omnipotence. For Luther there was no question that everything that happens upon earth is under God's control. God pushes everything along, as it were, as an internal driving force. God's working is revealed first in nature, so that no leaf falls from a tree unless God wills it. It is then revealed in the saving activity of God, inasmuch as nobody can obtain salvation apart from the effective working of God. Finally, God's working is evident in our daily lives, for apart from the will of God we could not even eat or drink. God is even completely efficacious in the course of history. All earthly authorities rest in God's hand and God can lead them wherever he wills. Earthly authorities and governments are not capable of thinking of anything unless it is suggested by God. Because God brings about and reigns over all things, he also holds power over the future. God alone knows what will happen in the future and can thus disclose the future to us.

This emphasis upon God's working of all in all entails many problems. It encourages us to view God as the sole actor who alone controls all things. If God alone is behind good and evil, fortune and misfortune, God can assume demonic characteristics. This danger is not completely absent from Luther's line of thought. Yet Luther is primarily concerned with an important theological problem—namely, God's authorship of all that is good. This is safeguarded only when God works everything. God is, accordingly, good, wise, just, truthful, and merciful. If we did not view God as working of all in all and as the sole actor, then the divinity of God—in the sense that God is the author of the good—would be jeopardized. God would then be only one (divine) power among many and salvation, in an ultimately effectual sense, could not be hoped for from him.

But alongside of this important theological concern, which we must affirm, there remains the danger that the emphasis upon the sole activity of God will lead to a doctrine of absolute predestination. In his book *The Bondage of the Will*, Luther especially wrestled with the doctrine of predestination. The assertion that humans can only do for their salvation that which God does in them appears justified so long as we apply this assertion only to the matter of our own salvation. But if the premise that God is the sole actor is also used to argue that some people are excluded from salvation, then the premise bears with it the danger that God will be made into a god above and outside of the law, and thus a demon or a tyrant. An additional problem of the doctrine of God's working everything is that one views every occurrence upon earth as determined by God. It would then be only a question of time before this divine pan-causality would be secularized, preparing the way for a mechanistic worldview.

These problems, however, did not present themselves for Luther. His understanding of God was not derived in a speculative manner but was oriented toward the God who had revealed himself as the Father of Jesus Christ. God's sole activity was seen by Luther in the revelatory Christ event through which God disclosed himself to human beings and enabled them to understand this self-disclosure. As aforementioned, Luther's emphasis on God's Godhead came from the existential realization that only God can and will save us—nothing and nobody else. To that end God had to be in absolute control. Luther thus stressed the personal character of the revelation of God in Jesus Christ as well as the uniqueness of this self-revelation. Yet Luther was unable to avoid another danger that arises from the concept of God's working everything. With God's sole activity and working of all in all, evil loses the potency of its reality because it appears as a sideline of God's saving activity. This dilemma has posed itself in recent times in the theology of Karl Barth (1886–1968), who also placed great stress upon the sole activity of God. If God works everything, then it is difficult to avoid the conclusion that God brings about evil or at least works through it and that evil does not possess an independent reality. This problem will be taken up in chapter 5. At this point, suffice it to say that Luther indeed recognized evil as an independent, antigodly reality.

The Divine Will Is Grounded in God's Own Being

If God is continually at work and is both almighty and works everything, then the question arises whether God's activity is guided by certain externally established rules, or whether God's will itself provides its own guidelines that inform the divine activity. For Luther it is obvious that we cannot inquire about the ultimate ground of God's will since the will of God is grounded in its own self and is the ultimate basis for its activity. "It is enough to know that God so wills, and it is becoming for us to reverence, love, and adore his will."[2] Luther presupposes here the ability of humans to know the will of God, and contends that we must submit ourselves to it. We are not to question—as people often do today—why God acts in a certain manner. Luther can even say that it is an abominable blasphemy to ask God why God does what he does, for in doing so one questions God and makes oneself out to be smarter and more knowledgeable than God. God's activity does not allow itself be steered by our reason but is to be unconditionally acknowledged, and those things that flow from God's activity are to be used with thankfulness. It is also useless to ask about the hidden ways in which God governs the world, for in doing so one enters upon the slippery surface of a speculative theology.

There remains only one possible response to God's activity: to entrust everything to God, conceding that God knows better than we do. But does not the challenge of Luther's demand imply a sacrifice of our intellect, since in regard to God and God's activity we must switch off our reason? Luther would deny that this is the case. His primary concern is with the divinity of God. The majesty of God cannot be fathomed but must rather be recognized as an awe-inspiring mystery. Additionally, the attempt to comprehend the divine will is condemned to failure because the divine and human wills are not on the same level. We can only comprehend that which is on the same level as we are, but not that which is on a higher level. We cannot unlock the mystery of God's will by beginning from the

2. Luther, ibid., 155.

human will since the divine will is complete in itself. The divine will needs no foundation. If one were able to explain or ground God's action, the majesty and perfection of God would be abrogated in the process. Hence for Luther the question about the *why* of God's action is pointless. One can only ascertain after the fact that God has acted in a certain way. The will of God is therefore always primary and cannot be grounded. God is not, however, capricious but has rather committed God's self to our salvation through his self-disclosure. It follows that God does not act high-handedly or irrationally and therefore does not work in a demonic way.

God as the Only Necessary Being

The will and being of God are grounded in God's own self. Only God is necessary. Nothing else need exist if God did not so desire. God is the unchanging being who alone is real. All other being is distinct from God because it is brought into being by God. It is derived being, while God is without foundation. God exists on the basis of God's own being and is clearly not an object among others. God is the power of being that is inherent in everything and that establishes all reality. God is not a God who refrains from doing that which is within the reach of his omnipotence, but he rather works all in all. This view is essential for Luther's conception of God. He takes up from tradition the idea that God is pure act, but adapts this idea so that God is not a disinterested will but is understood as working in a strictly personal way. God is, then, unchanging and unchangeable within God's own self, yet works continually for our salvation.

God is will and deed; God is the constant "mover" of the existing beings that God has created. It is seen here that Luther's dynamic understanding of God is oriented toward history. The contrast to speculative theology is likewise clear. Luther indeed takes up traditional philosophical ideas, but he always conceives of God in personal terms because he understands God from the perspective of God's revelation in Christ. Therefore Luther stresses that God is not an abstract being but deals with us continually according to God's love and goodness. Luther can even speak of a natural necessity by which God neither wills nor loves sin. But when God is the only necessary being this also means that God is always so close to us that we cannot fall out of God's hand. God is always with us and deals with us according to God's love. For Luther, God is not an impersonal fate or an unconcerned God of fatalism. Instead, God possesses the dynamic structure of a personal being.

God Is Truthful

If God is the only necessary being and God's will is grounded within God's own self, that does not mean that God acts capriciously and without any rules, for there is an important constant: God is truthful, even if one is unable to show this empirically.[3] God's faithfulness and truthfulness are extremely important for Luther. Because God is truthful one can rely on his promises and place oneself trustingly under God's protection. Every believer knows that God fulfills his promises and threats. If it were otherwise one could not rely on God and a relationship of trust with God would be impossible. We are able to trust God's word because God neither lies nor is capable of lying without transforming God's self into a demonic being. The distinction between the perfection of God and the imperfection of humans is clearly shown here. The truthfulness of God is not a theoretical postulate but is made concrete through Christ, who remained faithful to his mission. His promises, therefore, such as those he spoke in the institution of the Lord's Supper (cf. Mark 14:22–25), are true. Hence God's will is not without self-restriction and God

---

3. Luther on Genesis 27, *In Genesin Declamationes* (1527), in *WA* 24:476.4 *"Deus verax est."*

does not do evil or sin. This positive orientation is the foundation for our relationship to God. Yet the question remains open whether God is autonomous in God's will or whether God must, so to speak, inevitably act in a certain way.

God's Will as the Ultimate Criterion for God's Actions

Luther emphasizes that for God there is no rule, standard, or law and, therefore, nothing that God can violate. Luther illustrates this with the story of Pharaoh in Exodus 7–11.[4] The plagues that came upon Pharaoh were beyond doubt terrible, and if humans had brought such suffering upon him it would have been an evil deed. But since it was God who sent the plagues, we must call these actions good. We cannot judge God according to the appearances of God's actions so that these become the measure for good and evil. It is a mistake of many individuals to claim that God has a certain nature or character and then to judge him according to these preconceived notions. By making themselves the standard against which they measure God they offend his majesty. According to Luther, it is arrogant to suggest that God does something that is bad since where there is no law, there can be no sin. God is above every law and cannot, therefore, violate any law. Yet Luther admits that our reason is unable to comprehend this. Although God is not a capricious God, God's will remains the supreme law according to which everything is measured and judged and to which no other standard has anything to add. No one can either judge or justify God, for God is the eternally constant and unchanging justice and the supreme judge of all things.

---

4. Cf. Luther, *Predigten über das 2. Buch Mose* (1524–27), in *WA* 16:141.3–6.

God's Free Will Cannot Be Unjust

The justice of God is consequently not a principle that is attributed to God but is rather derived from his divinity. "God is not God because he is just, but rather, because God is God he is just. God's divinity is his justice."[5] The actions and will of God are always correct and are never arbitrary. Although the divine will is not determined by external criteria, God does not act according to constantly changing standards. What is good and what is evil is not subject to a capricious arbitrariness. God is much more the justice that is eternally constant and unchanging. According to God's own being God is just, even when, according to our human understanding, God does either good or evil. That does not mean that God is a good principle that must always do that which is good, but rather God wills the good and therefore God also does that which is good. God establishes good and evil through the will, and whoever acts contrary to what God wills is not good. Good and evil are determined according to God's will, but not vice versa, so that one cannot ethically judge God's actions according to our notions of good and evil. God's will is the ultimate criterion for all being and becoming. The divinity of God is to be seen in the fact that we can learn from God's actions what is good, yet we do not possess any other standard by which we could judge God's actions as good. In this way the priority of God—a priority that is also to be seen in God's creative activity—is safeguarded.

God's Activity in Creation

While today we rarely think of God still being active in creation, it was important for Luther that God is not just involved with history but also with present-day creation. God did not only create

---

5. So Heinz Zahrnt, *Luther deutet Geschichte: Erfolg und Misserfolg im Licht des Evangeliums* (Munich: P. Müller, 1952), 190.

everything that is but also sustains and preserves it in every moment of its existence.

God Creates and Preserves All Things

Nothing comes into being or continues to be apart from the active work of God. The relationship between God and the world is thus different from that between human beings and their creations. When a human-made product is finished it gains a certain independence from its maker, for it can continue to exist apart from the one who made it. The world, however, cannot continue to exist for a single moment apart from the sustaining activity of God. Luther wrote of God's activity in creation, "He did not therefore create the world like a carpenter builds a house and then goes away, leaving it stand as it is, rather he remains and sustains everything as he made it, otherwise it would neither be able to stand nor to continue."[6] This continuous divine work of preservation is at the same time an ongoing new act of creating. God is not yet finished with the work of creation but continually creates further.

Through God's active preservation and ongoing creating he is present in all reality. Luther can even maintain that God is present in a tree leaf since God preserves and keeps all things through his presence. "For he dispatches no officials or angels when he creates or preserves something, but all is the work of his divine power itself. If he is to create or preserve it, however, he must be present and must make and preserve his creation both in its innermost and outermost aspects."[7] The creative power of God is directly present in nature and in the entire creation. Though God is present in nature, God's all-present power is not identical with the course of world history,

---

6. Luther in a sermon on Rom. 11:33–36, *Crucigers Sommerpostille* (1526), in *WA* 21:521.21–25.
7. Luther, *That These Words of Christ, "This Is My Body," etc., Still Stand Firm against the Fanatics* (1527), in *LW* 37:58.

for the power of God transcends the world. With this distinction Luther is able to avoid every form of pantheism. He points out that God is not a thing with length or breadth that one could confine to a particular place and measure. God is rather incomprehensible and immeasurable; God is beyond and above all things and at the same time in all things. God's power is transcendent insofar as it is beyond all standards that one might attribute to it. God's power is its own dimension that is present in all things, while at the same time transcending all things.

Indirect Involvement of God

God's activity within creation is seldom carried out directly or immediately. Although God is everywhere active, he works mostly through the guise of forces that are visibly discernible to us. "All creatures are God's masks and costumes which God wants to work with him to help create all manner of things, yet he can and does also work without them."[8] God does not need any earthly cooperation, but out of his own free will God summons and asks for the cooperation of earthly forces. God requests us to accomplish our tasks with earnestness in whatever situation we find ourselves. We should do this not because God needs us, but because God has commanded it and will not bless us without our own effort. Nevertheless we should not view ourselves as the proper authors of the fruits of our labors and rely on them, since God produces them. Luther explains this in his *Small Catechism*, in the explanation of the Fourth Petition of the Lord's Prayer, "Give us today our daily bread." Luther writes, "In fact, God gives daily bread without our prayer, even to all evil people, but we ask in this prayer that God cause us to recognize what our daily bread is and to receive it."[9] Ultimately, all human success or

---

8. Luther in a sermon on Matt. 4:1ff.: *Fastenpostille* (1525), in *WA* 17/II:192.28–30.

results are God's gracious action, so that only in the foreground do they appear to show a causal connection between our effort and our success. Through God's command and promise work and blessing are connected and related to one another. Because the honor of "authorship" belongs to God alone we can rely on God in our labor. "Creatures are only the hands, channels, and means through which God bestows all blessings."[10] God's creative will not only provides human effort with meaning but it also sets its boundaries. God gives us nothing without our active readiness for cooperation, but our cooperation alone does not bring about the result.

Sovereignty of God's Activity

It is important to remember that God works everything through the word. "His command or speech is equivalent to creation."[11] Through the powerful word God brings about, for instance, the change of the seasons, as well as the historical communal life of humanity within the political order. When Luther speaks here of God's word he does not have in mind the gospel, but rather the creative and preserving word. Just as God called into existence that which was not at the beginning of the world through the word, so God continues today to work in a sovereign way through the word, so that no one can hinder or restrict him. Of course, one could ask whether Luther introduces a divine determinism that reduces all human freedom to nothing when he refers to God's sovereign activity in the creation. One must take into account, however, that Luther was an eminently praxis-oriented, in other words, an existential, theologian. The recognition of God's sole activity and his working all in all has immediate implications for

---

9. Luther, *The Small Catechism*, in *The Book of Concord: The Confessions of the Evangelical Lutheran Church*, ed. Robert Kolb and Timothy J. Wengert (Minneapolis: Fortress Press, 2000), 347.

10. So Luther in his explanation of the First Commandment in *The Large Catechism*, in *The Book of Concord*, 389.

11. Luther, "Psalm 147," (1532), in *LW* 14:124.

faith. If God is sovereign and continually active then we can put our confidence in what God promises.

Since God is active everywhere and in all things we are always in God's hands. We can go wherever we wish, but in the end we always encounter God (as so well described in Psalm 139). This inescapable and living presence of God is for humans either a frightening or a trust-inspiring reality, depending on their individual relationship to God. For the faithful this means heaven, but for those who distanced themselves from God it signifies hell. "He is present everywhere, in death, in hell, in the midst of our foes, yes, also in their hearts. For He has created all things, and He also governs them, and that they must all do as He wills."[12] Therefore we have nothing and no one to fear other than God. Those who put their trust in God are able to confidently believe that nothing can harm them. God is the almighty Lord of all powers. God's powerfulness in creation is the reason for the confidence of the faithful. They know that they are kept safe through God's works of creation and preservation, for to the very end they have to do with God himself and not a mere creature. It is otherwise for those who do not put their faith in God. Ultimately they cannot rely on anything and sooner or later will realize that their lives have no firm foundation.

Omnipotence of God

God holds humanity completely in his hand through omnipotence. Luther emphasized with particular clarity in his dispute with Erasmus of Rotterdam in *The Bondage of the Will* that free will is an attribute that belongs to God alone. Since God affects everything in human beings they can only desire and do what God does in them. God is the never-resting, driving force in God's creatures. For believers this

12. Luther, *Lectures on Jonah* (1526), in *LW* 19:68.

is a great comfort, for they recognize that even their faith in God is not their own work but is wrought in them by God. For those without God, however, God's omnipotence is a frightening reality, for they are moved to act in correspondence to their godless nature. "Hence it comes about that the ungodly man cannot but continually err and sin, because he is caught up in the movement of divine power and not allowed to be idle, but wills, desires, and acts according to the kind of person he himself is."[13] Luther even maintained that God can make the evil person even more evil, obstinate, and hardened. In contrast to this idea of obstinacy, which is only seldom mentioned by Luther and with which we cannot completely agree in this form, we must remember that Luther, although he knows humans to be entirely in God's hands, views them at the same time as existing over against God as those who are accountable and indebted to him and who will be finally judged by him. Through this accountability before God the conception of his working in everything is qualified.

Luther neither makes God's working in everything absolute, nor does he consequently draw from it every possible conclusion. He would never claim, for instance, that God causes people to sin. Although God also works in the godless so that they remain the way they are, God moves them only in a way consistent with the state in which he finds them. In connection with God's activity in creation Luther does not discuss where or how human guilt and sin originated. They are simply present and demand human accountability. Even the godless are not only moved by God to continue in their godless ways, but they are also preserved and kept by God as much as every other person. Luther has in view here not so much humans but rather God, upon whom everything in which

13. Luther, *The Bondage of the Will* (1525), in *LW* 33:176.

we can have confidence ultimately depends. This is also to be seen in God's redemptive activity.

Redemptive Work of God

The divinity of God is especially emphasized in redemption because the human certainty of salvation rests upon God's trustworthiness. God the Creator is not only responsible for the present existence of human beings but also for the accomplishment of their salvation. When we profess faith in God the Creator this also includes an admission of our own inadequacy and means that we rely upon God for everything. God's saving action occurs, as does the entire work of creation, out of nothing. The creation out of nothing (*creatio ex nihilo*) is not only a statement about the origin of the world, indicating that God works without prerequisites, but is also a statement about the saving activity of God directed toward humanity. If our salvation depended upon us or our cooperation in procuring salvation it would be very uncertain and would often turn into a disaster. With his emphasis upon a creation out of nothing Luther points toward God's activity under the guise of the opposite. Where God will exalt, God first humbles; where God creates life, God first brings about death. God accomplishes a foreign work, an *opus alienum*, in order to bring about the proper work, God's *opus proprium*. God's activity cannot be rationally predicted. Rather, we remain dependent upon God's word that makes his character and intent clear, so that we seek and recognize God where he wishes to be sought and recognized. In this way *sola fide* is also emphasized (that is, the fact that God justifies through faith alone). Only those who put their trust in God and honor him by allowing God to be God can hope for something from him.

The divinity of God consists in God alone being the Creator and the giver of all good things. We cannot come before God with any of our own works lest we question God's divinity by pointing to our own achievements. In every instant we are dependent upon God, even when our reason wishes to devise its own path to salvation. Reason argues religiously according to the notion that since God has given us something good we should also give something God in return. Such a reciprocal relationship between God and humanity, however, amounts to an assault against God's divinity, since we would thereby attempt to pay God back for what he has given us. "But that is to give His own back to God as though it were not His but ours. Even reason denounces as wicked and foolish the notion that someone who is generous not with his own property but with someone else's is doing anything special."[14] Human beings can only give God something that God has first given them. But this would make no sense. As far as God is concerned, no achievement of ours matters, but rather only our thanks. Yet even here Luther qualifies this by pointing out that even our expression of thanks to God is not possible without his help. Faith as trust remains the only human reaction that is appropriate in response to God.

The divinity of God is revealed in his creation when God creates out of nothing, indeed, under the guise of the opposite. Correspondingly, faith anticipates something from God precisely where there is nothing to be seen, and it perseveres against all adversity. Thus the divinity of God and faith correspond to one another. Faith is directed toward God alone and trusts God, from whom and to whom all things are and through whom alone justification is possible. Humans, therefore, will only act properly if they rely wholly upon God. Faith is not a turning off of our own

14. Luther in his exposition of Ps. 51:16 (1532), in *LW* 12:397.

power of reason, nor does it call for a sacrifice of one's intellect. Instead, it is a complete reliance upon God, without whom we can do nothing and to whom we are indebted for everything. Those who put their complete trust in God are not abandoned, but place themselves under the protection of God who is not only Creator and Sustainer but also Redeemer. Yet the question remains: To what extent are humans capable of professing faith in God?

5

Humanity between God and Satan

Luther shared the vivid belief in demons and the devil that was common in the late Middle Ages. Demons lived in forest and field, swamp and moor, ponds and clouds, and witches carried out all sorts of mischief. At the Diet of Augsburg (1530), according to Luther, each bishop had brought as many devils along with him "as a dog has fleas on St. John's Day."[1] But in contrast to this and similar popular opinions that Luther shared, one must not forget that Luther was also able to present the central themes of the Christian faith without making reference to the devil. In many of his sermons there is no mention at all to be found of the devil. But this also has to do with the fact that in the structure of the theology of the Middle Ages, the devil occupied no fixed place. Nevertheless, the devil played a large role in Luther's perception of life. His lively sense for evil and his aversion to it come together for Luther in the figure of the devil. Luther's devil has more "hellish majesty" than the medieval devil, for he is more

---

1. Luther in a sermon on St. Michael's Day: *Predigten des Jahres 1531*, in *WA* 34/II:264.16.

powerful and frightful and is to be taken more seriously. According to Luther one can say three things about the devil: First, he is God's adversary; second, he battles with God for humanity; and finally, he serves as an instrument of God.

Satan as God's Adversary

Luther speaks only occasionally about the devil's origin, fall, and the nature of his existence. Of much more importance for Luther is the devil's reign and activity in the world. Yet Luther does believe the devil to be a creature of God equipped with consciousness, understanding, and will; before his fall, he "was a very handsome angel and a decidedly outstanding creature. But . . . he was inflamed with envy, anger, and indignation against God."[2] He describes him as the powerful leader of the evil angels, whom he commands like a monarch. For Luther, therefore, the devil is not some cosmic principle but a personal being. Luther also speaks of him as the true archenemy of Christ and his kingdom, the one to whom all other enemies must serve as his instruments. He is the god of sin and death as well as the author and distributor of both. He is called "prince of sin" and "prince of death," "potent spirit and lord of the whole world" and "his power is greater than that of ten Turkish Kaisers."[3] In his hymn, "A Mighty Fortress," Luther writes of the devil, "With dread craft and might he arms himself to fight. On earth he has no equal."[4] The devil rules in the world through demons, evil persons, and heretics and has founded a kingdom of sin and disobedience from which only the power of God can rescue us. He is the embodiment of evil and can do only evil.

2. Luther in his exposition of Gen. 28:12–14, *Lectures on Genesis* (1535–45), in *LW* 5:221.
3. Luther in his exposition of Gal. 4:29, *In epistolam S. Pauli ad Galatas Commentarius* (1535), in *WA* 40/I: 678.26 (cf. *LW* 26:455); and in his sermon on St. Michael's Day, *WA* 34/II:232.28–233.16.
4. *Evangelical Lutheran Worship*, hymn no. 503.

As the great adversary of God, the devil is seen by Luther behind everything that opposes God's ultimate will for the creation and humanity. He is active in misfortune, in diseases and other life crises, and in death, for he is the master and holder of power over death. He tempted the first humans to sin and remains the tempter and inciter of evil. He is at work in history against God and Christ and against truth and the gospel. The devil hates Christ and persecutes him and all those who belong to him. Therefore the devil stands behind all the enemies of God, behind the misinterpretation of Scripture, and behind all heresies and pagan philosophy. He cannot bear the pure word of God and true doctrine and seeks to adulterate them, especially their all-decisive content, which is justification through faith alone. The devil brings all his forces to bear in order to destroy the doctrine of justification. He makes people blind to the clear word of God and he causes human reason to stumble over it. He hardens human hearts so that they do not fear the wrath of God and do not realize their true situation. He brings about human security, arrogance, and apathy, as well as the hopeless despairing of the mercy of God and Christ.

The threat posed by the devil and his seduction can be avoided by no one. The devil has a share in the dimension of the divine being so that he is omnipresent to every person. Hence God's power and that of the devil are opposed to one another; a great conflict ensues between them that permeates all of history and keeps it in a state of constant turmoil. History is therefore a witness to the battle of the devil against God, of God against the devil, and of the true God against the antigod. The devil desires to be God for he is the "ruler of this world" (John 12:31) and "god of this world" (2 Cor. 4:4).[5] He stands over against God as an opponent who is to be taken seriously.

---

5. Cf. Luther, *That These Words of Christ, "This Is My Body," etc., Still Stand Firm against the Fanatics* (1527), in *LW* 37:17.

Although his power and claim are so great that he can be called the god of this world, the singular divinity of the true God is never for one moment called into question. Luther limits the dualism between God and the devil through the omnipotence and sole activity of God. Nevertheless, God and the devil battle over humanity and for dominion of the earth.

God and Satan Battle over Humanity

"Each person either lives with Christ against the devil or with the devil against Christ."[6] The world is the kingdom of the devil and he is its lord, prince, and god. The world is subjected to his cruel tyranny, for he holds the hearts of humans captive in his bonds and afflicts them with all his power and might in order to force their subservience. His activity extends over body and soul. He plagues and torments the conscience and leads people astray into false doctrine as well as into either a state of false security or into the despair of unbelief. He strikes and punishes with sickness and countless evils in order to destroy human beings. This affliction of humanity reaches its climax in death, over which the devil holds power as master and butcher, even though death does not have its origin or power in him but in God, as we will later see more clearly.

Because there is no neutral territory in human beings' relationship to God relative to their salvation or condemnation, they are always either under the power of God or of Satan. "The human will is placed between the two like a beast of burden. If God rides it, it wills and goes where God wills. . . . If Satan rides it, it wills and goes where Satan wills; nor can it choose to run to either of the two riders or to seek him out, but the riders themselves contend for the possession and control of it"—so wrote Luther in *The Bondage of the Will*.[7] Moreover,

6. Luther in his exposition of Matt. 12:30: *Annotationes in aliquot capita Matthaei* (1527), in *WA* 38:545.28–29.

Satan works in human beings analogously to God when he gains power over them. Both push humans along through the dynamic of their wills without rest or quiet, the devil toward evil, God along the path of good. Whoever does not belong to Christ and is not living in the power of his spirit is ruled by the devil. The devil allows no one to be snatched away from him through any power other than the Spirit of God, that is, through the stronger one who, according to the saying of Jesus, overcomes the strong man, that is, the devil (cf. Luke 11:21–22). Through Christ, God snatches human beings out of the fangs of the devil.

In baptism humans are freed from the devil, since it is through baptism that they receive their portion of what Christ has accomplished upon earth, namely, the defeat of the devil. Yet this liberation from the devil's power can only be asserted in a life-long battle against him. Humans are confronted with an either/or: either fight against the devil or capitulate before him. "Choose, then, whether you prefer to wrestle with the devil or whether you prefer to belong to him. . . . If you refuse to be his, defend yourself, go at him!"[8] The weapon in this fight is God's word. This is true for the individual as well as for the church as a whole, for both must offer resistance to the devil through faith and the preaching of the word of God. Because faith is not found in everyone, the devil remains powerful in the world and in history. Hence Christianity awaits with anticipation the final judgment when Christ in his second coming will once and for all take away the devil's power. Yet at present the devil works all sorts of evil upon humans. He beguiles and seduces them through illusions, hallucinations, and other means, and brings bad weather, tempests, fire, diseases, and wars upon them. Through these afflictions he seeks to incite humans to sin, to distrust God, and

---

7. Luther, *The Bondage of the Will* (1525), in *LW* 33:65–66.
8. Luther, *That These Words of Christ, "This Is My Body," etc.,* in *LW* 37:17.

to strive with one another. The devil is the great liar who deceives humans into believing that those things are good that in reality are destructive and that cause the soul to descend into fear and misery.

Luther's understanding of the devil is also built upon the experience that external impressions and events often set evil impulses lose in human beings and bring upon them a multitude of evil, the origin of which is mysterious. In his thoughts about the devil he expresses the sentiment that evil is a unified force that penetrates the entire natural realm of life. The all-encompassing reality of human sin is also founded upon this destructive spiritual principle that holds power over the whole realm of nature. Through his concept of the devil, Luther gives drastic expression to the terrible, supra-human power of evil in the world. Luther seeks in this way to guard humans from self-assurance, since the knowledge of this antigodly destructive power prevents them from becoming set in their laziness and security. For Luther the devil is thoroughly evil; he is the adversary of God who battles God for control of creation. Yet the devil is at the same time God's instrument, as are all things in the world.

The Devil as God's Instrument

The brutal and frightening power of Satan is neither autonomous nor absolute. In his express rejection of a Manichaean dualism between God and anti-god Luther ultimately attributes the power and authority of the devil to God:

> Behold how wisely Moses [Psalm 90] speaks when he attributes such wrath directly to the creator; only that Manichaeus doesn't come with his great ideas and make two gods, one good and merciful, and the other evil. For he [Moses] does not say that the devil destroys people and brings them to nothing, but rather you (God) yourself. . . . It is his work and in the deepest sense his wrath. . . . He indeed makes use of the devil to torment and kill us; but the devil is not capable of this if God would not will to punish sin in us in such a way."[9]

This means that God uses the devil to punish our sinfulness. Thus Luther can also say that the devil has received his power and authority from God. He embodies the wrath and justice of God, since God uses him as his instrument and tool, indeed, as his executioner, in order to bring his punishment upon us. The hands and feet of the devil are the dreadful, atrocious claws of the wrath of God and of eternal death. The devil does not then rule unrestrictedly wherever he will, but only so far as the wrath of God extends. His authority is derived and limited and is contingent upon the ultimate authority of God, against whom alone we have sinned. Only in this way can we understand how Luther is able to often set God's wrath and the devil alongside of one another and can attribute to the later what he confesses to be the work of former. With reference to Eph. 2:3 and 2 Tim. 2:26 he says that we are "children of wrath, and . . . held captive at Satan's will," or, "We are swallowed up by the devil and God's wrath."[10]

Nevertheless, it would be an oversimplification to simply view the devil as cooperating harmoniously with God in this activity of punishment. Luther also contrasts the punishment of God with the destructive power of the devil. "He [God] is a merciful God and does not punish so as to annihilate or plow us under as the devil would do, so that neither help nor counsel would remain."[11] Or: "God is not a devil; He is not a devourer or a carnivore, as you [Satan] are, . . . He is merciful to sinners, perfect and incorruptible, faithful and righteous."[12] In this way Luther sets the devil who terrifies, kills, and slaughters, over against God, who alone brings life and comforts.

---

9. Luther in his exposition of Ps. 90:3: *Ennaratio Psalmi XC* (1534/35), in *WA* 40/III:516.25–517.14; 518.11–12.; 519.13–14.

10. Luther in his explanation of Gen. 4:8: *Lectures on Genesis* (1535–45), in *LW* 1:273; and in a sermon from May 20, 1532: *Predigten des Jahres 1532*, in *WA* 36:180.17.

11. Luther in a sermon on Deut. 4:29ff., *Predigten über das 5. Buch Mose* (1529), in *WA* 28:578.21–23.

12. Luther on Ps. 51:4 (1532), in *LW* 12:346–47.

Despite its relative independence the devil's might is subject to the far more encompassing power of God that punishes and judges even the devil and that leads to human salvation. Satan only has power when and where God grants him leeway, and this, contrary to outward appearances, is not without limits: "For if he had full power to rage as he pleased, you would not live for an hour."[13] The limits of satanic power are bound to the self-limitation of divine wrath based upon the love of God. The devil's might, therefore, serves only the purposes of God's wrath, and it extends as far as the wrath of God and is only unlimited to the extent that the wrath of God is unlimited. Yet Luther does not locate the limitation and contingency of the devil's dominion in either the wrath or power of God, but rather in God's overwhelming mercy. The power of God is the force that sustains, equips, and tirelessly moves human beings and all other creatures. Through this force the wrath of God provides the devil with the authority and space for the full development of his destructive power, and yields to the devil at the same time sin and death as unrestricted spheres of activity.

The love of God impedes the destructive activity of Satan and utilizes his powers, essence, and intent for its own purposes. While it is the devil's job to turn good into bad, the power, wisdom, and love of God are evident in that the devil, against his will, must serve the good and work toward the honor and salvation of human beings. God employs and uses even the devil and evil angels. Their goal is to corrupt all things, but God does not allow this unless it is for well-deserved punishment of humans. God lets pestilence, war, and other problems come upon human beings so that they might be humbled before God and fear him, and that they might abide by and call upon God. The devil must then ultimately serve God through the very

13. Luther, commenting on Gen. 32:1–2, *Lectures on Genesis* (1535–45), in *LW* 6:90.

means by which he sought to inflict damage. "For God is the kind of Master who can use the devil's wickedness, that he might bring forth good from it."[14]

According to Luther, we see in the devil's activity that God, despite his sole activity, does not act in a genuinely evil or demonic manner. God brings about good under the appearance of its evil opposite, and can also make such pedagogical use of evil that the end result is good. Because God is good, God does not condone evil as such but rather as a means toward the punishment of sinners so that their consciences are awakened to their guilt and helplessness. God works in this manner because God wills evil only as punishment, in order that the good that it opposes will stand out more clearly. Only in light of this presupposition is the following sentence of Luther's understandable: "God incites the devil to evil, but God does not do evil."[15] This statement can be affirmed when one continues further with Luther, "Because it pleased God so." Thus the wrath of God over sin manifests itself in the work of the devil. When God in wrath abandons humans, the devil attacks them according to the will of God and brings unbelief, despair, and death upon them or destroys the structures of human life in community. God need only take his hand from us or give the devil free reign and the punishment for sin comes upon us.

We do not, however, encounter God in fortune and some other power in misfortune, but rather in both *one* God remains ever faithful and is unwavering in steadfastness, neither quick to friendliness nor quick to anger but always merciful, even when he punishes us. Although Satan is active as the instrument of God, humans are confronted with God alone. What is accomplished through God's wrath and through Satan are largely one and the same, for the devil

14. Luther in a sermon on Matt. 18:1ff., *Predigten des Jahres 1531*, in *WA* 34/II:240.25–26.
15. Luther, *Predigten über das 2. Buch Mose* (1524–27), in *WA* 16:143.4–5.

is indeed God's devil. Yet at the same time he remains the devil, the enemy of God who seeks the opposite of all that God wills.

Yet how are the intention and activity of Satan related to the work of God, especially in connection with God's work of wrath? Luther explains this using the example of Job. This pious man is afflicted by genuine works of the devil. Nevertheless, Scripture attributes these ultimately to God. What does this mean? "God does not do evil things but uses instrumental means."[16] Two things are thereby to be observed. First, it is God who works through his instruments and, second, in that which God inflicts upon people one must distinguish between what God does and what is done by his instruments. It is God whom we recognize to be at work in everything bad that happens to us through the means of his instruments. Under no circumstances may we attribute misfortune or death to some separate, demonic power, for in doing so we would introduce a dualism. It is true that we must view the work of God and of Satan as one in order to guard against a dualistic worldview, but we must also distinguish dialectically between the two. But why make this distinction?

Luther clearly insisted that one must distinguish between the activity of God and of Satan, even though they are one and the same, because their intention and goal are radically different. Both assail and challenge human beings to the utmost. But God does it for salvation so that human beings can be freed from their own selves and all self-confidence, and flee to the arms of the merciful God. Satan, in contrast, seeks to snatch humans once and for all away from God through his activity. Hence Christians recognize through faith that everything that happens ultimately works toward their salvation, while others who are confronted with the same negative experiences despair of their misfortune and depart from God. Tribulation,

---

16. Luther on Ps. 51:8 (1532), in *LW* 12:373.

therefore, always has two faces: the face of God and the face of the devil. Although God is also the God of Satan, Satan continues to work ultimately toward the goal that human beings renounce their faith in God.

It is remarkable that in our thoroughly rational, enlightened world superstition is again exerting great influence. Horoscopes, which are founded upon a faith that the stars determine our fate, belief in witches and psychic persons, which assumes that some people have extraordinary powers and insights, and Satan worship, with its perverse and sometimes cruel and dangerous practices of animal and human sacrifice, are attracting people of all ages. At the same time Satan, as that power that is absolutely opposed to God, and other negative forces have fallen prey in official theology to a pervasive demythologizing so that they are either not spoken of at all or they are explained away psychologically.

One could, to be sure, claim that such negative forces are mere remnants of the Middle Ages that no longer have a place in our rational world. If they still occur today, then it might be argued that this demonstrates that certain groups within society that are trying to escape the modern world feel that they are pushed with their backs against the wall. Their attention to these negative phenomena provides them the opportunity to express their discontent with modern civilization. The interest in these forces might also be seen as an indication that some now wish to control these forces in order to master the future because other possibilities have not brought about the desired results. Occult practices would therefore be a further effort to control the world. In each of these efforts to explain the great interest in the occult and in the negative powers highlighted within the occult, there is certainly a measure of truth.

We must, however, concern ourselves with another, very different possibility. In the attempt to place all things under human reason an important part of reality could have been suppressed or simply forgotten. This neglect of an aspect of reality is to be observed in the following way. Just when we thought that we had achieved final mastery over the world and nature because the whole world had become comprehensible and manageable through technology and reason, precisely at this time our existence seems to be threatened as never before. The world that we mastered and controlled now threatens our own existence. As soon as we believe to have brought one problem under control, two new ones emerge. The world in and with which we live does not let itself be brought under control any more than we are able to permanently get around the threatening and negative powers. They announce their return with vehemence.

When we admit, however, that threatening and negative forces influence our world, does that make Luther's statements about the devil and demons more credible? In regard to this question we must consider the following:

1. The negative things that take place in the world and in the lives of individuals are of such destructive, antigodly character that one can neither attribute them to God without making him into a demon, nor simply credit them to human beings without belittling these events. There are such atrocious and beastly things going on in today's world that the influence of the forces of darkness must be reckoned with.[17] The reality of the antigodly, destructive powers that were self-evident for Luther is here to be acknowledged, even if Luther's naive and graphic anthropomorphic view of the devil is no longer tenable today. On account of the plurality of these powers it is better to

---

17. Next to figures of the last century, such as Hitler, Stalin, and Mao, who seem to have been obsessed by these powers in their drive to annihilate millions of innocent people, we could point to similar figures on the present scene.

talk here about antigodly powers, a term that also denotes the direction of their working.

2. Seen from the perspective of the divinity of God, it is not justified to introduce a second power that is equal to God but that has negative intentions. Such dualism would diminish God's godhead and impede our salvation. As Luther continually emphasized, Christ is greater than Satan. At the same time Luther affirmed that both God and Satan fight for supremacy. This both/and, between God and Christ on the one side and Satan on the other, is a paradox that cannot be resolved without making theology lopsided.

3. Consequently, the reality of the antigodly powers must be viewed as powers that, although operating destructively, are ultimately unable to impede the saving activity of God. This means that they must eventually, even if unwillingly, contribute to the glory of God.

4. That which is negative in this world is always ambiguous. On the one hand, it can be enigmatically understood as the just results of our estranged existence from God, but on the other hand, as the outcome of a chaotic activity.

5. The reason that God, in spite of his divinity, does not make it impossible for the negative to occur is to be found in part in the freedom that God grants everyone, and in part in the mystery of God's will, which cannot be fathomed. Immanuel Kant was correct when he called the attempt for a theodicy, meaning the attempt to find out why God's wisdom and justice does not eliminate evil in our world, "is essentially nothing but the issue of our arrogant reason which thereby forgets its limits."[18]

---

18. Immanuel Kant, *Über das Misslingen aller philosophischen Versuche in der Theodizee*, in *Werke in zehn Bänden*, ed. Wilhelm Weischedel (Darmstadt: Wissenschaftliche Buchgesellschaft, 1968), 9:105.

Hence we continue even today to stand within the context of a struggle between God and the antigodly powers, so that it is only due to the grace of God that we are able to survive. Where, we might ask, are these antigodly and destructive powers to be seen? Above all we experience them in the area of interpersonal relationships when, for instance, we "make life hell" for one another. The apostle Paul already recognized that for unexplained reasons he did not do the good that he actually desired to do, but rather the bad (Rom. 7:15). Since then nothing has changed in this regard. Instead of making life better for ourselves and others, we seek to pull others down, to spread negative things about them, and to use them for our own advantage. Also, in regard to the societal and international realm, there exists not only a permanent struggle over borders and resources, but completely absurd and incomprehensively cruel ethnic conflicts continually arise. To write all of this off as purely human barbarism diminishes the extent of these inhumanities. In this same context one must take into account the many environmental barbarisms, including the reckless overpopulation of the planet by humans. We are subject here to powers that we willingly serve and that transform God's good creation into a blasphemous chaos, while we also find satisfaction in their realization. This is truly a macabre mockery, which God, in his unfathomable patience, has not yet brought to an end.

6

The Ordering Activity of God
(The Two Kingdoms)

The Lutheran doctrine of the two kingdoms stands within a long tradition that can be traced back to the Gospel of John, in which the evangelist speaks on the one hand of the kingdom of God (John 3:3), and on the other hand of the rulers of this world (John 12:31) and their sphere of authority. Later, Augustine spoke of a "worldly city" and of a "city of God." Luther has often been accused of promoting a quietistic stance and silencing the church in regard to political, economic, and social problems through his doctrine of the two kingdoms. Some have even wanted to see a line running from Augustine through Luther to Adolf Hitler. As we shall see, however, this accusation does not do justice to Luther.

Historical Roots of Luther's Doctrine of the Two Kingdoms

Luther was neither an ethicist nor a political theologian. He was a biblical theologian keenly aware of what was happening around him and a preacher who sought to preach the gospel. His faithfulness to the Bible and his acute sense for relevant contemporary issues led him to the doctrine of the two kingdoms. Luther was aware that according to the testimony of the New Testament the redemption of the world was accomplished through the advent of Christ. The path back to God for his fallen creation was cleared, and its consummation was made possible. Yet he knew that sin and death would rule in our world until the final consummation of salvation. What was revealed in the life and destiny of Jesus continued to await universal implementation. The tension between the "already" and the persisting "not yet," which was most clearly expressed by Paul, was the starting point for Luther's doctrine of the two kingdoms.

Luther stood in the tradition of the Middle Ages in which a christocratic understanding of the state was prevalent. The dominion of Christ was to be realized through human dominion. During the period of the Reformation many leading theologians, and not only those coming out of sectarian circles, held such views. Martin Bucer (1491–1551), for instance, in his book *De regno Christi* (*On the Reign of Christ*) attempted to lay the foundations for a Christian ordering of society in England under the leadership of King Edward VI (1537–53; king 1547–53). Bucer's proposal, however, was quite utilitarian, for the proposed legislation was supposed to make the king responsible to the pattern of the law of Christ, but it resembled very much the social and political conditions already existing in England at the time. Luther, however, was suspicious of every christocratic approach, whether it was to be implemented by the church or by the state. Already in 1518 in his *Explanations of the Ninety-Five Theses* he questioned whether it was possible for the pope to hold both a spiritual and a secular *sword*. The Bible, according to Luther, spoke only of one sword, the "sword of the Spirit" (Eph. 6:17).[1] Luther concludes from this that a doctrine that claims two swords should be thrown into hell. But he was not the first to reject the idea that the pope was invested with two swords or two kingdoms. This doctrine, which was popular in the Middle Ages, held that Christ had entrusted the pope as his successor with the worldly and spiritual realm and that the pope gives the worldly realm to the emperor as a fiefdom. But already William of Occam (ca. 1285–1349) and Marsilius of Padua (ca. 1290–1342/43) indicated that this teaching was based upon a questionable allegorical interpretation of Luke 22:38. Even in Luther's time criticism against this doctrine had not been silenced.

In 1520, however, Luther went beyond the traditional polemic against the teaching of the pope's two swords. In his writing *On the Papacy in Rome*, he took up the question whether the authority of the pope was of divine or human character. He concluded that the pope's authority was, beyond doubt, of a worldly and not a divine nature. But Luther was also aware that the external structure of Christendom could not be abandoned, even though this structure could not be equated with true Christianity, which is spiritual. Both aspects of Christianity, external structure and inner substance, must be clearly distinguished, yet cannot be separated from one another, or in one form or the other held to be absolute and definitive. They belong together just as the soul belongs to the human body. It becomes clear here why Luther moved ultimately toward a doctrine of two kingdoms with entirely distinct structures. He was concerned about the inner spiritual life of Christianity and believed that without a genuine distinction between the secular and spiritual realms the latter would be overwhelmed by the worldliness of medieval christocracy in the long run. In this manner, the distinction between the two kingdoms serves to make possible the proclamation of the gospel,

---

1. Martin Luther, *Explanations of the Ninety-Five Theses* (1518) on thesis 80, in *LW* 31:244.

unhindered by secular interests. On the other side, it has thwarted the attempt of enthusiasts to spiritualize the world and to erect in the present a "kingdom of God" in the world.

Because of the unique historical situation of Luther's time, he was not able to follow the two kingdoms doctrine of Augustine in the development of his argument. For Augustine, Christians were still a small group of people who were under constant threat from the all-powerful pagan state. Even after the Emperor Constantine (ca. 285–337, emperor 306–337) had adopted the Christian faith and suspended the persecution of Christians, the majority of the influential families in Rome defended their traditional religion. Therefore Augustine equated the kingdom of the world with the realm that had fallen away from God. For him, this kingdom contains antigodly tendencies and can sometimes even be called the city of the devil. As we see in Luther's work *On Temporal Authority: To What Extent It Should Be Obeyed* (1523), Luther initially largely accepted this view. Humanity must be divided into two groups. One group consists of the true believers in Christ who realize the kingdom of God under the headship of Christ. The other group has no Christians in its midst, and is the kingdom of the world and of the law. The world is essentially a sinful place in which Christians suffer as a small minority. It is the enemy of God and is ruled over by secular princes. But Luther soon abandoned the Augustinian distinction, which had become outdated. In Luther's new version the worldly kingdom included not only the state, but everything that we view today as secular, such as marriage, property, vocation, and so forth. This means that Luther could no longer apply the distinction between law and gospel to the two kingdoms without qualification. The kingdom of the world (or the secular kingdom) encompasses everything that is necessary for the sustenance of daily life and is understood as something good.

Unity of the Two Ways in Which God Rules the World

It would be wrong to equate Luther's teaching of the two kingdoms with his doctrine of the kingdoms of God and the devil. Although he was absolutely convinced of the opposition that existed between God and the devil, as aforementioned, Luther did not think in dualistic categories. In the New Testament, however, especially in the Gospel of John, an opposition between the kingdom of God and the kingdom of the world can be seen in which the latter is understood as a fallen world ruled by sin, death, and the devil. Though Luther distinguishes between Christ's kingdom and the kingdom of the world, the kingdom of the world is not just the domain of the devil. It also attests for Luther to the ordering and sustaining will of God. This can be seen, for example, in the ordering of nature and in political legal systems. Luther acknowledged the world as God's good creation, but did not naively mistake it for being a world without serious problems. In contrast to the Gospel of John or to Augustine, Luther does not see the destructive work of the devil as being confined to the kingdom of the world or to the secular realm. The battle lines are now drawn through both kingdoms, and Satan seeks to transform them both into a God-opposing chaos. Luther confesses, "Against this rule of God, however, Satan rages; for his sole purpose is to crush and destroy everything that God creates and does through this rule."[2] It is God's will that both of his kingdoms or means of governing serve as a bulwark against the destructive attacks of the devil. This points also to the inner unity of the two kingdoms, as Luther wrote,

> God has established two kinds of government among men. The one is spiritual; it has no sword, but it has the Word, by means of which men are to become good and righteous, so that with this righteousness

2. Luther on Zech. 1:7, *Lectures on Zechariah* (1527), in *LW* 20:173.

they may attain eternal life. He administers this righteousness through the Word, which he has committed to the preachers. The other kind is worldly government, which works through the sword so that those who do not want to be good and righteous to eternal life may be forced to become good and righteous in the eyes of the world. He administers this righteousness through the sword. And although God will not reward this kind of righteousness with eternal life, nonetheless, he still wishes peace to be maintained among men and rewards them with temporal blessings.[3]

This quotation from 1526 clearly shows that the same God stands behind both kingdoms and is active and present within both in different ways. Since God is active in both kingdoms according to his goodness and love, Luther concludes that God bestows a twofold blessing on humans: a material blessing for this life and a spiritual blessing for the life eternal. We can see, therefore, an expression of God's love in the unity that exists between the two kingdoms.

This unity, however, is not only to be understood theocentrically. Luther also says that God has "three outward rules and in addition three outward ways or means for his own divine rule."[4] Elsewhere he wrote, "God has therefore established three hierarchies against the devil: the family, the political order, and the Church."[5] Although God's lordship ultimately ties the two kingdoms together, the unity is also visible in human activities since humans live simultaneously in both kingdoms and in all three hierarchies. As responsible coworkers with God, humans encounter both forms of God's government, namely, God's *law* (as it comes to expression in the political realm, the family, and ecclesial structures) and God's *gospel,* as it is proclaimed to them in the preached word.

---

3. Luther, *Whether Soldiers, Too, Can Be Saved* (1526), in *LW* 46:99–100.
4. Luther on Zech. 1:7, in *LW* 20:172.
5. Luther, *Die Zirkulardisputation über Matth. 19,21* (1539), thesis 52, in *WA* 39/II:42.3–4.

Distinction and Mutual Permeation of the Two Kingdoms

Although Luther was convinced of the fundamental unity of the two kingdoms, he never tired of emphasizing that we must distinguish properly between them. The worldly and spiritual kingdoms must be distinguished as clearly as heaven and earth. The one is concerned with faith and eternal salvation, the other with external peace and the prevention of evil. The secular kingdom serves the earthly life and is, like our life on earth, finite, while the spiritual kingdom is related to life eternal, which is the ultimate goal of God's activity.

The worldly kingdom is ostensibly subordinated to the spiritual kingdom. God rules in the secular realm with the left hand while God reigns over the spiritual kingdom with the right hand. This is God's actual work and he cannot allow that anyone else to reign over souls. Christians are indeed aliens in the kingdom of the world, for they are guided by faith. Yet those who are not Christians cannot be guided by faith and love. They belong to the kingdom of the world and are instructed in proper conduct by earthly rules and by the sword. Because Christians are already leading their lives as the sword, that is, the worldly order, requires, the keeping of laws within the secular realm poses no difficulty for them.

Luther correctly observed that Christians cannot escape from the kingdom of the world; we "are all caught within it, indeed, born into it, before we become Christians. Therefore we must also remain within it so long as we live upon the earth, but according to the external bodily life and existence."[6] According to our worldly needs, we are citizens of the kingdom of the world, but according to our spiritual existence, we are citizens of the spiritual kingdom. This

---

6. Luther in a sermon on Matt. 5:38–42, *Wochenpredigen über Matth. 5–7* (1530–32), in *WA* 32:390.15–18.

demonstrates that despite all their differences, an organic and mutual permeation of the two kingdoms exists.

Luther especially emphasizes one point at which our dependence upon the kingdom of the world is manifest when he says that the spiritual kingdom requires peace and order in the world, which are results of the secular realm, in order that the word and the sacraments can be properly administered. Christians cannot lead a sheltered existence and escape from the world. This dependence is further made clear in the encompassing character of the worldly kingdom. As we have seen, the kingdom of the world encompasses not only human authority and government and the orders of nature, but also the means that serve to sustain our life on earth such as marriage, family, property, business, and different vocations. These various human undertakings are carried out according to the law, or according to the sword, which are for Luther synonymous.

But how can one know the divine law if one is not even a Christian? Luther himself admits realistically that already "since the beginning of the world a wise prince is a mighty rare bird, and an upright prince even rarer."[7] Luther even writes that princes, for the most part, have been the greatest fools and the worst scoundrels. How, then, can they know the law of God? Here we must once again recall the great trust Luther placed in the natural reason that God has given to all persons. The kingdom of the world is ruled through reason, and political and economic decisions are not made according to the Bible but according to reason. Luther observes that Christ never preached about economic issues, but left this field to reason so that it could instruct us as to how goods should be divided and trade conducted.[8] Luther's understanding of reason, however, does

---

7. Luther, *Temporal Authority: To What Extent It Should Be Obeyed* (1523), in *LW* 45:113.
8. Cf. the illustration given by Luther in a sermon on Matt. 5:1ff., *Wochenpredigten über Matth. 5–7* (1530–32), in *WA* 32:304.21–32.

not correspond to the Enlightenment conception that understood reason as the autonomous possession of humans. For Luther, even natural reason is a gift of God, for the proper use of which humans are ultimately accountable to God.

The function of reason in Luther's doctrine of the two kingdoms is clarified for us when we turn to the distinction between general and special revelation. It is obvious for Luther that God has revealed certain things to all people through general revelation, while other things are only accessible through the special revelation in Jesus Christ. The regulations and laws of this world are not given through Christ but are already available through the natural law, which is a source of general revelation. Luther is, however, aware that in this world the knowledge of the will of God, which is made possible through general revelation, is often distorted and obscured as a result of human sinfulness. Yet he is convinced that it is not Christ, but rather the law of each particular nation that answers the social and cultural questions concerning what a parent, teacher, politician, or judge should do in certain situations.[9] Of course, these laws are historically conditioned and have undergone many revisions. Luther challenges us, therefore, to use our reason to investigate whether these historically evolved laws still constitute an adequate expression of the natural law that they are supposed to represent. Luther does not equate the natural law with the laws of a particular nation. The natural law is, moreover, the wellspring from which the other laws flow and upon which basis they are to be criticized and interpreted. Yet we normally encounter the natural law in the form of a positive law, which we find in the laws and usages of a particular nation. Although Luther distinguished between the positive law of a given

9. Cf. Luther's distinction between the worldly and spiritual regiments, along with all the examples that he provides, in his explanation of Zech. 1:7, *Lectures on Zechariah* (1527), in *LW* 20:172.

nation and the natural law, he sometimes identified the two—an identification that, in light of human sinfulness, is not without problems.

Christian Existence in the Kingdom of the World

Luther consistently maintained that Christians could also be responsible citizens. Although Christians should not exercise any secular authority among themselves, they must make use of this authority in order to preserve the peace for others. For themselves, however, they should simply obey those who exercise worldly power, thus submitting themselves to secular laws. Luther also believed that Christians should not oppose evil if this opposition benefited only them. When Christians, however, occupy a secular office, as for example as a parent, teacher, politician, judge, and so forth, they must oppose evil to the extent that this opposition is a function of their office. Otherwise, they would neglect their responsibilities and in the long run endanger others. We have the responsibility to enforce the rules connected with our positions with the necessary resolution, yet in love. For example, I must help the neighbor who is in difficulty, and when I am a judge and anyone has injured him or her I must punish them to the full extent of the law. But even as a lawbreaker, the person who injured my neighbor remains my brother or sister. Evildoers must indeed be punished and their crimes condemned, but the punishment must be executed with compassion. This means that I must distribute punishment only in my role as judge and not as a private individual. I enforce the law out of my responsibility toward God's own order, not because I hate the lawbreaker.

The validity of the law is not limited to the kingdom of the world but also has its appropriate place within the spiritual kingdom, yet only as a function of an office in which the law represents

God and his order. The law should never be degraded to a means toward personal revenge, because it must ultimately be an act of love toward one's neighbor. Luther can therefore encourage Christians to seek a secular office. If politicians and judges are necessary and one believes oneself to be qualified to fill one of these positions, then one should strive to achieve this office; otherwise the necessary authority of the office would be held in contempt and weakened. Although Luther counsels against using force either too freely or too sparingly he admits: "To err in this direction . . . and punish too little is more tolerable, for it is always better to let a scoundrel live than to put a godly man to death."[10] Just how far Luther is from the idea of a power-hungry secular order can be seen in his advice that Christians who hold secular office should imitate Christ. Just as Christ as supreme prince came and served us without seeking to increase his own power and honor, Christians in their offices should also not strive for their own advantage but serve those placed under their authority protecting and defending them.

Luther's attitude toward property serves as a good example of his understanding of the service-oriented character of Christians. Luther maintained that all property, with the exception of that which is needed for personal use, is unjustly possessed and has actually been stolen from God and, therefore, should be used to help others.[11] God demands of us to give generously to others. Maintaining possessions becomes theft when we do not use all resources that go beyond our personal needs to alleviate the suffering of others. Luther, therefore, criticized business people who took interest from hard-working persons. Without the slightest investment of their own and without concern for others, they profit from ambitious, hard-working men

---

10. Luther, *Temporal Authority*, in *LW* 45:104–5.
11. So Luther in a sermon on Luke 16:1–3, on August 17, 1522, *Predigten des Jahres 1522*, in *WA* 10/III:275.7–10.

and women who are exposed in their work to a variety of dangers. To alleviate this injustice, Luther proposes that those who finance a loan receive no set annual amount of interest but rather a percentage of the profits earned by the one who took out the loan. If the profits are high then both will fare well. But when they are low then both will suffer. In this way those who loan money can exhibit a genuine interest in the people to whom they have made a loan and in their work. Here again Luther's emphasis upon the service-oriented nature of secular structures is to be seen. These structures should serve people and not the free-reigning power of capital.

The emphasis on service to others Luther expressed with particular clarity when he described the principles according to which (Christian) princes should exercise their office.[12] They must in the first place turn to God with good faith and deep prayer. Then they must handle those under their authority out of love and an attitude of Christian service. Third, they must treat their counselors and officials with a spirit of openness and nonpartisan opinion. And finally, they should confront evildoers with responsible force and severity. These arguments show that although one cannot serve both God and mammon (or wealth), one can serve both God and emperor. It even appears that one can better serve the emperor in the secular realm if one also serves God in the spiritual realm. Yet one might rightly inquire to what extent Luther's position goes beyond a simple advocacy of the status quo and strives for a transformation toward a more just society.

Critique of the Doctrine of the Two Kingdoms

Lutherans have faced the accusation that their doctrine of the two kingdoms supports the status quo and hardly allows for any creative

12. Cf. for the following Luther, *Temporal Authority*, in *LW* 45:126.

innovation. Of course, Luther's doctrine of two kingdoms should not be uncritically applied to our own day, just as Augustine's concept of a city of the world and a city of God could not be applied to the medieval situation without decisive modifications. The modern form of societal structure in which the authority to govern comes from the people was unknown to Luther. His emphasis upon the sword and punishment through rulers must therefore be seen today as outdated. In the Western world, public order can only be maintained through a basic consent that must, however, be oriented toward specific values and objectives. In this regard Luther's insistence upon order, justice, and mutual concern is certainly of continuing value.

It is precisely the ordering function of authorities, however, that has been met with much criticism in light of the rule of injustice in the Third Reich, as well as in formerly communist regime in East Germany, which existed in the heartland of the Reformation. Was not Luther's doctrine of two kingdoms partly responsible for the rise of the Third Reich? As an answer to this question, we must remember that Hitler started out in the predominantly Roman Catholic city of Munich. Only much later did his movement engulf Protestant Prussia, since there was Berlin, the capital of Germany. Further, one must point out that the Lutheran nations of Scandinavia sought to offer resistance to the Nazi occupation, albeit with little success. Indeed, so many factors came into play with the rise of the Third Reich that one cannot simply lay the blame directly upon the Lutherans. Additionally, one must also understand Luther's argument historically. Over against the medieval feudal system and its spread of terror, Luther stressed the king's peace and its preservation through every available means. One cannot speak either of a pure pacifism or of quietistic inaction in regard to Luther.

As a second area of criticism against the Lutheran doctrine of the two kingdoms, the accusation is often brought to bear that it contradicts the New Testament understanding of the kingdom of God. For this reason one is particularly inclined in Reformed circles to replace the two-kingdom view with the reign of Christ in the one kingdom. Although such terminology can make very good sense inasmuch as it is oriented to the New Testament Gospels, it must not be forgotten that in this world true believers, nominal believers, and unbelievers live with one another in the same world. Christians do not yet enjoy an eschatological community of believers, even if the New Testament understanding of the kingdom of God presents this as having already been inaugurated. If one does not wish to make the church into a duplicate of the world or, vice versa, to place society christocratically under the explicit reign of Christ, then one must distinguish between that realm of society that allows itself expressly to be governed by God's word, and all other areas, in which God is not mentioned or even deliberately excluded, and that must therefore be governed by God in an indirect manner.

Despite all the criticisms three aspects of Luther's doctrine of the two kingdoms remain especially important for us today:

1. *The world is not only a place of sin and evil, but it stands also under the rule of God.* To simply write off the world as bad not only goes against the prevailing sentiment of most people but it also contradicts the conviction of the Bible. The description of this earth as a valley of trouble, drudgery, and tears, and as the domain of the devil from which Christians will soon be delivered when they reach heaven, represents only one aspect of the biblical truth. If one sets up this partial truth as absolute, one gets the impression that the gospel cannot say anything positive about the world. Yet it is the understanding of the Old as well as the New Testament that God cares for this fallen world, protecting and preserving it. Luther's emphasis upon

the reign of God within the secular realm reminds us that the world, even in its God-alienated state, is not without God. God's presence in the self-disclosure in Jesus Christ is merely the special way in which God is with his creation. If we reject the notion of a general revelation, which in hidden and faint ways always expresses itself in specific situations, we would deny the divinity of God. The result would be an unbiblical, dualistic worldview in which the world, as it were, would exist without God. Humans, however, have always had an awareness of God and a concept of good and evil. It would also be difficult to explain the persistent religiosity of humans, through which religious themes continue to occupy our attention despite all the secularization of the day-to-day world, apart from a general revelation.

2. *If we do not want to perish with the world, then it must be a place of mutual compensation and concern.* The natural law, which Luther correctly saw expressed in the Golden Rule, is fundamental for the survival of a society. If the Golden Rule is denied as the fundamental principle of community life (for instance in the family, in a people, or in the whole of humanity), then human relationships will suffer in the long run. This can be recognized in the state capitalism of former socialist nations, as well as in Western-style individualistic capitalism. Both forms of life together show too little mutual consideration and concern for fellow human beings. In both cases society is not able to bear the long-term results. The increasingly obvious North-South discrepancy on our globe functions in a similarly disturbing fashion. One can even demonstrate that humans ultimately destroy themselves if they do not exhibit sufficient care of creation as a gift of God but rather only selfishly exploit its resources. The natural law functions as regulator, in order that

we might recognize our own exploitative tendencies toward other humans and toward nature and correspondingly correct these. Since humans are creatures blessed with reason, there is also cause for optimism that we will not mutually and permanently destroy our God-given environment in which we live, but rather live peacefully with one another upon the earth. Yet in our striving for mutual concern, we should realistically remember that the earth is only God's worldly realm and that dreams of heaven on earth are utopian and unjustified.

3. *Power always brings with it a demonic temptation toward its misuse.* In contrast to many great religious figures both before and after him, Luther was very much aware of this temptation. When Luther chided evil princes and held their abuses before them, he knew that humans were by their sinful nature centered upon themselves; they are beings estranged from God. For this reason Luther turned often to Christian princes and encouraged Christians in general to take up public office. Although Christians know the natural law and are willing to obey it, they are not guided by its often only hazy precepts. They live according to the example of Christ and by his grace. Therefore they can establish signs and pointers to God's will in a demonic world. As the community of the body of Christ, their aim is to proleptically actualize the future provided by Christ. They need not despair because they are only a minority or because no one seems to take notice of their efforts. They can and must announce the future that Christ has provided, because they know the One who was the first to live as God intended humans to live. Therefore, both symbolically and literally they should represent mutuality in their communal structures. Christ has overcome the disunity and contradictory ways of humanity by dying the death of this world and beginning a new life.

Yet Christians can at present only realize this new life in a fragmentary fashion. They actively and anticipatorily await with the whole creation the universal coming of the new creation and the final redemptive act of God. At this future point the two kingdoms or forms of God's administration will be fused into God's one world. In the contemporary world, however, we continue to live within two distinct kingdoms.

4. *Luther always had a healthy mistrust of authority.* In contrast to the Anabaptists, he did not close himself off from the world, but called instead for Christian engagement within the world. Hence his criticisms of the sociopolitical relationships of his time were not destructive and did not reflect a mistrust of the ruling powers as such, but he was always conscious of his responsibility toward the entire community. He followed no particular "party line." During the Peasants' War, for example, he initially took up the complaints of the peasants who were being exploited by the nobility and upper classes, and warned the ruling class, "For rulers are not appointed to exploit their subjects for their own profit and advantage, but to be concerned about the welfare of their subjects."[13] Yet he also warned the peasants: "The fact that the rulers are wicked and unjust does not excuse disorder and rebellion, for the punishing of wickedness is not the responsibility of everyone, but of the worldly rulers who bear the sword."[14] He warned both sides: "For God's sake, . . . take hold of these matters properly, with justice and not with force or violence and do not start endless bloodshed."[15] However, when the peasants took up arms, Luther reminded the princes of their duty: "For in this case a prince and lord must remember that

13. Luther, *Admonition to Peace. A Reply to the Twelve Articles of the Peasants in Swabia* (1525), in *LW* 46:22–23.
14. Luther, *Admonition to Peace*, 46:25.
15. Ibid., 46:40.

according to Romans 13[:4] he is God's minister and the servant of his wrath and that the sword has been given to him against such people."[16] Christians, whether in a ruling position or as ordinary citizens, must therefore always look to what is right, and take the side of what is right, and seek without resorting to violence to help that which is right to gain the victory, using all means at their disposal, so that the well-being of the entire community will be promoted.

In many of Luther's letters, he took a stance regarding the political issues of his day. In so doing, he did not seek to become involved in political life by virtue of his reputation, as if he knew better than others. Rather, he saw it as his Christian duty not to let the political events of the day pass by without comment. Luther almost always rejected advising anyone to resist the powers that be, although as evidenced by his very clear criticisms, he did not seek to shelter them. If the governing authority is influenced by speaking the truth to it, Luther writes, "well and good; if not you are excused, you suffer wrong for God's sake."[17] We owe the governing authorities the word of truth, whether that be criticism or affirmation, even though we should not count on its being accepted. Luther was convinced that an irresponsible governing authority would not go unpunished, for God overthrows the powerful from their thrones and is able to "eradicate their roots along with their name and the memory of them."[18] God reigns and will in God's own good time abolish an insubordinate government.

Luther's fear that those faithful to the Roman Church who rejected his reforms might brand him as a leader of rebellion also played a

---

16. Luther, *Against the Robbing and Murdering Hordes of Peasants* (1525), in *LW* 46:52–53.
17. Luther, *Temporal Authority*, in *LW* 45:124–25.
18. Luther, *Den 82. Psalm ausgelegt* (1530), in *WA* 31/I:193.24–25.

role in regard to his disapproving attitude toward opposing authority by force. He feared that under the pretext of putting down what they would label as "Luther's rebellion," they could roll back the reforms that he had set in motion. In order not to give them any excuse to go on the offensive, Luther was very concerned to maintain order. This attitude had a lasting effect. For instance, for this reason it was very difficult for those influenced by Luther—such as the lawyer Hans von Donanyi (1902–1945), the lawyer and former mayor of Leipzig, Carl Friedrich von Goerdeler (1884–1945), and General Ludwig Beck (1880–1944)—to finally make the transition to active revolt in the July 20, 1944 attempt to overthrow Hitler. Following the thought of Luther, they understood Rom. 13:2 ("Whoever resists authority resists what God has appointed, and those who resist will incur judgment") as a warning against every self-proclaimed uprising against authority. They asked themselves, therefore, whether Hitler could still be considered the legitimate authority.

After the war, there appeared an important book on political ethics by the Lutheran theologian Walter Künneth (1901–1997), *Politik zwischen Dämon und Gott* (Politics between the demonic and God),[19] in which Künneth portrayed politics as existing in tension between Romans 13 (authority as the ordering power of God) and Revelation 13 (the demonic state), and conceded the right to rebellion against the state under certain, carefully considered conditions. One should not, therefore, rise up against anything and everything in the opinion that, as a Christian, one knows better than others what is best for the general good. Luther himself had a healthy mistrust of attempts to Christianize the world:

> If anyone attempted to rule the world by the gospel and to abolish all temporal law and sword on the plea that all are baptized and Christian,

---

19. Walter Künneth, *Politik zwischen Dämon und Gott* (Berlin: Lutherisches Verlagshaus, 1954).

and that, according to the gospel, there shall be among them no law or sword—or need or either—pray tell me, friend, what would he be doing? He would be loosing the ropes and chains of the savage wild beasts and letting them bite and mangle everyone, meanwhile insisting that they were harmless, tame, and gentile creatures; but I would have the proof in my wounds. Just so would the wicked under the name of Christian abuse evangelical freedom, carry on their rascality, and insist that they were Christians subject neither to law nor sword.[20]

Because there are sinful people in this world, one cannot dispense with a political order that judges according to the principles of justice. But such systems need the cooperation and engagement of Christians who should further the principle of justice and peace and oppose all injustice.

---

20. Luther, *Temporal Authority*, in *LW* 45:91.

7

Scripture Alone

Luther was a biblical theologian. Scripture alone (*sola scriptura*), therefore, became the basic premise of Lutheran theology. Bible translation and the broad availability of Bibles were of great significance for the spread of Luther's teaching. Johannes Gutenberg (ca. 1394/99–1468) had revolutionized the production of books by using reusable metal letters in a printing press. It fell to Luther to revolutionize Bible translation. He worked from the original languages, rendering the Old Testament from Hebrew and the New Testament from Greek. But first of all, he had to acquire adequate knowledge of both languages. This task was made more difficult because at his time the study of Greek and Hebrew in the German universities was still in its early stages and reliable lexicons and grammars were rare. Luther therefore had to rely upon the counsel of well-informed friends and experts. For the first translation of the New Testament, the so-called September Bible of 1522, Luther frequently relied upon Melanchthon's knowledge of the Greek language. With the Old Testament Luther turned for advice to the

Jews, who were particularly helpful to him in his translation of Old Testament laws into German. Additionally, the Wittenberg Hebrew scholar Matthäus Aurogallus (ca. 1490–1543) assisted him. To the very end of his life, Luther worked on his translation of the Bible, so that later editions contained many improvements.

Luther was not the first one to translate the Bible into German. But each of the earlier translations depended upon the Latin version of the Bible known as the *Vulgate.* Hardly any of these translations found their way into the hands of the people because, according to the official opinion of the church, the word of God in the language of the people did not belong in the hands of laypeople, since they would not understand it properly. Additionally, these translations were difficult to read because they often followed too rigidly the structure of the Latin on which they were based. Martin Luther was the first to insist that one must "look the people in the face," that is to say, one must bring the biblical texts to the people. To this end, Luther used the diplomatic language of the Saxon court, which was largely familiar to Germans living in the center and the south of Germany, but less to the people living in the north, who often spoke Low German, which is akin to the English language. Johannes Bugenhagen, hailing from Pomerania and therefore fluent in Low German, translated Luther's translation of the Bible into Low German. But the people there preferred Luther's own version. This means that Luther's Bible translation helped to forge a unified German language, early High German.

Although Luther was especially careful to render the objective meaning of the biblical text in unabbreviated form into German, he also succeeded through his choice of words in conforming the text to contemporary thought and language patterns. Luther's translation of the Bible was an important linguistic work of art that was even praised by his opponents. Hence he reported in a table talk, "I have this testimony from Duke George that he once said: If only the monk would put the whole Bible into German and follow it where he should go [meaning, into hell]!"[1] Duke George of Saxony, who clung to the old faith, was an irreconcilable opponent of Luther. But even he wished that Luther would complete his translation of the Bible.

As soon as Luther's translation appeared it became an absolute bestseller. Between 1522, when the September Bible appeared, and 1546, the year of Luther's death, more than three hundred full or partial editions of the Bible were published. Even if each printing only ran to about two thousand copies, then altogether there were probably at least 750,000 copies of Luther's translation of the Bible sold during his lifetime. This incredible number of Bibles is all the more astounding when we consider that very few people at that time could read and that the price for Luther's translation of the Bible, as for all books at that time, was very high. For the translation of the New Testament published in 1522, the price was between a half and one and a half guldens, a price that, compared with the average yearly wage of a domestic maid at one and a half guldens, would be considered very expensive even in our time.—Nevertheless the relatively high printing of three thousand copies of the 1522 translation was sold out within three months, and in December a new edition was published.—Luther, however, did not receive a single cent for his Bible translation. The profit went entirely into the coffers of the publishers.

For Luther, the translation of the Bible was indispensable, for the Word of God and Scripture belong together. The Word is only to be found in Scripture and must always be measured by it. Because we are each responsible for our own faith, we cannot rely upon other people's interpretation of Scripture and believe on the basis of their

1. Luther, "Table Talk" no. 2790a (1532), in *WA TR* 2:661.16–18.

authority. Rather, every single Christian depends on Scripture, but must thereby be first of all familiar with it. Although Luther clearly differentiated between different biblical writings in view of their varying theological content and weight, the Scripture as a whole had only one content for Luther, which was Jesus Christ.

Christ as the Sole Content of Scripture

Christ is the Word of God become human. It is for this reason that the Bible can be the Word of God only when its single and entire content is Christ. To be sure, Luther knew that the Bible contained more than words from and about Jesus. It also included the Old Testament law, but nevertheless, according to Luther, it also pointed to Christ, who is the one who is freed from the law and is the content of the gospel. Therefore, either directly or indirectly, Christ is the content of Scripture. Luther was aware that the biblical canon was formed within the church over a period of time. This, however, does not allow the church to place itself above Scripture, for the contents of Scripture are authenticated by Christ and not by the church. As the content of Scripture, Christ himself attests to the truth of Scripture. Just as John the Baptist did not stand over Christ, although he pointed to him, so also according to Luther, the church, which points to Scripture, cannot rule or stand over it. No human institution can authorize Scripture, that is, can lend it credibility. It bears its authority within itself through that which speaks from within it, namely Jesus Christ. Only to the extent that the church places itself under Scripture and satisfies its requirements can the church itself be authorized by Scripture. "The gospel is not believed because the church confirms it but rather because people sense that it is the Word of God."[2] The self-attestation of Scripture corresponds to its self-interpretation.

2. Luther, *De potestate leges forendi in ecclesia* (1530), in *WA* 30/II:687.32–33.

Martin Luther rejected the usual fourfold interpretation of Scripture common at his time and stressed that Scripture should always be interpreted *literally*. It should not be translated *allegorically*, that is, in the sense of the church and its teachings; nor *tropologically*, meaning as related to ethics and morals; nor *anagogically*, as pointing to the eschatological fulfillment. Scripture must in the first place be understood literally, in the sense that its original authors meant it. Because this sense comes to the fore nowhere so directly and vitally as in Scripture itself, this means that Scripture must interpret its own self. Luther pleaded therefore for an interpretation that originates from Scripture and is not imposed upon it. If another authority would interpret Scripture, this authority would authenticate it and the character of Scripture as final authority would be lost. "Scripture, therefore, is its own light. It is good, then, when Scripture interprets itself."[3]

The principle of Scripture's self-interpretation is, on the one hand, directed toward Rome, where it was argued that only the teaching office of the church is able to authoritatively interpret Scripture. On the other hand, Luther also used this principle against the enthusiasts who contended that a special gift of the Spirit enabled them to correctly understand Scripture. Luther, nevertheless, suggests that only people who are moved by God's Spirit can interpret Scripture. Yet the Spirit comes to them alone through Scripture. If we expect such a spiritual gift through institutions and events external to Scripture, then we elevate these above Scripture and ultimately interpret Scripture according to our own wishes. For Luther, this ultimately means that Scripture should always be interpreted according to its literal sense. One should only make exception to this principle when the text itself forces one to adopt a figurative

---

3. Luther, in a sermon from July 25, 1522, *Predigten des Jahres 1522*, in *WA* 10/III:238.10–11.

understanding. If Scripture, on the contrary, is interpreted "spiritually," then everyone can impose his or her own spirit upon the words and Scripture loses its clarity.

The self-interpretation of Scripture, however, presupposes that Scripture is in itself clear and understandable. Luther was firm in this belief, especially in view of the Roman Church's teaching that Scripture is unclear and can only be rightly interpreted by the teaching office of the church. The clarity of Scripture is seen already by Luther in the fact that Jesus and the apostles referred to Scripture, that is, what we now call the Old Testament, in their teaching; in doing so, they testify to the general clarity of Scripture. For Luther it is not a dogmatic postulate that Scripture is clear and understandable. This recognition was reaffirmed through Luther's own study of the Bible. The fact that many people either do not understand Scripture or understand it incorrectly was explained by Luther by indicating that these persons were either held captive by Satan or, in the case of the pious, that God allowed them to continue in error for a certain time in order to show them that only God could enlighten them.

The interpretation of Scripture must always occur from its center, that is, from Christ. Of course, the ruling scholastic theology of the time also knew that Christ was the center of Scripture. Yet Christ was usually understood morally as a law-oriented teacher of virtues, as we see in Erasmus or the legally minded reformers of the late Middle Ages. For Luther, however, Christ as the center of Scripture is synonymous with the free grace of God, on whom alone human salvation depends. Luther's view of Christ comes primarily from the New Testament proclamation, especially from the writings of Paul and the Gospel of John. But he also found testimony to Christ already in the Old Testament: "Therefore what is preached about Christ is all one Gospel, although every writer has his own distinctive literary style. . . . But whenever it deals with Christ as our Savior and states that we are justified and saved through faith in Him without our works, then there is one Word and one Gospel."[4]

The christocentric exposition of Scripture is an interpretation of the biblical message that is derived from the gospel of justification through faith alone. In the event that a passage of Scripture contradicts the evangelical meaning and stands in opposition to the rest of Scripture, seen as a whole, then this passage has no authority as word of God. This was applied by Luther, for example, in the case of the Letter of James. Luther declared that one must interpret this letter according to the rest of Scripture, and must not derive any theological propositions from it that would oppose the plain and clear direction of Scripture as a whole. If this method of interpretation is not followed, then one would have to reject James as unbiblical. Hence Luther's principle of the gospel-centered exposition of Scripture also becomes biblical criticism when the text does not appropriately represent the gospel.

Limits of Biblical Criticism

Luther occasionally expressed criticism of the biblical documents when he pointed to contradictions and discrepancies within them. Nevertheless, it would be inaccurate to view him as one of the founders of historical biblical criticism, because he made such critical observations only very occasionally and did not give any great weight to them. Decisive for Luther was that we have the right understanding of Scripture and the right articles of faith, that is, the hermeneutic key to understand the Bible. Questions of historical criticism were, in contrast, secondary for him. Even when Luther criticized theologically individual parts of the canon, the standard he judged them against was either Christ or the gospel of free grace and

---

4. Luther, in his preface to his exposition of 1 Peter, *Sermons on the First Epistle of St. Peter* (1523), in *LW* 30:3.

justification through faith alone. One could also say that for Luther what was apostolic was decisive. That meant for him, by way of content, that Christ as Savior must be proclaimed loud and clear: "It is the office of a true apostle to preach of the Passion and resurrection and office of Christ."[5]

The apostolic character of a New Testament author is witnessed to in the contents of his writing, namely, in the clarity of his testimony of Christ. This is the standard that Luther used to classify a book as canonical. "All the genuine sacred books agree in this, that all of them preach and inculcate Christ."[6] If this characteristic is deficient or entirely missing in one of the canonical writings, then its author cannot be an apostle. In applying this criterion, Luther determined in his "Preface to the New Testament" in 1522 which books are the truest and noblest in the New Testament. They are the Gospel of John and the First Letter of John, the letters of Paul (especially the Letters to the Romans, Galatians, and Ephesians) as well as the First Letter of Peter.[7] Although the Gospel of John only reports a few miracles, it is truly the chief of the Gospels and is far ahead of the others. The others report many miracles, but they do not proclaim the gospel as clearly as John. Luther recognized the intention of the Letter of James— it is directed against those who would put their trust in faith without works. Yet he criticizes that the letter was not fully up to this task. In regard to the Letter to the Hebrews, Luther points out the great difference in its content with that of the other apostolic writings, yet he has a great appreciation for it precisely because of its witness to the priestly office of Christ and its interpretation of the Old Testament.

---

5. Luther, "Preface to the Epistles of St. James and St. Jude" (1522), in *LW* 35:396.
6. Ibid.
7. Ibid., 361–62.

In 1522 Luther wrote concerning the Revelation of John that he could sense no inspiration of the Holy Spirit in this book. Hence he placed it at the end of the Bible, together with the Letter of Jude. In 1530 he wrote a new critical preface to the book of Revelation in which he interpreted the book in relation to the history of the church, and in this way highlighted its continuing value to the church.[8] But he was still not able to recognize it as one of the chief books of the Bible.

Luther's assessments of individual books of the New Testament are significant because, if for no other reason, they show he applied criticism to the canon and did not understand the Bible and all of its parts as a divine law book all having the same weight. He pointed to differences within the canon in terms of whether a book stood nearer or further from the center of Scripture. He also indicated varying degrees of evangelical clarity and thereby varying degrees of authority and significance for the church. Hence for Luther there existed a canon within the canon. He did not, however, express any criticisms in the name of reason by claiming, for instance, that one could no longer accept certain views of Scripture in light of a particular scientific worldview or on the basis of some modern self-understanding. Only in those places where he detected a clouding of the proclamation of the gospel did he question the character of a writing or a text as God's word. Decisive for Luther is that which empowers Christianity, and not what does or does not make sense to reason. Luther's biblical criticism is kept within clear boundaries and is pre-Enlightenment.

---

8. Luther, "Preface to the Revelation of St. John" (1530), in *LW* 35:401.

Relationship between the Two Testaments

It is important to Luther, in regard to the word of God, to distinguish between law and gospel. This distinction, however, is not identical to that between the Old and New Testaments. In the Old Testament there is gospel, namely in the promises, just as there is also law to be found in the New Testament, as in the Sermon on the Mount. Nevertheless, the Old Testament is primarily law, while the gospel dominates the New Testament. The Old Testament mainly teaches the law and convicts of sin, whereas the New Testament brings grace and peace through the forgiveness of sins. The Old Testament, therefore, is primarily a law book and the New Testament a gospel, or good news. Both Testaments are related to one another in the same way as are promise and fulfillment, for the Old Testament points toward Christ and salvation, while the New Testament testifies to these promises as fulfilled.

The entire truth of the New Testament is already contained hidden within the Old Testament, so that it must only be opened up and revealed. Thus Luther can say,

> Everything that the apostles have taught and written they have derived from the Old Testament, for everything has been proclaimed in it that would take place in the future in Christ and would be preached. . . . For this reason they based all of their preaching upon the Old Testament and there is no word in the New Testament for which one does not see behind it the Old Testament in which it was previously proclaimed.[9]

Christ opens up for us the Old Testament. In his word Christ unveils the meaning of the First Commandment as a witness to the resurrection of the dead: God is a God of the living and not of the dead. Luther is even able to contend that the New Testament has no

---

9. Luther, "Evangelium in der hohen Christmesse. Joh. 1,1–14," *Kirchenpostille 1522*, in *WA* 10/I/1:181.15–22.

other function than to open up the Old Testament and to reveal the gospel hidden within it.

New Testament proclamation is by its very nature interpretation of the Old Testament. Luther took notice of the fact that Jesus wrote nothing at all and the apostles very little, for they referred to and grounded themselves upon already existing writings, namely the Old Testament. The Old Testament, then, according to Luther, becomes the swaddling clothes and crib "in which Christ lies."[10] This is also the testimony of the angel to the shepherds in the nativity story. The New Testament is entirely founded upon the Old Testament, even though the Old Testament is only first unveiled in the New Testament and can only be understood through it. To the extent that the Old Testament bears the gospel within it and has to do with Christ, it points beyond itself. The Old Testament is not complete within itself but points instead to the New Testament.

Binding Nature of the Old Testament

The Old Testament, in the form in which we have it today, is first of all the testament that God gave to Israel. The law that is contained within it is likewise only applicable for Israel. Hence Luther can say that the Old Testament is "the *Sachsenspiegel* of the Jews, that is to say, their law book."[11] As such, it is not directed toward Christians and is not binding for them. Luther distances himself from the enthusiasts and Anabaptists, who often turned to Old Testament regulations to justify their actions and in doing so continued to regard the law of Moses as the binding word of God for them. Luther responded to this view, saying, "One must not only consider whether it is the Word

---

10. Luther, "Preface to the Old Testament" (1523), in *LW* 35:236.
11. Luther, on Exod. 19f., *Predigten über das 2. Buch Mose* (1524–27), in *WA* 16:378.9. The *Sachsenspiegel* was the most influential and one of the oldest German legal code of economic and social laws, written by Eike von Repgow (ca. 1180/90–after 1233) between 1220 and 1230.

of God, whether God has said it, but much more, to whom he has said it, whether it applies to you."[12] In the law, God has spoken first of all to Israel and not to Christians. "For Moses is given to the Jewish people alone, and does not concern us Gentiles and Christians."[13] This applies not just to the Mosaic ceremonial law and legal code but also to the Decalogue.

The Decalogue, or Ten Commandments, is the source and center of all the laws of Israel. Even the ceremonial law and legal codes depend upon it. Christ, however, is the end of the law. The ban against images (Exod. 20:4) and the Sabbath laws (Exod. 20:8) are therefore abolished. Nevertheless, the Old Testament law and the law of Moses does not remain exclusively related to Israel. It is also a special form of natural law written in the hearts of all people. To the extent that the Mosaic law and this natural law correspond, it is also applicable to non-Jews. It is not binding for them as the law of Moses, but rather obligates them through its content in their hearts and consciences. Moses is not the author but only the interpreter of the laws that are written in the hearts of all people.

When Christians teach the Mosaic law, particularly the Ten Commandments, then it is because "the natural laws were never so orderly and well written as by Moses."[14] We must not, however, according to Luther, accept the Decalogue in its historical form without reflection, but must clearly distinguish between what is binding and what is not binding within it. The fear of God, for instance, remains binding, for as Luther says, God should be "feared, loved and trusted above all things." The Sabbath ban, on the other hand, as Luther's reformulation of the third commandment shows, is declared to be no longer applicable. It loses the status of binding, but

12. Luther, on Exod. 19–20, in *WA* 16:385.7–9.
13. Luther, *Against the Heavenly Prophets in the Matter of Images and Sacraments* (1525), in *LW* 40:92.
14. Ibid., 98.

continues to be recognized as an example in the form of "you shall keep the day of rest holy."

In the law of Moses, there are also many other regulations that can serve as examples to other peoples without being binding. As examples of these, Luther mentions the Tenth Commandment, the jubilee year, the Sabbath year, and the law on divorce. He would have been pleased if these and other ordinances of the Mosaic law would have been taken over by secular law, not by compulsion (as if they were divine laws) but freely, based upon the reasonable insight that these regulations are simply exemplary. Luther was of the opinion that frequently throughout history a people would take over laws from another people when they recognized that these laws were good. Thus, the law of the Old Testament has manifold continuing relevance for non-Jews. Luther also admits the history of Israel, as we find it in the Old Testament, has a certain relevance for us. We can learn from its example how people either obeyed the law of God or were disobedient, and how God responded either with grace or wrath. Even Christians can learn from such examples, for human beings remain the same in their nature throughout the ages. Christians, in their own individual histories with God, will continually be confronted with similar questions and decisions. The history of the people of Israel, therefore, has an exemplary significance for all people.

Christ and the Old Testament

According to Luther the Old Testament is a book that testifies of Christ. As law it points to Christ and is filled with him, inasmuch as it promises and points proleptically to Christ and his church. Moses taught the law so that the people would recognize their reluctance toward the law and would strive toward grace. With these observations Luther took up the interpretation of the law as the disciplinarian that leads us to Christ (Gal. 3:24–25.). Similar to Moses, the prophets point beyond themselves. Luther interprets them as both proclaimers of the promise and advocates of the law. They demonstrate how God has in a very firm and strict manner confirmed his command. The proclamation of the prophets, therefore, is to be understood christocentrically.

The Old Testament, however, does not simply lead us to Christ, for Christ is already present within it. In his actions and promises he is already present in the God of the Old Testament. In the Old Testament we do not encounter some abstract God, but rather God the Father, who lets God's self be found in certain places and under certain signs, and who gives the people his promises. These promises all point to Christ, whereby one must distinguish between the immediate promise of Christ and the anticipation of him. First of all, Christ is promised in the prophets, Psalms, and the well-known messianic passages of the historical books. Even if the prophets often erred in the predictions of future historical events, which Luther concedes, they were nonetheless on the mark with the decisive sense and content of their proclamation that announced Jesus Christ and his kingdom in advance.

Limits of Luther's Interpretation of Scripture

Alongside the Old Testament's promise of Christ and its leading to him, there is also an anticipatory depiction of Christ and his church. Luther finds this above all in the Levitical law, the priesthood, and the sacrificial system, but also in the monarchy. Luther follows here the typology of the Letter to the Hebrews. The Old Testament "pointed to Christ, while the New Testament now gives us what was promised and prefigured in the Old Testament."[15] Christ is, then, present in the

---

15. Luther, *Sermons on the First Epistle of St. Peter* (1523), in *LW* 30:19.

figures of the Old Testament. Hence the Old Testament law has a double function as a model that, on the one hand, points far beyond Christ, and on the other hand, is abolished through Christ and is no longer binding for Christians. Luther applies here a "spiritual interpretation" to the Old Testament that differs from the allegorical only in that it is grounded in salvation history and explains the relevant texts as pointing to Christ.[16]

Such an interpretation goes beyond the literal meaning of the text. Because Luther does not view these texts as on the same level as the Christian faith, he believes they must be understood in a completely different sense that finds its basis elsewhere. In contrast to the allegorical interpretation, Luther appreciates the literal meaning in his spiritual interpretation because the history these texts deal with is prophetic. Luther is able to place the original literal meaning and the spiritual interpretation together and bring them into living relationship with one another through the concept of symbol, or model. Luther sought to initially interpret a Scripture passage historically in relation to its own contemporary situation and then to relate it to the New Testament community. So, for example, he saw the Passover Feast of the Old Testament as a symbol and model of our Easter feast.[17] In this way, Luther seeks to make the eternal presence of Christ and his salvation meaningful for believers along with the temporality of salvation history, which includes the coming of Christ in time. In so doing, he intends to show the essential simultaneity of all believers both before and after Christ, as well as their historical and temporal differentiation.

This interpretation of the Old Testament, however, is no longer comprehensible today, just as we can no longer repeat the interpretation of the early Christians. The discovery and introduction

16. Cf. Luther, "Preface to the Old Testament," in *LW* 35:247–48.
17. Cf. Luther, *Der 111. Psalm ausgelegt* (1530), in *WA* 31/I:396–97.

of historical exegesis stands between us and these periods. One cannot today simply interpret the prophetic texts of the Old Testament christologically, for our understanding of their concrete historical meaning has been sharpened. Their originally intended meaning was not simply fulfilled in Jesus Christ. The meaning was often expanded and changed in order to apply to new situations and finally to Christ. Therefore, the relationship of the Old Testament to Christ and to the New Testament has become more complicated for us. Nevertheless, we as Christians can agree with Luther that the history of Israel moves toward Christ. If today we want the Old Testament to be meaningful for us Christians, then we must interpret it christologically, that is, as pointing to Christ. Otherwise it remains a document of another religion. This means that, in contrast to Luther, we must emphasize the historical difference between the two testaments; but in agreement with Luther we must also emphasize their continuity in which they build upon one another.

8

Law and Gospel

Initially, the distinction between law and gospel sounds typically Lutheran. In the Reformed and Pietist streams of Protestantism, which seem to exclusively stress the liberating power of the gospel, one hears of the binding demands of the biblical message so much that the gospel is overshadowed and even obliterated. One could say here that the law is merely the flip side of the gospel that is used to guide the Christian toward a Christlike life. Luther, however, learned firsthand about the disadvantages of the ethos of obligation and compensation of the late Middle Ages, first through his upbringing in popular piety and then through his own experience of monasticism. For this reason, he stressed that God has freed us from all obligations of the law through the gospel. In order not to exchange this newly won freedom for a new legalism and in order to emphasize the priority of God's activity, Luther distinguished sharply between law and gospel, but without separating one from the other. He stressed that the Word of God encounters human beings in the twofold form of law and gospel.

Antithesis and Unity of Law and Gospel

As aforementioned, the law has always been known to humans since God has inscribed it into their hearts at creation. Luther holds this position, as we have seen, in agreement with Paul. Even if the written law had never been given through Moses, the human spirit would have known through its very nature that one should worship God and love one's neighbor. The Spirit of God, according to Luther, dictates the law perpetually into the hearts of all people. But the will of God, which expresses itself in the law and enlivens and enlightens human understanding, has been misunderstood ever since the fall through the sinful desires of human beings. God was forced, therefore, to give the Israelites a written law through Moses that would remind them of the natural law in their hearts. Moses is not the proper author of the Decalogue, but simply the one who interpreted the natural law more clearly.

The law is the embodiment of the eternal will of God and, as such, is what condemns the sinner. One needs to distinguish between the *content* of God's law and the *form* in which this content encounters human beings. According to its *content*, the law represents the eternal will of God, and its fulfillment leads human beings to salvation. This means nothing other than that humans shall not impugn or offend God's divinity. If humans conduct themselves accordingly, God will be gracious to them. The law meets human beings already in their original condition and it will continue to be valid in the new world to come, where it will be completely fulfilled. Consequently it has protological (original) *and* eschatological (final) significance. The law is always and eternally the unchanging will of God. With the fall, however, the relationship fundamentally changed between humanity and the law as the eternal will of God. God's eternal will became for sinful human beings what we now experience as law. The content remained identical but the form has changed. This form of the will of God, that is, the law, must now be more thoroughly examined.

Today, the concept or *form* of law carries with it a twofold meaning.[1] It has a secular use and a theological or spiritual use. In its first or secular use, it guards against serious transgressions and crimes and protects the public peace in this world, which stands under the influence of the devil and is prone to sin. The law is applied through the offices established by God—namely, worldly authorities, parents, and teachers—and also through secular, societal laws. As it manifests itself in this form, humans can essentially fulfill the requirements of God's law and achieve a secular righteousness. It is possible for one to live within the framework of commonly accepted laws without becoming a lawbreaker. One must, however, distinguish this from a second sense or use of the law that Luther characterizes as the *true* use. This second use convicts people of their sins. Jesus illustrates this use of the law in his Sermon on the Mount. Through his exposition of the law, he greatly intensified the will of God. A pure heart and perfect obedience are required of humans before God and not just outward conformity. The law, which humans were once able to fulfill, has become for sinners utterly unfulfillable. Instead, the law reveals to them and even intensifies their sinfulness. While beforehand people thought of themselves as being fundamentally good, the proclamation and knowledge of the law makes them aware that this is pure self-deception. Hatred of God and despair result from the sinner's knowledge that the requirements of the law cannot be fulfilled. This understanding of the law continually accuses us and delivers us over to wrath, judgment, and eternal death.

---

1. On the twofold use of the law see Luther, see the *Smalcald Articles* (1537), in *The Book of Concord: The Confessions of the Evangelical Lutheran Church*, ed. Robert Kolb and Timothy J. Wengert (Minneapolis: Fortress Press, 2000), 311–12.

All persons are to some extent aware of this accusing law of God, but they do not have a genuine knowledge of its power since they have not yet experienced it. In order for this to be possible the law must first be preached. Humans will then be startled out of their state of ignorance as they perceive the power of the law that calls them to repentance. The law, intended as a sign of God's love that was meant to guide us in a God-pleasing life, has become an instrument of God's wrath. This theological aspect of the law shows human beings the extent of their estrangement from God.

Those who wish to preach only the gospel and not the law because they are afraid that it frightens people refuse to hear God's truth about themselves. For this reason, Luther opposes the Antinomians, who dispute the theological use of the law and want it to be applied only in the city hall, that is, in the civil domain.[2] For Luther the law is necessary for salvation, since without it humans remain far off from God, because they have not recognized just how alienated they already are from God. Through the confrontation with God's wrath and the recognition of their own failure, humans are driven to God and the gospel, for alongside the law stands the gospel, which is the other side of God's word.

Law and gospel have entirely different, even opposing functions. The law establishes what one should do and what one is not allowed to do, and as a consequence of human failure, it accuses and condemns. The gospel, on the other hand, has as its content God's promise in Christ. It announces that everything that the law requires has already been accomplished for us by Christ. The gospel preaches, therefore, the forgiveness of sins. "The preaching of the forgiveness of sins through the name of Christ, that is the gospel."[3] With Paul,

---

2. Cf. Luther, *Die Thesen gegen die Antinomer* (1537–1540), in *WA* 39/I:344.30, where he cites the theses of the Antinomians, to which he responds with his own series of theses; cf. especially *WA* 39/I:349.39–40.

3. Luther, *In epistolam Pauli ad Galatas commentarius* (1519), in *WA* 2:466.12–13.

from whom Luther has taken over the characterization of the gospel as promise, Luther contrasts law and gospel with one another. The gospel as good news announces the grace of God that for the sake of Christ, God no longer counts our past failures against us. As Christians we can begin a new life. The law leads to death, but the gospel gives eternal life through the liberation provided by Christ. The law places us under the wrath of God; the gospel, however, brings grace. Law and gospel stand against one another, in that through the gospel the justification of the sinner occurs, contrary to what is possible through the law. It is the liberating gospel that must be believed, not the law that demands our condemnation. Justification takes place, as Paul says, *apart* from the law. Luther goes still a step further than Paul at this point and says *against* the law.[4]

Law and gospel, however, are related to one another even in their opposition. Law and gospel must indeed be clearly distinguished from one another but they cannot be separated, just as they can also not be blended together. They are inseparably connected and bound together. The gospel, which brings with it the forgiveness of sins, presupposes the law and its exposition. Sin is thereby presupposed, but it can only be recognized when one knows the law. Therefore Luther, in his dispute with the Antinomians, could say, "If the law is dismissed, so is sin. If sin is dismissed, so is Christ, for there would be no more need of him."[5] The good news of Christ's saving work and the redemption from sin can neither be understood nor desired if one has not recognized the extent of human estrangement from God, as seen from the vantage point of the law. The gospel needs the law, for it is the preaching of the law that is the indispensable and

---

4. Cf. Luther, *Die Promotionsdisputation von Palladius und Tilemann* (1537), thesis 36, in *WA* 39/I:219.23–24.
5. Luther, "Die dritte Disputation gegen die Antinomer," (1538), in *Die Thesen gegen die Antinomer* (1537–40), in *WA* 39/I:546.14–16.

necessary presupposition of preaching the gospel. Without the law, humans cannot realistically judge their own abilities, but remain self-confident and even arrogant in the assessment of their moral capacity. As a gracious God, God effects with the law that which is alien to God (God's alien work) in order to arrive at what is proper to God (God's proper work).

The preaching of the law alone, however, does not lead us to true repentance or to belief in the gospel. God's Spirit must work together with the preached word, so that we are able to experience the gospel. When the law convinces humans of their sin and they perceive the wrath of God, it drives them to despair. If people hear only the law, they remain in their despair and do not experience salvation. It is therefore important that the word of the gospel be added to the law, so that they realize that the law is not God's last word but rather points to God's forgiveness and salvation. The law precedes the gospel, so that humans find the gospel and, so to speak, flee to Christ. There are not, however, two gods, as believed by Marcion in the second century, one being responsible for law and the other offering us the good news of the gospel. Both law and gospel are the work of the same God.

Law and Gospel as Expressions of the Same Word

The law is neither exclusively to be found in the Old Testament, nor the gospel in the New Testament. The law includes everything that reveals to us our sin, accuses our conscience, and terrifies us, regardless whether we encounter it in Christ or in Moses. Luther represents a perspective-like understanding of the law, for by law he understands not only the expressed imperatives, meaning the accusing and condemning word of God, but he is also able to characterize the Lord's Prayer as "full of the teaching of the law," since whoever prays it earnestly confesses that he or she has sinned against the law and stands in need of repentance.[6] When we pray, for example, "Hallowed be your name," we also admit that we have not yet fulfilled this challenge. Thus the Lord's Prayer exercises upon us the work of the law.

The preaching of the gospel is, likewise, at the same time the preaching of the law. The preaching of Christ, who should be our example, can take on the character of the preaching of the law, since it manifests the will of God that we are to fulfill. Even the proclamation of Christ as redeemer can become the preaching of the law, since redemption presupposes sin. Yet the gospel also testifies to the goodness of God. Humans recognize their ingratitude and contempt for the goodness of God, for which they remain indebted to God. The recognition of sin comes either from the law in the strict sense, that is, from the biblical admonitions and prescriptions, or from the gospel, insofar as it becomes law. Whatever points toward my obligation and shows me that I remain guilty—that is the law. The word of God cannot, consequently, be divided into the words containing law and the words containing gospel, for it is one and the same word that the sinner encounters as law and as gospel. The center of the gospel, being the word of the cross, exposes human sin and lostness more deeply and painfully, for instance, than any law could do. Nevertheless, one can give no other advice to those who have recognized their sin in the face of God's love than to point them to the crucified Christ who bears the sin of the world and brings good news to the poor. This same Christ, to whom we find ourselves ever again indebted, is then preached as savior, as the mediator between God and humanity and the comforter of the distressed. The gospel leads to repentance, as well as to faith; it leads to despair and to peace. It is true that law and gospel have two distinct and contrary

---

6. Luther, "Die dritte Disputation gegen die Antinomer," thesis 17, in *WA* 39/I:351.1–2.

functions, but both are functions of the same word of God and occur simultaneously.

Faith is a movement from law toward gospel, a movement that cannot be reversed. As gospel, however, it is a word of comfort, and therefore the movement comes here to rest. The law is taken up into the gospel, but never vice versa. The God and Lord, to whose mercy we are indebted, never ceases to be merciful. The contrast between law and gospel in the life of the sinner indicates, therefore, a transitional stage on the way to the original unity of the two. It also points to the paradoxical situation that the Christian, who has not fulfilled the law and thus stands accused, believes nevertheless in the gospel and fulfills the commandment of God, despite his or her sinfulness. Until now, we have spoken only of sinners. But since the Christian is at the same time sinner and saint, the question arises whether the law has a continuing function for the Christian.

Christ as the End of the Law?

We have seen that Christ is the end of the law. Through him, the will of God, which we are unable to fulfill on our own, is fulfilled vicariously for us. Christ has liberated us from the power of the law so that we are no longer delivered over to the wrath of God and to death. The law as the demand of God, which requires eternal separation from God and thereby death because of our sins, is now fulfilled. The law no longer applies for those who are justified inasmuch as it accuses and condemns for past offenses. But God's holy will remains in force for them. Yet Christians do not experience this as a requirement of the law, for they do freely that which the law requires. Through God's Spirit who abides in Christians they willingly fulfill the law. They no longer stand under the demands of God's law, but live their lives in accord with it through an act of love brought about by the Holy Spirit. The law has recovered its original function. It no longer condemns but yet continues to express God's will.

Although the law meets believers as neither demand nor accusation and, to a certain extent, no longer applies to them, it nevertheless has significance for them. First, Christians continue to live their lives upon this earth. At the same time, as both believers and sinners, they live sometimes according to the spirit and sometimes, as Paul says, according to the flesh. To the extent that Christians still belong to their former humanity according to the flesh, the law cannot be invalidated for them but rather reigns accusingly over them. Christians live without the law but also under it. The law, for them, is partly invalidated, and in part still valid.

For Christians the decisive event has already taken place, for they have been justified. Yet to the extent that they remain or turn back to their former selves, the law continues to exercise its spiritual or theological function over them and convicts them of their sins. It summons them to overcome their former humanity. Luther makes this clear in his explanation of baptism: "It signifies that the old creature in us with all sins and evil desires is to be drowned and die through daily contrition and repentance, and on the other hand that daily a new person is to come forth and rise up to live before God in righteousness and purity forever."[7] The law serves to overcome the entrenched state of humans and prods them to continually struggle against what leads them astray from God. On earth the struggle for cleansing from sin is never completely successful. We are on the way to fulfilling the law, but this goal will never be accomplished completely. Only at the final resurrection will the law have fulfilled its task and be completely abolished. Concerning the theological function of the law for Christians, however, one must remember that

---

7. Luther in his explanation of baptism in *The Small Catechism*, in *The Book of Concord*, 360.

they are already moved by the Spirit of God and repentance is no longer an adverse and difficult matter for them, but rather, as Luther said, "something easy and enjoyable."[8] Yet how does one know what one should do? Do not Christians also need the information transmitted through the law so that they can know the will of God? To this Luther says two things:

1. If the Holy Spirit moves Christians they no longer depend upon the law. By the power of the Holy Spirit Christians can establish a new Decalogue, as did Jesus and the apostles.[9] They need no spelled-out precepts, since the Spirit teaches them what to do.

2. Yet Luther qualifies this assertion, admitting that not all Christians possess such a measure of the Spirit that they can be their own lawmakers. In such individuals the flesh continues to struggle against the spirit and impedes a clear judgment about the content of God's will. For this reason it is good for Christians that they orient themselves on the apostolic imperatives of the New Testament. For the Christian, however, these are no longer law but rather apostolic commandments or mandates, that is, directives.[10]

There is, therefore, no theological aspect of the law for Christians, who as those who have been justified fight no longer against sin but struggle rather to live positive, Christlike lives. For this the New Testament instructions are important, for they lead the Christian to a proper knowledge of good works. To this end, the Decalogue is also useful for the Christian, not in its word-by-word formulation but in the continuing relevance of its content.

---

8. Luther, "Die erste Disputation gegen die Antinomer," in *WA* 39/I:398.15–16.

9. Cf. for this and the following Luther, *Thesen de fide* (1535), in *WA* 39/I:47.25–36.

10. Cf. here the distinction made by Paul Althaus (in the vein of Luther) between law and commandment in Althaus, *The Theology of Martin Luther*, trans. R. Schultz (Philadelphia: Fortress Press, 1989), 271–73.

As we see in his catechism, Luther expounded the Ten Commandments, freely supplementing and applying them in agreement with biblical admonitions. The Commandments are hence not only a mirror in which we recognize sin, although they retain this function for the Christian; they are a much-needed and wholesome instruction in that which God expects from us by way of good works. In contrast to the opinion of later Lutheran orthodoxy and of the Reformed tradition, there is, according to Luther, no so-called third use of the law applicable to the one who has been justified. The commandment of God, not the law, provides the Christian with guidance for the right way to live.

9

Church and Sacraments

The Reformation of Martin Luther took place in the context of the struggle with the church of his day. Luther not only opposed the physical reality of a largely corrupt and superstitious church—he also opposed the Roman, hierarchical, and centralized view of the church. He did not lead the fight on the basis of a churchless, individualistic view of piety, but on the basis of a clear understanding of the gospel, on which his view of the church was based. Although the institutional element seems at first to be missing in Luther's descriptions of the church, it has a solid and important place.

The congregation is called together through the Holy Spirit. The church is built by the gospel and is nothing other than the congregation, which is itself gathered around the gospel. The word of God and the sacraments are distinctive marks of the church: "Where you see baptism, the [Eucharistic] bread, and the gospel present, in whatever place and through whatever persons, you must not doubt that there is the church."[1]

The church is not bound to a particular manifestation, as for instance to the Church of Rome, but rather to the proclamation of the word. The apostolic church lives from the apostolic gospel and therefore stands in true apostolic succession. Luther even goes so far as to state that there can be no salvation outside the church when he says, "I believe that no one can be saved who is not found in this congregation, abiding with it harmoniously in one faith, word, sacrament, hope, and love."[2] Faith and community belong inalienably together. One and the same church is visible and invisible, hidden and revealed. It is an institution, as well as the communion of saints. No one can see faith. Therefore, it is only Christ as the good shepherd who knows his sheep. On the other hand, the congregation of believers becomes visible as it gathers around word and sacrament, as it follows Christ, and as it is led by its pastors.

Church as a Community of Saints

Luther inherited the already-existing conviction that the church is the communion of saints. For the church of his time the connection and relationship between the earthly and the heavenly church was important, as seen for example in the veneration of saints and the use of their merits. In contrast to this, the community of saints within the earthly church receded sharply into the background, because the biblical word *saints* was primarily reserved for communion with saints in heaven in a meritorious, moralistic manner. Luther brought the communion of saints down from heaven to earth when, in agreement with the New Testament, he did not understand "saints" as a particular elite group within the community, but rather as all

1. Luther, *Ad Librum eximii Magistri Nostri Magistri Ambrosii Catharini, defensoris Silvestri Priertatis acerrimi, responsio* (1520), in *WA* 7:720.36–38.
2. Luther, *Eine kurze Form der zehn Gebote, eine kurze Form des Glaubens, eine kurze Form des Vaterunsers* (1520), in *WA* 7:219.6–8.

members of the community, because they are all made holy by God and are all chosen to serve God. Luther no longer distinguished saints from everyday Christians, but rather only deceased saints from living saints. Although Luther unambiguously concluded that "no saint has adequately fulfilled God's commandments in this life," he attributes a living and present significance to the saints for the church, because a living power of faith goes forth from them.[3] They function, therefore, as examples for others to follow.

There is, however, no treasure from the life of the "traditional" saints, no excess of merits that they could apply to other Christians, for they lived, suffered, and worked as members of a body together with all other Christians. All petitions directed to the saints in the piety of the time did not, according to Luther, signify that they could achieve something *with God*. They signify instead a gracious work of God *for us* in which God draws us to himself through the service of our fellow saints. To be sure, Luther believed that the angels in heaven pray for us, as does Christ, but the saints on earth do that as well and perhaps also those in heaven. But Luther will not for this reason call upon the angels and saints in the worship service. In the same way, we do not venerate our brothers and sisters on earth who pray for us. Because the justification of believers takes place through God's free and gracious turning to us, our acceptance by God is worked by God alone and needs no intermediary.

The church as communion of saints is at one and the same time gift and responsibility. Luther summarized the gift of the communion of saints as follows: What belongs to Christ and all the saints belongs also to me, and my burden, distress, and sin is that of Christ and the saints. The faith and prayers of others become a helping force in the powerlessness of my Christian life. I am alone neither in life

---

3. Luther, *Explanations of the Ninety-Five Theses* (1518), thesis 58, in *LW* 31:213.

nor death, for Christ and the church are at my side. Living for myself ceases in the Christian life, which becomes a life of living for one another through love in the community of life. The helping, warning, disciplining, and guiding word of spiritual care we receive in conversation with one another is important, as is the comfort we have from others. Luther was thinking here not only of conscious intervention on behalf of one another, but also of possible models for our own life.

The community is also a responsibility, for all the members shall take the burden of Christ and of his church on themselves. Christians fight for the truth and against injustice; they work for the renewing of the church and its members. They intercede on behalf of the poor with their possessions and on behalf of the sick with their own lives, as well as on behalf of sinners with their own righteousness before God and humankind. Just as Christ took on our human form out of love, so we should convert others through the same loving devotion. "Everything we have must be available for service; if it is not available for service, then it is a theft."[4] Every gift and power, as well as possessions, health, and peace, belong to love and to the service of the community. This also holds true in regard to the sinner, from whom we cannot separate ourselves, but whom we must rather seek to lead to Christ. We do not run away, but must come running to the center of the church to work for its renewal. That is how Luther understood the path one should take, and it was also the path he sought to follow in his relationship to the Church of Rome. Luther saw the community as obligatory, for the unity of the church is to be protected despite its sin and degeneration.

The term *communion of saints* means the evangelical priesthood, that is, service that begins from the gospel. Luther is able to describe

---

4. Luther, sermon on Luke 19:29–34, *Predigten des Jahres 1523*, in *WA* 12:470.40–41.

his understanding of the church as communion of saints in such a way that he can characterize the priesthood as a way of life for the church. When Christ bears our burdens and intercedes for us with his righteousness, that is a priestly sign from which the mutual upholding and acting on behalf of one another in Christianity is derived. The foundation of the church is the priestly office of Christ, and its inner constitution is the mutual and common priesthood of Christians. Through baptism, all Christians receive their portion of the priestly office. Priesthood means to come before God, to pray for others, to intercede and offer oneself to God, and to proclaim the word of God to one another. One is never a priest for oneself but always for others. The point of departure for the priesthood of believers, therefore, is the community of saints and not some religious individualism. Public teaching within Christianity is restricted to those called through the congregation. Individuals may come forward without such a calling, on the other hand, only when allowed in mission situations or in emergency, as for example when a called teacher fails or falls into error.

In the private realm, however, each one is called to proclaim the word of God to others. Luther recognized no congregation that did not proclaim the gospel, and that did not call everyone to give Christian witness, or to give spiritual care with a word of comfort to one's neighbors in their time of need. The entire congregation and each of its members have also been fully empowered to declare the forgiveness of sins. This is experienced in private confession and absolution. "When my neighbor comes and says: 'Friend, my conscience is heavy laden, speak the word of absolution to me,' I may of course do that."[5] Luther rejected, to be sure, the churchly obligation of private confession, yet he nonetheless saw in private

---

5. Luther, sermon on April 25, 1522, *Predigten des Jahres 1522*, in *WA* 10/III:97.10–12.

confession the indispensable form of the gospel. The hearing of private confession is a priestly service that can be performed by any Christian. Even when we turn to a called servant of the word in this regard, we are asking for a brotherly or sisterly service.

Office and Authority

Although all the baptized are authorized and called to the service of word and sacrament on the basis of their priesthood, not every member of the congregation can publicly perform these duties for the entire congregation. Such individual self-appointments would lead to chaos in the congregation. In order to guard against this, the congregation must assign these public tasks to a particular person who performs them in the name of the church. In this regard, Luther argued that, according to the New Testament example, Christ has given various people different gifts and has therefore chosen some to be apostles, some to be prophets, some evangelists, and others teachers. The preaching office, therefore, is an office commanded, founded, and ordered by God.

Twofold Foundation of the Pastoral Office

Both these foundations, from below and from above, are placed by Luther impartially alongside one another, without connecting them to one another. Although he does not see them as opposites, we must nevertheless be firm in our belief that the pastoral office is founded upon, and is a consequence of, the priesthood of all believers. On the other hand, the pastoral office is founded directly by Christ without reference to the priesthood of believers. Both foundations, however, presuppose that the gospel must be proclaimed and the sacraments administered so that the church remains as long as the world continues. When one asks who should hold that office, Luther responds with rational and sociological considerations.

The twofold foundation points to a dilemma that Luther was most likely aware of, namely, that he could not trace the pastoral office back solely to the fact that it was established by Christ. If he were to do that, then it would remain inexplicable why it is through baptism that all Christians are made priests. The establishment of the office through Christ would indeed be sufficient in itself. Luther, however, in all of his arguments, is a very practically minded theologian. He recognizes that the preaching office is established by Christ. But from the perspective of proper order, the congregation must now call individual Christians to this special office, to the service of word and sacrament. In this way the authority that the entire congregation and each individual in it possess is delegated to a single individual chosen out of its midst and called to perform the duties of the office. No one can of his or her own accord claim the authority to carry out this ministry in the congregation. Someone must be called to do so with the consent of the congregation. If these conditions are met, then that person carries out the duties of the office on behalf of the whole congregation.

The pastor is the representative of the congregation who acts in the name of all of its members in the proclamation of the gospel and in the liturgy. Luther explained how he conceptualized this in his description of the evangelical Mass:

Publicly and plainly he [the pastor] sings what Christ has ordained and instituted in the Lord's Supper. . . . We, who want to receive the sacrament kneel beside, behind, and around him [the pastor] . . . all of us true, holy priests, sanctified by Christ's blood, anointed by the Holy Spirit, and consecrated in baptism. . . . We let our pastor say what Christ has ordained, not for himself, as though it were for his person, but he is the mouth for all of us and we all speak the words [of the institution] with him from the heart and in faith.[6]

The representative action of the pastor, therefore, does not exclude but rather includes the cooperation of the congregation. It is similar with the proclamation of the word. The public preaching of the pastor to the members of the congregation does not excuse them from their priestly duty to speak the word of God to one another.

Nonhierarchical Understanding of the Pastoral Office

The pastoral office has no other content and no other authority than that of the priesthood of all believers, which is founded through baptism. Those who bear the ecclesiastical office act in the name of Christ, their word is the word of Christ, and they represent Christ to the members of their congregation. Yet this is also true of every Christian who exercises spiritual care to other Christians in private confession or ministers to them in some other way. Individual Christians are entrusted with the care of their neighbors; the bearers of the pastoral office, on the other hand, are entrusted with the care of the entire congregation because their office is of a public character. When Luther speaks of the service of the word, he characterizes it as the highest office in the church. But he does not think of it in hierarchical terms, because he sees it as the task of all Christians.

Luther rejects a special priesthood consecrated through a liturgical rite and emphasizes instead the priesthood of all the baptized. In this way he also deviated from Jewish practice, which retains special priests. In the New Testament, Luther could not find that the apostles or any other followers of Jesus were designated as priests. This title was instead applied without distinction to all Christians. This strict functional understanding of the pastoral office also highlights its inalienable character; there is no special priestly class.

---

6. Luther, *The Private Mass and the Consecration of Priests* (1533), in *LW* 38:209–10.

Proper Calling

Decisive for the pastoral call is the proper liturgical action with which one is called to be a preacher of the gospel. One cannot take the office upon oneself, but receives it through proper and public appointment. Luther emphasizes the proper calling, as it is expressed in the *Augsburg Confession* of 1530, especially over against the enthusiasts who believed themselves to be appointed directly from God.[7] He also sought thereby to defend himself against Roman Catholic accusations that his Reformation would bring about chaotic conditions.

Yet Luther distinguished between two types of calling: an internal immediate call (as when God called the prophets and the apostle Paul directly) and an external mediated call (which comes from God through human beings). An immediate call must be capable of being demonstrated through external signs and evidences. Luther applied this against Thomas Müntzer and the enthusiast peasants. When God breaks through the pattern of the historical order, then this must be confirmed through external signs and wonders. The external call mediated through other people, on the other hand, does not need these signs, for it takes place when someone is sought out by other Christians to preach and is given the pastoral office. Of course, it is ultimately God who calls someone to be a pastor through other Christians.

The proper calling of a pastor is not only necessitated for the sake of churchly order, but also for the sake of the pastor. In this way pastors are able to know that their office is not self-appointed but has been entrusted to them. Luther speaks here from personal experience. In his work as a reformer, he was comforted by the knowledge

---

7. Cf. *The Augsburg Confession*, article 14, in *The Book of Concord: The Confessions of the Evangelical Lutheran Church*, ed. Robert Kolb and Timothy J. Wengert (Minneapolis: Fortress Press, 2000), 47.

that he did seek out the pastoral office but was called to it. "For I would surely in the long run lose courage and fall into despair if . . . I had undertaken these great and serious matters without call or commission."[8] If one appoints oneself to be a preacher, then that is disobedience against God. "It is the calling and commission that make the parish pastor and preacher. . . . God doesn't want anything done by one's own choice or notion, but by command and calling, especially in regard to the pastoral office."[9] Luther is aware that many rebel against this rule because they believe themselves to be especially well-suited to the pastoral office. Yet Luther challenges such people to consider that if God needs them, then God will call them.

How the call takes place for each individual is not important. What is important is that the call comes according to human order and not a divine order. It is also important for Luther that the congregation has the power to choose their servants of the word. At the same time, the bishops, according to the example of the New Testament, should also play a role in this process when they take their office seriously. Yet they dare not appoint someone without the consent of the congregation: "Calling is done legitimately by the church," whereby the church always assumes the cooperation of the local congregation.[10] Luther, therefore, shows that he is no longer interested in a special liturgical act of ordination. Ordination, in principle, is nothing other than the calling and commission to the pastoral office.

Church and Tradition

For Luther it was clear that the Protestants were not building a separate, new church, but "are the true old church, and with the

---

8. Luther, *Infiltrating and Clandestine Preachers*, in *LW* 40:387–88.
9. Luther, in his exposition of Ps. 82:4, *Den 82. Psalm ausgelegt* (1530), in *WA* 31/I:211.19f.31–32.
10. Luther, *Against the Thirty-Two Articles of the Louvain Theologians*, article 41, in *LW* 34:357.

entire holy Christian church are one body and one communion of saints," for God has wonderfully preserved the true church even in the midst of its Babylonian captivity.[11] Even through the decline of the papacy Luther did not believe the true church would be lost. For instance, alongside what was contrary to the gospel, he also found what was genuinely Christian in the Roman Mass, and he took up these elements in his German Mass. He also took up many Latin hymns and sung portions of the liturgy and translated them into German. An example of this is the Advent hymn, "Savior of the Nations, Come."[12] He approached the German hymns of the Middle Ages in a similar manner, cleansing them of thoughts contrary to the gospel and sometimes substituting new verses. This can be seen, for example, in the Christmas hymn, "All Praise to You, Eternal Lord."[13]

Luther was especially brought to reflect upon the authority of tradition in the church in his disputes with the Anabaptists. He stressed that a consensus of the whole church was binding, so long as the teaching or practice in question did not contradict Scripture. He objected, for instance, against the spiritualistic interpretation of the Lord's Supper by Müntzer and Zwingli, and argued that the testimony of the entire Christian church was already sufficient reason to remain with the Reformation understanding of the Lord's Supper. He found it dangerous and frightful to abolish something that had, as a basic consensus, "existed harmoniously throughout all the world for more than 1500 years."[14] Luther restricted neither Christian dogma nor the teachings of the church to that which is expressly found in the Bible. In contrast to the Reformed camp of Calvin and Zwingli, he did not reduce the truth content of Christianity to biblical teaching alone, because he recognized that the Holy Spirit has also been

---

11. Luther, *Wider Hans Worst* (1541), in *WA* 51:487.3–5.
12. Cf. *Evangelical Lutheran Worship*, hymn no. 263.
13. Cf. *Lutheran Book of Worship*, hymn no. 48.
14. Luther, *Sendschreiben an Herzog Albrecht von Preußen* (1532), in *WA* 30/III:552.14–15.

active in the church since the time of the apostles. On this basis, the validity of Christian tradition is established, yet this must be critically examined to be sure that it does not contradict the clear truth of the gospel found in Scripture. Whatever stands up under this examination should continue to be retained. In this sense, Scripture is the standard against which the tradition of the church is measured, and not vice versa.

If, however, in particular cases tradition is not able to be harmonized with Scripture or stands in obvious contradiction to it, then it must be rejected. Such a no to tradition was especially painful for Luther because, by rejecting tradition, he brought the entire development of the church into question and was confronted with the dangerous possibility that he was opposing the church of Christ and even Christ himself. Luther confessed that "no one likes to say that the church is in error; and yet, if the church teaches anything in addition or contrary to the Word of God, one must say that it is in error."[15] The question remains, nevertheless, what precisely Luther understands by "Word of God" in this context. We remember that his enemies often used Scripture passages as the "Word of God" to defend their teachings which Luther then rejected.

Authority of the Word of God

Neither the Bible, nor the canon as such, nor individual Scripture passages are able to serve for Luther as the final authority and binding standard. Instead, only the center of Scripture, the gospel as understood through Christ, can serve this function. As we have already seen, Luther viewed the canon as a piece of the tradition of the church that must be subject to the scrutiny of the word of God. This canonical criticism is to be distinguished from subjective

15. Luther, *Lectures on Galatians* (1535), in *LW* 26:66–67.

and arbitrary decisions that pick out individual words or verses and hold them to be absolute. Luther, in contrast, argues on the basis of the core of the Bible, namely, the theocentric character of the gospel. From this perspective the glory of God, who creates without preconditions out of nothing, is to be defended.

Alongside of and apart from the word of God, there is no authority in the church, for Luther, that has unconditional validity. When someone calls upon the opinion of the church, the decisive point is whether this opinion is based upon the center of Scripture or is only being passed off as the true opinion of the church. The first has authority, the later has none. The teachings of the church, the opinions of the church fathers, and the traditions, offices and office bearers of the church cannot have unconditional authority, because the church can err. According to Luther, this is demonstrated by the Bible itself, for David and Nathan in the Old Testament erred, and the apostles often sinned or failed. In Luther's view, the church remains "a submissive sinner before God until the day of judgment and is holy alone in Christ its Savior by grace and the forgiveness of sins."[16] A Christian cannot offer unconditional obedience to the church, but rather only to the gospel proclaimed by the church. Luther observes that already in New Testament times, Paul reproaches Peter because of his deviations from the gospel (Galatians 2). Authority and the duty of obedience toward the church have both their foundation and their limits in the gospel: "To err is human" goes also for the church, for in this point, just as earthly authorities, the church has no privileged position. Even in regard to the proclamations of councils, it must be determined and not taken for granted that they attest the truth, even though the entire church

---

16. Luther, *The Private Mass and the Consecration of Priests* (1533), in *LW* 38:171.

speaks through them. They attest the truth only when they are grounded on the gospel.

For Luther the true church of Christ and historical Christianity are not the same thing. The true church is hidden and is not identical to the official church and its history. Often it is not even recognized by the official church. The true and hidden church is nevertheless ruled by the Spirit of Christ. It cannot err, because Christ remains by it and it remains with Christ until the end of the world. Yet the historical church and the hidden church have the same focal points of identity: the gospel and the sacraments. Even in the often erring official church, the true church continually becomes visible when the former holds firm to the gospel and allows it to work unhindered.

The Sacraments

Martin Luther largely follows Augustine in his understanding of the sacraments. He describes a sacrament as a visible sign of God's invisible grace. Although every invisible action has some meaning and can be understood as a picture or image of an invisible reality, this does not mean that every symbolic action is a sacrament. A symbolic action has sacramental character only when it is instituted by God and is connected with a promise. Where there is no divine word of promise (as in the case of marriage or confirmation), one cannot, in Luther's view, call these sacraments. On the other hand, there are divine promises, such as prayer and the cross, for which there are no corresponding signs or actions. These, too, are not sacraments. According to Luther's understanding, therefore, only baptism and the Lord's Supper are sacraments in the strict sense. In them signs instituted by God and a promise, namely the forgiveness of sins, meet.

It has seemed proper to restrict the name of sacrament to those promises which have signs attached to them. The remainder, not being bound to signs, are bare promises. *Hence there are, strictly speaking, but two sacraments in the church of God—baptism and the bread* [the Lord's Supper]. For only in these two do we find both the divinely instituted sign and the promise of forgiveness of sins.[17]

The sacrament is a sign of God's promise. The special quality of a sacrament is found in its visibility. The visibility of the sacraments is an aid to faith, for in them one can see through their symbolic character the promises of God for individuals. Luther explains how signs and promise work together in *The Small Catechism*. In regard to baptism he wrote, "Clearly the water does not do it, but the Word of God, which is with and alongside the water."[18] Similarly he wrote concerning the Lord's Supper, "Eating and drinking certainly do not do it [the forgiveness of sins], but rather the words that are recorded: 'given for you' and 'shed for you for the forgiveness of sins.'"[19] The promise that joins with the sign invites one to faith. Hence a sacrament does not function automatically through its occurrence, but it demands and fosters faith.

In contrast to the Roman Catholic teaching of his time on sacraments, Luther stressed that the sacraments were not necessary for salvation. Yet a Christian will never despise them. If one is able to receive baptism then one should be baptized. If conditions, however, prevent someone from being baptized, then that person will nevertheless be saved if they believe in the gospel. Baptism is "only" a particular form of offering the gospel. The same is true with regard to the Lord's Supper. Over against the Anabaptists and the spiritualists, it was necessary for Luther to point out that the sacraments are not mere external matters one can reject, but that they are instituted by God, who has commanded that they be made use of appropriately. One dare not tear sacrament and gospel from one

17. Luther, *The Babylonian Captivity of the Church* (1520), in *LW* 36:124.
18. Luther, *The Small Catechism*, in *The Book of Concord*, 359.
19. Ibid., 363.

another, putting one down as mere "external trapping" while lifting up the other. Word and sacrament, or gospel and sacrament, are two ways God relates to us.

Baptism

Baptism by water is first of all a human action. Yet humans do not baptize in their own name but in the name of God. Baptism brings a complete salvation, as Luther says in *The Small Catechism*: "It brings about forgiveness of sins, redeems from death and the devil, and gives eternal salvation to all who believe it."[20] Baptism is singular and unrepeatable. Yet although it is a one-time act, it remains present throughout one's life and must continually be accepted. "The Christian life is nothing other than a daily baptism; once begun we keep going back for more."[21] The new life given through the external act of baptism must be continually turned into a reality. God makes a covenant with human beings in baptism and agrees to forgive all their sins. The symbolic action in baptism, being immersed or washed with water, is, to be sure, a one-time occurrence, but it must be continually actualized. "The old creature in us with all sins and evil desires is to be drowned and die through daily contrition and repentance, and on the other hand that daily a new person is to come forth."[22] Luther, building upon Romans 6, emphasizes the lifelong realization and fulfillment of baptism. While Paul speaks of a baptism of the converted, Luther has in mind infant baptism, in which the great moment of decision and insight into life are missing, and the emphasis is upon the fact that baptism should be realized throughout the whole of one's life. If one falls from baptism, then repentance is

20. Ibid., 359.
21. Luther, *Vom Sakrament der Taufe* (1529), in *WA* 30/I:220.22–23.
22. Luther, *The Small Catechism*, 360.

not a new, supplemental means of grace, but rather effects a return to one's baptism and to the promise that took place within it.

Infant baptism was especially opposed by the Anabaptists. Luther brought forth all manner of arguments against their rejection of infant baptism. He argued, for instance, that God would not have allowed it to continue so long if it were not right.[23] He was also of the opinion that Christianity would not have existed if infant baptism were false and against God's will, because in such a case there would have been no legitimate baptism. But this, however, would contradict the confessional statement: "I believe in one holy Christian Church." Luther referred to the force of tradition that says we should not eliminate or change anything unless there is clear scriptural witness against it. Luther conceded, however, that infant baptism was not expressly instituted or commanded in Scripture. Instead, baptism alone is commanded, an instruction that does not limit itself to adult baptism. Because the Anabaptists are a more recent development, the burden of evidence rests upon them, and they need clear scriptural testimony for their rejection of infant baptism. For those who retain infant baptism, it is sufficient that Scripture does not say anything against the baptism of infants and that it is in accordance with Scripture. Also in regard to infant baptism, Luther does not back away from the generally accepted conviction that the sacraments are only effective when they are received in faith. The faith and confession of the baptismal sponsors contribute nothing to the sanctification of the one baptized, because no one is saved through the faith of other people but only through one's own faith.

Luther never based the validity of infant baptism upon the presence of faith in the infant, although he did for a time argue that such faith existed. Infants are to be baptized, not because it is clear that they

---

23. Cf. Paul Althaus, *The Theology of Martin Luther*, trans. Robert Schultz (Philadelphia: Fortress Press, 1966), 359–61, for this and the following.

believe but because it is in accordance with Scripture. One can also not baptize infants on the basis of their future faith. Luther ultimately argues that baptism calls one to faith, and the reality and validity of baptism do not depend upon the faith of the one being baptized. Baptism is entirely the God's work in which God, nevertheless, expects the assent of the one baptized. Even in the case of a "believers' baptism," where baptism is made dependent upon the faith of the baptismal candidate, it remains unclear when one should baptize. One can never know with certainty whether the one to be baptized truly believes. There is no reliable sign of faith, not even the free decision to present oneself for baptism nor the confession of faith of the candidate. One always builds upon a foundation of uncertainty with regard to believers' baptism. To baptize and to have oneself baptized on the basis of one's own faith makes not only for uncertainty, but it is also idolatry, for one relies upon one's own work rather than the action of God through which God accepts us. So it is, according to Luther, that the baptism of the Anabaptists is reduced to a mere sign of their piety. Yet faith and baptism nevertheless belong together. Faith clings to the promise of God that one may baptize and that through baptism God receives the one baptized into his covenant. Faith, however, is also the consequence of baptism in which one affirms that which has taken place in baptism.

The Lord's Supper

In the development of his doctrine of baptism, Luther in principle only separated himself from the works righteousness of the Anabaptists and often also from those who held to the so-called old faith. In his understanding of the Lord's Supper one can distinguish between two very different lines of his thought. Up until about 1524, Luther's argumentation was directed against Rome, and its teaching of the sacrifice of the Mass. After this time, he battled against the enthusiasts who rejected the sacraments altogether, and the Swiss, that is, against the Reformed camp and their symbolic interpretation of the Lord's Supper. The Roman Church held to a doctrine of transubstantiation that teaches that in the Eucharist, the inner substance of bread and wine is transformed to body and blood, while the outer form remains the same. Luther, in contrast, maintained a doctrine of consubstantiation, which affirms that the body and blood of Christ are present in unchanged bread and wine. Yet he did not place any great weight or significance upon this difference. As late as 1520, he said that whoever wished was free to retain the doctrine of transubstantiation, but that he would not tolerate anyone making this opinion an "article of faith" that others must accept.[24] Important for Luther was that in the eating and drinking of bread and wine, union with Christ and all the saints took place. The resultant actual presence of the body and blood of Christ (real presence) was important for Luther inasmuch that, as a sign of Christ's sacrificial death, it assures us of the forgiveness of sins.

Words of Institution

The eucharistic words of institution were decisive for Luther. Important in this regard is not only the New Testament text itself but also Luther's understanding of the gospel, which he used to interpret the text—an understanding that itself confirmed the gospel's promise of grace. In our understanding of the Lord's Supper, reason must not be made to rule over the text, because God, who makes God's self understood in the text, is greater than our reason. The text must take precedence as God's word of promise. Faith also means that we must cast our own thoughts and desires behind us and hold on, as if we were blind, to the word and will of God. Luther writes,

---

24. Luther, *The Babylonian Captivity of the Church* (1520), in *LW* 36:35.

A faithful, God-fearing heart does this: it asks first whether it is God's Word. When it hears that it is, it smothers with hands and feet the question why it is useful or necessary. For it says with fear and humility, "My dear God, I am blind; truly I know not what is useful or necessary for me, nor do I wish to know, but I believe and trust that thou dost know best and dost intend the best in thy divine goodness and wisdom. I am satisfied and happy to hear thy simple Word and perceive thy will."[25]

Luther stressed the sovereignty of the word and will of God over against all human insight into religious necessity and the meaning of divine actions. That which God's word says and gives is useful to us, and we cannot measure God's word according to that which we determine to be its usefulness. We must follow the literal meaning of the text and not some human interpretation, for the wording of the text is in all events given by God.

Real Presence of Christ

Luther fought with unexpected stubbornness for the real presence of Christ in the Lord's Supper. His specific interest in the issue was the same as that which he championed against Rome: the sacrament must be understood as a genuine gift of God that comes to us without human assistance, and that means also without the help of faith. What is essential in the real presence is that Christ encounters us in such a way that pure passivity and pure reception dominate the action on the human side. Although Christ is likewise personally present in the oral proclamation of the word, in Holy Communion he is, according to his word, physically present for the individual. Analogous to the Word become flesh, this bodily presence is at the same time a spiritual presence, because faith receives Christ's presence and everything that takes place in faith is spiritual. Spiritual

25. Luther, *That These Words of Christ, "This Is My Body," etc., Still Stand Firm against the Fanatics* (1527), in *LW* 37:127.

eating means not only savoring something that is spiritual, but also partaking of something that is a genuine reality that comes from the Holy Spirit and that desires to be received spiritually, that is, in faith. There is, therefore, no pure, inner, spiritual presence of Christ. Christ's presence manifests itself instead in what is outwardly visible, in bread and wine. Whoever despises this external presence also denies that God has revealed himself to us outwardly in human history. When Luther's opponents felt the real presence of Christ in bread and wine on the altar was unworthy of God, Luther could only understand this as a rejection of God's becoming flesh in the incarnation.

Through the power of the word of Christ, his body and blood are present in Holy Communion. The body of Christ is present in the bread and wine, and is received by all, not only by those who believe. But only for the latter does it work for their salvation; in those who reject Christ, it works for their damnation. The "concretizing" of grace in the bodily presence of Christ thus brings either life or death. In the sacrament of the altar, the believer receives the forgiveness of sins because the sacrifice of Christ is present in the sacrament. In believers, the gospel effects "forgiveness of sins, life, and salvation," as Luther puts it in *The Small Catechism*.[26] Luther doesn't speak at all in this regard of the real presence. It is instead a fundamental presupposition of the efficacy of the sacrament, for someone can only be efficacious when that person is really present. The real presence, therefore, is not an object of faith but rather a presupposition of the salvation that one receives in Holy Communion.

---

26. Luther, *The Small Catechism*, 362.

Excursus 1: Additional Accents in Luther's Theology

As we now turn our attention away from our survey of Luther's teachings, some might ask, "But didn't Luther have anything to say about human sinfulness, the person of Christ and his work of reconciliation, or eternal life?" Of course, Martin Luther made many comments on these areas in his writings and in so doing set out important new accents in their treatment. Yet for the most part they are developed out of his Reformation perspective, as we have seen in the preceding treatment. We highlight here only a few points:

1. *In his understanding of the figure of Jesus Christ, Luther largely followed ancient Christian dogma.* It is a noteworthy quality of Luther that, as a former Augustinian monk, he not only took up Augustine in many facets, but he also took up many suggestions from the whole of the ancient church in his understanding of the message of the New Testament. For Luther, it was clear that Jesus Christ was truly human and truly divine, and he held fast to the two-nature Christology of the ancient church. Nevertheless, it was essential for him that Jesus, as the human face of God, allows us a direct look into the "heart" of God. Luther conceded that Muslims—the only world religion apart from Judaism with which he was familiar—knew much about God, such as that he is Creator, Sustainer, and Redeemer. Yet he maintained that we can have certainty that this God is also our Redeemer only through Jesus Christ. Luther's interest in the nature of Jesus Christ was not speculative but directly existential. Christ opens for us the entrance to the heart of God and thereby to God's own self. In such statements, we see a turning toward an understanding of Jesus as redeemer and moving away from the medieval understanding of Christ as judge of the world.

Luther did not see in Christ a figure that evoked fear, but rather the Son of God who offered himself for us and who brings us salvation. This salvation is necessary for us human beings, because in our estrangement from God there are no possibilities for us to be justified before God.

2. *In his understanding of humanity, Luther emphasizes that human beings, in relation to the created order, possess a large degree of freedom.* As creatures of God endowed with reason, humans can move in the world conscious of their responsibility, and can lead happy and successful lives. But because they are estranged from God, their success in the world, whether brought about through human self-elevation or through denial of the world, does not bring them a single step closer to God. In principle, all human works lead to a heightening of human sinfulness. They are an expression of human self-affirmation and do not give glory to God but to human beings. Through them we seek to forget that we ultimately owe everything to God. This complete dependence upon God is also emphasized in Luther's doctrine of justification.

3. *Together with Augustine, Luther affirmed that because of our sinfulness we have earned nothing but eternal death and eternal alienation from God.* Yet Christ has died on account of our sins. He placed himself where, by all rights, we should have stood, in a state of estrangement from God and damnation. Through this wonderful exchange in which he took our place, an alien justification has been attributed to us and as undeserving sinners we have been pronounced justified. Jesus Christ bridges the horribly wide chasm between us and God. As the human face of God, he takes our side so that we can once more find ourselves on the side of God and inherit peace with God and eternal life. This saving event is so unexpected and unusual that it is not

able to be deduced from any empirical facts, but can only be comprehended in faith alone through the gospel, that is, through trust in God's promise. Because this unexpected gift of eternal life is opened up to us, Luther is able to look with different eyes upon eternal judgment and the end of the world, a subject that also drew the attention of most of his contemporaries.

4. *The piety of the late Middle Ages was characterized by the fear of the last judgment, because there we are met by the stern judge of the world before whom we are not able to endure.* Luther, in contrast, was able to speak of the "dear last day," the advent of which he longingly awaited.[27] At the end of the world there is no merciless day of accounting that awaits us, but we encounter instead the same Jesus Christ as judge whom we have already experienced in faith as our redeemer. To be sure, Luther took repentance seriously and even heightened its importance by stressing that the entire life of a Christian must be one of continual repentance, and that we must ever anew flee to the grace of God. Yet he did not live under the anxiety of a manufactured illusion that, to the very end of his life, he had to make himself appear acceptable to God through radical penitential exercises. Luther knew that such efforts were useless and put his trust, instead, in the grace of God offered to us apart from any human merit. A life of repentance should demonstrate that our life upon earth is one of continual new beginnings and is always in need of improvement. He also saw himself inspired to this Christlike life because humans live *from* the grace of God that makes daily life possible, and they live *toward* the grace of God that opens for them the fullness of new life. The Christian life should be one of thankfulness, marked by many and great good works. The ethical orientation of the

27. Luther, in a letter to his wife from July 16, 1540, in *WA BR* 9:175.17, and in many other places as well.

Christian life is not the prerequisite but rather the result of faith. This practical consequence will be elucidated in the following chapters, in which we examine some areas of ethical reflection.

Before we do this, however, we want to briefly touch upon one point in Luther's writings which is often seen as a very dark spot: Luther's relationship to the Jews.

Excursus 2: Luther and the Jews

Since the attempt in the Holocaust to exterminate the Jewish race, the claim has often been made that there is a straight line from Luther to the persecution of the Jews during the German Third Reich. But this is simply wrong. If one has written as much as Luther had, one can always find quotations that affirm one's own opinion or one's own prejudice. With Luther, too, we must see him in the context of his own time to do justice to him. We will then quickly notice that even with his most outlandish remarks with regard to the Jews, he "was taking up suggestions long made from another side. They are neither original nor harsher than those that others at his time had made, and across all ecclesiastical and spiritual persuasions."[28]

On the eve of the Reformation, the Jews in Europe had a very hard time. Already in 1290 the Jews had been expelled from England by King Edward I (1239–1307). In 1492 they had been evicted from Spain, and in 1506 in Lisbon, Portugal, approximately two thousand Jews had been killed. The learned Erasmus of Rotterdam lauded France in 1517 because, in contrast to other countries, it "remains not infected with heretics . . . with Jews, with half-Jewish marraños [i.e., converted Spanish Jews]."[29] The legal safety of Jews was always in

---

28. Bernhard Lohse, *Martin Luther's Theology: Its Historical and Systematic Development*, ed. and trans. Roy A. Harrisville (Minneapolis: Fortress Press, 1999), 344.

jeopardy and could only be granted by the emperor or a prince who then demanded a special tax for that privilege.

In the German empire in the fifteenth century, the expulsion of Jews from cities or districts increased as well. At the eve of the Reformation the urban expulsion was nearly completed. In Wittenberg, for instance, there was still a street named *Judengasse* (Jewish lane).[30] But when Luther settled there no Jews were left in this town. "After 1520 the Jews were only expelled from a relatively small number of cities, while in the preceding period from 1388 (Strasbourg) until 1519 (Regensburg, Rothenburg ob der Tauber) nearly 90 expulsions had been conducted."[31] For instance, in February 1519 in Regensburg, Balthasar Hubmaier (1485–1528), the former member of the cathedral chapter and later Anabaptist, was instrumental in having the Jews expelled from the city. The Jewish ghetto, including the synagogue, was destroyed and in its stead a pilgrimage church was erected for "The Beautiful Mary." In other cities, too, such as in Nuremberg (1349) and Würzburg (1349), once the ghetto and the synagogue were destroyed, churches dedicated to Mary were erected where the synagogue had stood. Martin Luther lived in this milieu that was so antagonistic to the Jews.

In 1523 Luther composed a pamphlet with the title *That Jesus Christ Was Born a Jew*. He defended the Jews there against various slanderous accusations, and then writes,

If the apostles, who were also Jews, had dealt with us Gentiles as we

29. Erasmus of Rotterdam, "Letter to Riccardo Bartolini" (no. 549, March 10, 1517), in *The Correspondence of Erasmus: Letters 446 to 593, 1516 to 1517,* trans. R. A. B. Mynors and D. F. S. Thomson, notes by James K. McConica (Toronto: University of Toronto, 1977), 279.

30. See Thomas Kaufmann, *Luthers "Judenschriften." Ein Beitrag zu ihrer historischen Kontextualisierung* (Tübingen: Mohr Siebeck, 2011), 156. Kaufmann also shows that Luther had hardly any firsthand experience with Jews.

31. So Heiko A. Oberman, *"Luthers Beziehungen zu den Juden: Ahnen und Geahndete,"* in *Leben und Werk Martin Luthers von 1526–1546. Festgabe zu seinem 500. Geburtstag,* ed. Helmar Junghans (Göttingen: Vandenhoeck & Ruprecht, 1983), 1:520.

Gentiles deal with the Jews, there would have never been a Christian among the Gentiles. Since they dealt with us Gentiles in such brotherly fashion, we in our turn ought to treat the Jews in a brotherly manner in order that we might convert some of them. For even we ourselves are not yet all very far along, not to speak of having arrived.

When we are inclined to boast of our position we should remember that we are but Gentiles, while the Jews are the lineage of Christ. We are aliens and in-laws, they are blood relatives, cousins, and brothers of our Lord. Therefore, if one is to boast of flesh and blood, the Jews are actually nearer to Christ than we are, as St. Paul says in Romans 9.[32]

Three items are important for us here:

1. Luther agrees with Paul that the Jews are closer to Jesus according to their descent than we are, because we come from paganism. Therefore they merit our special attention.
2. Luther concedes here that we can hope for their conversion only if we treat them in a brotherly way and in humility.
3. Luther hopes that at least some of them will convert to Christianity. Conversion, however, cannot be conducted by force, but must occur by the power of the gospel and the love of the Christians. In addition he contends that the Jews unjustly wait for the Messiah, because he has come already with Jesus Christ.

In 1536 the Saxon elector John Frederick (1503–1554) issued an edict forbidding the Jews to take up residence and work in his territory. They were also not allowed to traverse his territory. Josel of Rosheim (1476–1554) from Lower Alsace, a well-known representative of Judaism, intervened. Luther wrote to Josel calling him "his good friend" and told him that he himself had done much for Judaism. "Yet because your people misuse my service in such a bad way and also do things which we Christians cannot tolerate from them, they

32. Luther, *That Jesus Was Born a Jew* (1523), in *LW* 45:200–1.

themselves have deprived from me all support which I could have done with regard to the princes and lords."[33] Luther further writes that it had been his hope that through this friendly treatment God would bring them "to their Messiah." Yet this friendliness has only strengthened them in their error. Therefore he cannot do anything for them and will not intercede with the elector for them. Luther's hope that at least some of them would accept Jesus as their Messiah had not come true. He then became increasingly irate.

Finally, in 1543, Luther's pamphlet *The Jews and Their Lies* appeared, which is often regarded as typical for Luther and his attitude toward the Jews. Again one must read this treatise in context. The first sentence reads, "I had made up my mind to write no more either about the Jews or against them. But since I learned that these miserable and accursed people do not cease to lure to themselves even us, that is, the Christians, I have published this little book, so that I might be found among those who opposed such poisonous activities of the Jews and who warned the Christians to be on their guard against them."[34] Since Luther had heard that the Jews tried to convert Christians it made no sense to wait for the conversion of the Jews to Christ. The only hope consists in that "they reach the point where their misery finally makes them pliable and they are forced to confess that the Messiah has come, and he is our Jesus. Until such a time it is much too early, yes, even it is useless to argue with them about how God is triune, how he became man, and how Mary is the mother of God."[35] Luther then concludes,

> Thus we cannot extinguish the unquenchable fire of divine wrath, of which the prophets speak, nor can we convert the Jews. With prayer and the fear of God we must practice a sharp mercy to see whether we

33. Luther, "*An den Juden Josel*" (letter no. 3157 of June 11, 1537), in *WA BR* 8:89.4–8.
34. Luther, *The Jews and Their Lies* (1543), in *LW* 47:137.
35. Ibid., 139.

might save at least a few from the glowing flames. We dare not avenge ourselves. Vengeance a thousand times worse than we could wish them already has them by the throat. I shall give you my sincere advice.[36]

Luther still has not abandoned the hope that the Jews would recognize Christ as their Messiah. He wants to take no vengeance on account of their stubbornness and their boasting that they have the true faith, because vengeance is alone God's business. But then comes his awful "advice":

First to set fire to their synagogues or schools and to bury and cover with dirt whatever will not burn, so that no man will ever again see a stone or cinder of them. . . . Second, I advise that their houses also be razed and destroyed. . . . Third, I advise that all their prayer books and Talmudic writings, in which such idolatry, lies, cursing and blasphemy are taught, be taken from them. . . . Fourth, I advise that their rabbis be forbidden to teach henceforth on pain of loss of life and limb. For they have justly forfeited the right to such an office by holding the poor Jews captive with the saying of Moses (Deuteronomy 17[:10 ff.]) in which he commands them to obey their teachers on penalty of death, although Moses clearly adds: "what they teach you in accord with the law of the Lord." Those villains ignore that. They wantonly employ the poor people's obedience contrary to the law of the Lord and infuse them with this poison, cursing, and blasphemy. . . . Fifth, I advise that safe conduct on the highways be abolished completely for the Jews. . . . Sixth, I advise that usury be prohibited to them. . . . Seventh, I commend putting a flail, an ax, a hoe, a spade, a distaff, or a spindle into the hands of young, strong Jews and Jewesses and letting them earn their bread in the sweat of their brow, as was imposed on the children of Adam (Gen 3[:19]).[37]

As we already said at the beginning of the excursus, this advice was not new for the time of Luther. It was not an appeal to people in the street to attack the Jews. Even if heresy drew capital punishment—we remember that Luther as a heretic was declared to be an

36. Ibid., 268.
37. Ibid., 268–72.

outlaw—Luther did not demand this for the Jews, but still hoped for their conversion. Moreover, he thought that the rabbis had misled them. He even wrote, "Even when one persuades them out of Scripture, they retreat from the Scripture to rabbis and declare that they must believe them, just as you Christians (they say) believe your pope and your decretals. That is the answer they gave me."[38] According to Luther's opinion the Jews were misled by the teachers. Therefore one should prohibit them from teaching because they spread wrong doctrines. Luther was especially offended that the denied any christological interpretation of the Old Testament, meaning that the Old Testament did not foretell Jesus as the Messiah. This stubbornness, as Luther saw it, infuriated him.

In the context of that time even Luther's opinion that the Jews be expelled is understandable, because in one given territory there could only be one religion. In the Holy Roman Empire of the German nation, it was not until the Diet at Augsburg in 1555 that the estates, but not the people, were finally given free choice to decide between the old religion and the Augsburg Confession. This possibility of choice for the estates, meaning the princes, was an unheard-of innovation. Before that the respective religion had to be uniform in the whole empire. This means up to 1555 even those territories in which the Reformation had taken roots were actually outside the law. Religious tolerance came only very gradually, and in many countries today, even in Europe, it is far from being accepted.

Furthermore, Luther was of the opinion that Christians would be held accountable at judgment day if they permitted the Jews to publicly blaspheme Christ by stubbornly rejecting Jesus as the Messiah. Christians would also incur divine wrath if they were to

---

38. Luther, "Against the Sabbatarians: Letter to a Good Friend" (1538), in *LW* 47:66.

"protect and shield them."[39] Blasphemy cannot be permitted. This was common opinion at the time of Martin Luther.

Today, we can neither repeat Luther's advice, with his reference to judgment day, nor approve of it. These words are from a different time and in our view they can only be regarded as regrettable. They are also in stark contrast to Luther's writing of 1523 *That Jesus Christ Was Born a Jew*. Therefore it was appropriate that in 1994 the Church Council of the Evangelical Lutheran Church in America rejected Luther's anti-Semitic writings. We can be thankful that we live in a different time and should avoid everything to fall back into this earlier era. Yet on two points we still must heed Luther's line of thinking: Jesus is the Messiah for all people, even for the Jews. This obliges us not to withhold the gospel from the Jews. Luther, however, emphasized in this respect a sisterly way of conduct with the Jews. This kind of conduct is more pressing than ever, especially in Germany with its history of the "final solution of the Jewish issue" during the Third Reich. (Yet we should also not overlook the fact that the National Socialism of the Third Reich was a religious, neo-pagan ideology. Not only Jews ended up in the concentration camps, but also many confessing Christians.) Yet when church administrations find it doubtful to baptize Jews, even if they wish to be baptized, then this can only be equated with the denial of the gospel,[40] not only a denial of Luther and the church that has learned from his essential insights. For instance, the Bethel

---

39. Luther, *The Jews and Their Lies*, in *LW* 47:279.

40. We want to refer here to an "Announcement Concerning the Development of the Christian-Jewish Relationship" of the Fall Synod 2008 of the Evangelical Lutheran Church in Bavaria (November 26–27, 2008). There it states, "Activities which have as their goal a conversion from Jews to Christianity are unthinkable for the Evangelical Lutheran Church in Bavaria." In the discussion that ensued from this statement (cf. *Korrespondenzblatt* 124, March 3, 2009, 48–50) it says that "the comprehensive mission of the church remains without doubt. . . . The issue concerning the statement of the Synod in the city of Straubing is the way of this mission. An active missionary approach towards the Jews is unthinkable for the Evangelical Lutheran Church in Bavaria because of historical reasons."

Confession (*Betheler Bekenntnis*) of 1933 affirmed, "The church cannot be exempted from its duty to call Israel to repentance and to baptism disregarding any cultural and political considerations. Neither can Christians stemming from heathenism separate themselves from Christians coming from the people of Israel."[41] We cannot deny the gospel to anybody.

41. *Das Bekenntnis der Väter und die bekennende Gemeinde (Das sog. Betheler Bekenntnis)*, in *Die Bekenntnisse und grundsätzlichen Äußerungen zur Kirchenfrage des Jahres 1933*, ed. Kurt Dietrich Schmidt (Göttingen: Vandenhoeck & Ruprecht, 1934), 128.

10

––––

Love, Marriage, and Parenthood

When Martin Luther and Katharina von Bora were married in 1525 a new age began. On the side of the Reformation the parsonage was started from which many important persons hailed such as Eberhard Nestle (1851-1913), the editor of the Greek New Testament, or the philosopher Friedrich Nietzsche (1844-1900), According to Luther's understanding even a marriage of clerics was blessed by God and therefore holy and pure.

Sexuality and Love

It is, according to Luther, the good will of God and God's own work that humans exist in this world as male and female. Because both sexes are the good work of God, one sex should not attempt to belittle or hold the other in contempt, but instead each should honor the other as a good work that is pleasing to God. God has ordered things so that men and women are mutually dependent upon one another. Even the attraction and desire for the other, that is to say, sexual love, is a work of God. "And that is the Word of God, through the power of which in the human body seed becomes fruit and the intense natural attraction to the woman is created and preserved. This cannot be hindered either with vows or with laws for it is God's word and work."[1]

This has been true since the beginning of the creation and remains unchanged today. Luther speaks with lofty words of the love between the sexes, for it is the greatest and purest among all the various types of earthly love. He contrasts it not only to false love that seeks egoistically after its own self, but also to the natural love that exists between parents and children and among siblings. "Every other love seeks something besides that which it loves, but this love alone desires to have only the loved one. And if Adam had not fallen then the loveliest thing imaginable would have been a bride and groom."[2]

But Adam did fall and humanity thereby fell into sin. This also affects sexual love, which is no longer pure. It is no longer a pure giving to the other but now also seeks to satisfy its own lusts on the other. Fleshly lust has even had its effect upon procreation. Luther understands Ps. 51:5, "Indeed, I was born guilty, a sinner when my mother conceived me," as evidence that the transmission of original sin is connected with the human act of procreation and not (as is common in present-day exegesis) as a statement concerning the historical fate of Israel.[3] Luther remained trapped, therefore, in the traditional Augustinian contempt for sexual lust. Yet despite the limitations of this viewpoint, Luther recognized that there is a demonic element of egotistic desire in sexual love in which the one partner only uses the other instead of loving and honoring the other, as Luther explained in his explanation of the Sixth Commandment.[4]

---

1. Luther, *Christliche Schrift an W. Reißenbusch, sich in den ehelichen Stand zu begeben* (1525), in *WA* 18:275.25–28.

2. Luther, *Ein Sermon von dem ehelichen Stand* (1519), in *WA* 2:167.33–34.

3. Cf. Luther in his wedding sermon on Heb. 13:4 from January 8, 1531, *Predigten des Jahres 1531*, in *WA* 34/ I:73.3–10.

Luther understands marriage, therefore, within the framework of this complex of problems brought about by original sin.

Marriage

Luther determined first of all clearly and firmly that marriage was the will and work of God already before the fall. It was not an emergency measure meant to limit human sinfulness. God established marriage so that the world would be filled with human beings. Although for Luther it was clear that marriage and children belong together, he in no way saw the meaning of marriage as restricted to procreation. In our fallen world, marriage also means assistance for us sinners and a means of healing in the face of the promiscuity of the sex drive, and also help against the disorder that comes over us because of sin. Marriage harnesses the sexuality distorted by sin and defends body, goods, honor, and friendship from the harm that unbridled sexuality brings upon us. According to Luther, marriage can no longer be lived without sin, because sensual desire continues within marriage. Nevertheless, marriage is the will and work of God, a holy order that stands under God's blessing.

Marriage, Sensuality, and Celibacy

God does not judge those who stand in faith and wish to do God's will in spite of the sensual desires that take place in marriage. Hence despite the sin associated with it, marriage (if not by its nature then by the grace of God), receives God's gracious word of creation, forgiveness, and justification. Even though in sin, it remains a godly and holy estate. Luther sees sexual love, therefore, from a twofold

---

4. Cf. Luther, "The Sixth Commandment," in *The Small Catechism*, in *The Book of Concord: The Confessions of the Evangelical Lutheran Church*, ed. Robert Kolb and Timothy J. Wengert (Minneapolis: Fortress Press, 2000), 353.

perspective: from the perspective of God's good creation, and from the perspective of its distortion through sin.

Marriage, according to Luther, is the fundamental order of God from which all other orders and states are derived. It is commanded through God's creative will, for humans are driven to it by their very nature. Marriage cannot, therefore, simply be understood as God's command, but rather, by design of the Creator, it is a necessary part of being human. Whoever does not enter into the estate of matrimony at some point, according to Luther, inevitably falls prey to a loss of sexual discipline, prostitution, or self-abuse. These opinions are colored by Luther's own experiences with and observations of celibacy and contain a great deal of criticism specific to his time. (Just by way of illustration, there was an ordinance in the city of Regensburg that young girls should not come too close to the entrance of a monastery for fear of being grabbed and pulled inside. Conversely, in a women's convent excavations brought to light a number of baby skeletons.) So it is that Luther can also contend that the one who withholds himself from the estate of matrimony tempts God and does the will of Satan. Only within marriage is sexuality not a destructive force. Hence everyone should enter into the estate of marriage, if for no other reason than out of necessity and because of the sin inherent in our sexuality.

Yet Luther is aware of exceptions to marriage that are conceded by God. In the first place, there are some people who by their very nature are simply not suited to marriage. Likewise, there are others to whom God gives the exalted and supernatural gift of abstinence so that they are able to live a chaste life without being married. Such persons, however, are very rare. According to Luther, we would not find one among a thousand, for such persons are a "special miracle of God."[5] The Roman church leaders lost sight of this fact when they made priestly celibacy into law. Yet if some genuinely have this gift from God, they should be thankful. All others, however, should not put their trust in such abstinence and attempt the celibate life unless God has called them specially to be single, or unless they feel God's gracious gift of abstinence very strongly in themselves.

Luther, therefore, conceded the possibility of a celibate state and emphasized its special function and worth. While it was a sin in the Old Testament to be without wife and child, this no longer applies for the New Testament. In agreement with Paul, Luther is even able to admit that the single state is better inasmuch as one, without the responsibilities of marriage, "may better be able to preach and care for God's Word. . . . It is God's Word and the preaching which make celibacy—such as that of Christ and Paul—better than the estate of marriage. In itself, however, the celibate life is far inferior."[6]

This means, then, that from the moral perspective there is no higher estate than that of matrimony. Luther rejected, therefore, the qualitative supremacy of the priestly estate. The marital estate, according to Luther, through the burdens that God lays on those who are married, contributes toward putting to death the old nature and is the advanced school of patient humility within God's will. Marriage provides innumerable opportunities to express patience and love that a single person does not have. Hence marriage is the rule and the celibate life the exception.

One should enter happily into marriage and should remain happy in marriage because we know that God is pleased with marriage and with those who are married. The marital estate is adorned and made holy with the word of God. Hence marriage is a powerful source of joy in the midst of all burdens, crises, and disappointments. In marriage one finds peace in suffering, desire in apathy, and happiness in sorrow. "It is an art to see this estate according to the Word of God

---

5. Luther, *The Estate of Marriage* (1522), in *LW* 45:21.
6. Ibid., 47.

that alone makes both the estate of matrimony and those who enter into it lovely."[7] Luther therefore rejects the secular view of marriage that sees it only as a human and worldly institution that has nothing to do with God. Though a worldly matter, marriage is sanctified through God's will and word.

Seen from the perspective of human beings, however, marriage can only be holy when it is lived in the knowledge of God's involvement, that is, in faith. This does not contradict the characterization of marriage as an external, physical, or worldly thing, because according to Luther, "Weddings and the married estate are worldly affairs."[8] Marriage belongs to God's natural created order and not to Christ's redemptive order. Hence marriage is not a sacrament but is instead an institution that stands under God's blessing. Marriage is a holy estate even with those who are not Christians. Because it falls under the natural order, however, the church is not responsible for marriage as a legal institution. Marriage should not be subject to ecclesiastical laws and judgments but rather to those of the secular order. So it is that in those lands that adopted the Lutheran Reformation the legal aspects of marriage are administered by secular authorities. The church cannot establish laws in regard to this natural order of God any more than did Christ or the apostles, explained Luther. The only exception found in those matters is when the issue at hand is one of conscience. Here there is also a place for the pastor to counsel and, if necessary, comfort people when they are uncertain about something in their own conscience and are confused, or when then have violated the true estate of marriage.

One sees the consequences of the doctrine of the two kingdoms in Luther's understanding of marriage. Marriage is part of the created order and is therefore a worldly thing that belongs to the kingdom

7. Luther, sermon on Heb. 13:4, January 8, 1531, *Predigten des Jahres 1531*, in *WA* 34/ I:67.5–7.
8. Luther, *A Marriage Booklet for Simple Pastors*, in *The Book of Concord*, 367.

of the left. It is not a part of God's redemptive order, for one can also be sanctified without marriage. Hence the question of what form marriage should take (patriarchal, partnership based, or egalitarian), is a question that must be solved in the secular realm and one to which the church is not able to contribute any special knowledge. The form of marriage is determined by the social conditions of different ages. Hence Martin Luther's wife, Katharina, was alone responsible for the family's home, property, and finances while her husband pursued his theological responsibilities. Both parents were responsible for the upbringing of the children, Katharina mostly during the day and when her husband was away on business, and Martin mostly after he came home from work and when his wife was sick, although the children were also allowed to play around his desk while he was working. There was no clear separation of household duties, for during his many years before marriage—he was forty-one years old when he got married—he had learned, for instance, to mend his own clothing, a practice he happily continued after his marriage despite the protests of his wife. It was clear, however, according to the custom of the time, that he would represent the family in important external matters, as for instance when a salary increase needed to be sought from the elector. Katharina, on the other hand, was mostly responsible for internal matters, which included supervision of those employed in the house and outside in her small farm. Except for the nobility, women were not public persons. We have, for example no paintings of the women of the reformers, with the exception of Katharina. Moreover, when the husband died women were assigned a legal guardian since they could not inherit the estate. Luther, however, consulted lawyers and wrote his will accordingly to avoid the assigning of a legal guardian if he would die before his wife did. Nevertheless, to her great dismay a guardian was assigned to Katharina when her husband died.

Luther had little to do with the worldly estate of marriage in his pastoral duties, as this was the responsibility of the secular authorities. Nevertheless his advice was often sought out as a theologian, a pastor, and a friend in order to give counsel to the conscience. He frequently dealt with marital problems in his letters in a pastoral manner. According to Luther, the real responsibility of the pastoral office in regard to marriage was to proclaim to those who had entered into this estate not only the gospel but also God's will for marriage. It should, therefore, announce to them the power of faith and of love, without which one cannot have a good marriage.

The Practice of Marriage

In the practice of marriage, Luther continued the traditional steps into marital union. The actual marriage, that is, the exchange of the vows, the exchange of the wedding rings, and the pronouncement of the couple as husband and wife, took place at the door of the church, since this was all considered a worldly affair.[9] (That the "worldly affair" was too worldly was already a problem at Luther's time, since he complained that people think it is "a joke or child's play to get married or to have a wedding."[10]) Inside the church, at the altar, the spiritual ceremony took place in which God's word concerning marriage was proclaimed, God's blessing announced, and the prayers of the congregation for the young couple sought. "The pastor in this way blesses the bride and groom, confirms their marriage, and testifies that they have accepted and publicly acknowledged each other."[11] The so-called church wedding is therefore only a

---

9. Ibid., 369. In Germany today, all marriages must officially take place at a government registrar's office before those couples who so wish are allowed to proceed with a church wedding. The church wedding, then, usually follows the secular wedding by one or two days.
10. Luther, *A Marriage Booklet*, 368.
11. Luther, *Exempel, einen rechten christlichen Bischof zu weihen* (1542), in *WA* 53:257.8–10.

confirmation of the marriage that has already taken place and is a belated act of ecclesiastical blessing.

The public nature of marriage belongs to its very essence. Luther was careful to ensure that marriage as a public estate was always celebrated with a wedding before witnesses and the local congregation. A secret engagement and marriage, according to Luther, provides no certainty and the testimony of both the parties is not sufficient to recognize their marriage. A marriage should also not take place without the knowledge and consent of the parents, for this would violate the Fourth Commandment. On the other hand, parents should not force their children into a marriage against their will, nor should they forbid them to marry when they fall in love with someone.

Marriage has a twofold meaning: in the relationship of the couple to each other and in their responsibility to procreate and rear children. Husband and wife are first of all there for one another. The happiness of a marriage is secured when "husband and wife cherish one another, become one, [and] serve one another."[12] Sensual love alone is not enough, for it can quickly cool. Marriage is much more a covenant of faithfulness. "That is the ground and the entire essence of marriage that a person gives him or herself to another and promises to remain faithful to them and not to turn to another. Meanwhile the one, therefore, is bound to the other and gives him or herself over captive to the other."[13]

Within this covenant of faithfulness, sexuality has a different context than outside of marriage, for it is no longer driven by self-seeking lust but by the desire to serve the other. The physical relationship of a couple need not be limited only to that which is necessary to produce children. God allows couples sexual intercourse

---

12. Luther, *The Estate of Marriage*, in *LW* 45:43.
13. Luther, *Ein Sermon von ehelichen Stand* (1519), in *WA* 2:168.38–169.2.

beyond what is necessary for procreation as an expression and consummation of marital love. Here Luther provides a corrective to Paul by contending, "Although Christian married folk should not permit themselves to be governed by their bodies in the passion of lust, as Paul writes to the Thessalonians [1 Thess. 4:5], nevertheless each one must examine himself so that by his abstention he does not expose himself to the danger of fornication and other sins."[14]

Marital love and faithfulness guards itself above all in cases of disappointment in one's spouse, in times of conflict, and in the event that one's spouse is unbearable and mean-spirited. Luther viewed marriage very soberly and recognized that it is always endangered when it is lived only by its own power. A Christian, however, does not draw superficially upon happiness, but upon the will of God. Luther argues similarly when he speaks of the illness of a spouse that prevents the fulfilling of conjugal duty. In this situation one should not separate from the spouse but should serve God in the person of the one who is sick. "Blessed and twice blessed are you when you recognize such a gift of grace and therefore serve your invalid . . . [spouse] for God's sake."[15] We can trust God that we will not be given more than we are able to bear. Everything depends on whether one enters and continues in marriage with God, or self-confidently, that is, without God.

A first love or an initial falling in love is not, according to Luther, a sufficient foundation for a marriage. "It's easy enough to get a wife, but to love her with constancy is difficult."[16] It is an act of the devil that one becomes weary of one's spouse and casts his or her eye upon others. One should arm oneself against this danger by beginning and leading a marriage under the eyes of God and praying for God's help.

14. Luther, *The Estate of Marriage*, in *LW* 45:36.
15. Ibid., 35. Luther's original German here reads *Gemahl*, that is, "spouse," or even "husband," but not "wife" as the English version has it.
16. Luther, "Table Talk" no. 5524 (1542/43), in *LW* 54:444.

If another woman seems to me more beautiful and desirable than my own wife, wrote Luther, then I say to myself, "I have at home a much more beautiful ornament in the person of my own wife who God has given me and made beautiful above all others, whether or not she is physically attractive or whether she is otherwise frail."[17]

The other aspect of marriage, according to the word and will of God, is its fruitfulness. Here the mother serves the loving will of God for his creature. She is made worthy with her whole being to be the tool and hand of God. This is true in pregnancy as well as with birth, seen in light of the crisis and danger of death associated with child-bearing that Luther poignantly experienced, as a result of the state of medicine and hygiene in his time. What the natural person sees as pure burden, limitation, and hard work, the eye of faith sees as a unique calling to serve God's gracious will and to foster new life. God therefore calls parents as apostles, bishops, and pastors of their children.

Parenthood and Family

Parents, according to Luther, represent God and deserve to be seen by their children as the highest authority on earth. All other human authority, including that of the secular rulers, is derived from parental authority. Parental authority extends across both regiments. The parents are the rulers of their children in the secular regiment. By virtue of the priesthood of all believers, however, they are also the spiritual authority for their children and are responsible to proclaim the gospel to them. Hence parents should not only love their children and prepare them for success in secular society, but they should also provide for them spiritually as they are able. Through a good

---

17. Luther, in a sermon on Matt. 5:27–29, *Wochenpredigten über Mt. 5–7* (first printed 1532), in *WA* 32:372.18–21.

upbringing, parents can earn blessedness for their children—or through neglect, damnation.

Luther did not think much of the opinion, popular today in many places, that one should not seek to influence children; that is, that they should decide for themselves what they wish to believe. Although he constantly stressed that one cannot and dare not force someone to believe, he was well aware of the role parents have as models and of the truth of the proverb, "The apple does not fall far from the tree." If the parents have no positive relationship of faith, then the children, whether consciously or not, will be brought up with an attitude of religious indifference. God, however, has established parents as his representatives. For this reason children should see their parents as representing God. Hence Luther wrote in *The Small Catechism* that children should hold their parents in honor, for to honor is greater than to love.[18] To honor, however, love also belongs, and beyond love respect. Love should not occur apart from respect, and respect not apart from love, for both should be given to one's parents, just as to God. To do justice to the parent-child relationship we must first of all remember that parents are the highest unified authority their children know. This authority, however, is not grounded in any parental claim to power, for this authority finds its limits in the divine commission of the parents.

Luther attributes broad powers to the father as head of the household. In addition to the parents and children, a family of the late Middle Ages frequently included servants, journeymen, and apprentices of the craftsmen, or boarders, all under one roof. In the relationship between husband and wife the husband is the head, as Luther deduces from the physical and spiritual situation of both parties. Yet none of the normal tasks of wives are below the dignity

---

18. Luther, on the Fourth Commandment, *The Small Catechism*, in *The Book of Concord*, 352.

of a husband to perform when necessary. Hence Luther can describe how the husband at night rocks the children, washes diapers, and cares for and works for his wife.[19]

The wife is the companion of the husband. She carried out the normal, lower middle-class functions of her day—as Luther knew them—at home and on her property, and did this independently, and not under the supervision of her husband. The routine of the father of the house was coordinated with that of the wife and was not limited in regard to other household duties. Although the household is subjected to the rule of civil authorities, its internal structure and the functions of its members among themselves follow an order that is unique to each household and is appropriate to the order of creation. The father of the house, therefore, does not derive his authority from civil authorities, nor does he exercise it on behalf of them. Within the household he is independent of any government.

The primary concern of the wife is economic. The father, on the other hand, is primarily responsible for the religious aspect of family life. According to the preface of Luther's *Large Catechism*, "It is the duty of every head of a household at least once a week to examine the children and servants one after the other and ascertain what they know or have learned of it [that is, the *Catechism*]."[20] The father takes on the same function within his household as a pastor does in the parish. He exercises the role of a catechetical instructor in his spiritual care for the family, and receives this through the position given him by God within the family as a baptized Christian, not by delegation from the church.

The special function of the father is to be seen in that he cares for his children together with the mother, for they, at least until a certain age, are dependent upon parental care, as Luther asserted. Children,

19. Luther, *The Estate of Marriage*, in *LW* 45:40.
20. Luther, preface to *The Large Catechism*, in *The Book of Concord*, 362.

therefore, stand in a similar relationship to their parents as all persons do to God who created them. The natural love for one's children, which arises from the biological connection to them, corresponds to the will of the Creator. Yet this love dare not lead to a physical love, for the parents rear their children for God and in God's stead. Hence parents should be just as concerned about the well-being of their children's souls as they are about the well-being of their bodies.

To bring up children for God does not mean, however, that they should be sent to a monastery. It means, rather, that they should be brought up so as to learn to serve in caring for others, in fulfilment of their vocation, in availability for their congregation, and under the authority of God. The stubbornness of a child who resists the authority of its parents is, according to Luther, the preliminary stage of the antisocial behavior of an adult and must be prevented through wise and if necessary strict discipline. "One should bring up children with great enthusiasm to have a healthy fear so that they fear those things for which one should have respect, but not so as to make them fearful, as many parents do, which hurts them throughout their life."[21]

Unnecessary severity toward children is therefore foolish because it very easily has the opposite effect as what was intended. It is also a sin against the nature of children who, in their simplicity, are nearer to the original condition of our first parents than are adults. Luther therefore reprimands parents who do not compensate for the natural childlikeness of their children or who are unwilling to recognize their individuality.

One sees in Luther's view of the relationship between parents and children a fundamental ethical relationship built upon mutual interaction. Also, one cannot accuse Luther of a patriarchal conception of the family in which the father is the unrestricted

---

21. Luther, *Decem praecepta Wittenbergensi praedicata populo* (1518), in *WA* 1:449.35–39.

lord and master, even though Luther assumes the priority of the husband over the wife in the family, which was the accepted family order at his time. He based this view on natural law as interpreted by tradition. Katharina was responsible for the family budget, for hiring servants, getting boarders to help with the budget, etc., while Martin cared more for the external affairs. It was not just in jest that he addressed her occasionally as "Lord." But Luther's analogy between parents and secular authority is no longer functional for us, due to our democratically constituted government, even though we occasionally speak of a "father of the nation." Luther's insistence on the obligation of the father for the religious upbringing of the children certainly needs to be reconsidered, as well as his emphasis that the raising of children is not a private affair but is done in God's place.

Although our historical distance to Luther becomes very clear in this chapter, we should not overlook the seemingly modern characteristics in his understanding of marriage and family. The rights of parents, for example, find their limits in the First Commandment. And Luther himself went against the express will of his parents when he entered the monastery. Also, as can be seen in Luther's own marriage, a wife had a certain amount of freedom that was not subject to the rule of her husband. One could even speak here of a partnership marriage in the sense of an "intellectual and spiritual partnership of the wife,"[22] whereby husband and wife are dependent upon one another and are each concerned for the well-being of the other.

---

22. So Ingetraut Ludolphy, "Frau VI. Reformationszeit," in *Theologische Realenzyklopädie*, 11:443, in reference to Luther.

11

Vocation

Luther's teaching concerning vocation has had an incredibly broad impact, extending well beyond the ecclesiastical and religious spheres. The combined influence of the Protestant church and the middle-class world of seventeenth- and eighteenth-century Germany produced an understanding of carrying out one's vocation as direct service of God. Vocation became the focal point of human activities done in response to God's grace. Vocational loyalty was not just understood as loyalty to one's employer, but primarily as loyalty to God. In the periods of the Enlightenment and German Idealism in the late eighteenth and early nineteenth centuries, vocation ultimately became a fundamental concept in the ethical teaching about duty. Thus, according to the German philosopher Immanuel Kant (1724–1804), the universal moral law is fulfilled in vocation. It is for this reason that Frederick the Great (1712–1786), who ruled Prussia as king from 1740 to 1786, proclaimed, "The prince is the first servant of his state." This description of vocation as duty rubbed off on the Prussian officials and government workers who were known for their conscientious fulfillment of duty. Prussia's supremacy in Germany led to the development of an efficient and incorruptible bureaucracy that, in the community of nations, is still to this day exemplary in many ways.

For Luther, of course, such far-reaching ramifications were unintended. In his teaching about vocation, he was primarily concerned to dispel the view common in his time that priests and monks, through their vocation within a spiritual order, possessed a higher level of sanctification than those who had a secular vocation. In his 1521 writing, *On Monastic Vows*, Luther rejected the vocational privilege of monasticism, which held that monastics and priests held a vocational status superior to that of all others. From 1 Cor. 7:20, "Let each of you remain in the condition in which you were called," Luther concluded that even an ordinary working person, without having to belong to a monastic order, can carry out here on earth an occupation that is good and commanded by God. For Luther, vocation no longer means to be called out of the world to a better and higher vocational status, but is seen rather as a calling to and within that place where one does his or her work.

Luther's rejection of the idea of a religious vocation being more worthy also follows from his conviction that all persons are justified, that is to say accepted, through trust in God and not by being able to demonstrate certain good works before God. Because we have already received everything from God our Creator, it would be a contradiction to want to be rewarded by God for one good work or another. Good works, therefore, have nothing to do with our justification. "Those things we do for God are not called good works, but that which we should do for our neighbor, these are good works."[1] The fact that we perform works here on earth is entirely

---

1. Luther, in a sermon on John 20:21–23, April 27, 1522, in *WA* 10/3:98.26–27.

motivated by the fact that our fellow human beings need our help, that is, our works. Those who perform some worldly task do it to the glory of God and as a service to their neighbor. One should even view the pastoral office from this perspective, because here, too, the service to one's neighbor and the glorification of God is expressed.

In our industrialized, urbanized society, however, this conception of vocation has largely disappeared. The modern understanding of one's "job" is characterized by maximizing investment and profit and by the ability to exercise control. But employers and employees today are increasingly taking notice of the fact that without personal engagement, what is simply a job eventually amplifies the meaninglessness of life over the long run. Health problems, lack of motivation, and a decreasing quality of work are only some of the results. For more and more people, the level of remuneration and the shortness of the working week are no longer decisive, but what matters is the fact that the work is interesting, challenging, and personally engaging. A few years ago, I heard the dean of the Harvard Business School saying in his address to the graduating MBA students, "If you take your first job just because of the money it pays, you will love it. But after a while you will hate it. So look for more than just money." So it is that Luther's emphasis on vocation as service of one's neighbor takes on renewed significance today. As we turn now to the task of briefly outlining Luther's understanding of vocation, we must first view it in light of his understanding of one's status or station within society, which to some extent parallels his understanding of vocation.

Stations in Society

One cannot equate Luther's concept of *station* with the concept of class in the modern sense of the word. For Luther, one's station is first of all a general concept of order that makes it possible to group together all those persons who in one way or another share something in common that distinguishes them from all others. In 1630 the German hymn writer Johann Heermann penned words that reflect the thought of Luther: "Give me the strength to do with ready heart and willing whatever you command, my calling here fulfilling."[2] Such a calling or station could define a group (such a young girls), a social class (such as peasants), or a churchly estate (such as monks). Luther sees the various stations (in German, *Stand*) as standpoints for our actions. They are beyond our own arbitrary decisions, for the Creator has established them and placed us within a particular station. For example, I am the father of our children, I am a university professor, I am a member of my congregation, etc. These stations are places to which God calls us so that we can carry out a specific and unique vocation. Stations have a stabilizing function, but they cannot be compared to castes, which are closed in on themselves and do not allow any mobility from one station to another.

Tradition generally recognized three general stations: the teaching station, the economic station, and the political station. Luther accepted these on the whole, but understood the economic station quite differently and described it as the station of family life.[3] Under the category of the station of the family, Luther understood first of all marriage, then the family in the narrower sense, that is, the community of parents and children, and also the family in the broader sense that included domestic servants as well. Finally, Luther was able to classify the socioeconomic and civic-societal relations of human beings under the category of the station of the family. Of importance for Luther in regard to this station are the economic relationships of people to one another who all belong to the same social structure. For

2. Cf. *Evangelical Lutheran Worship*, hymn no. 806, stanza 2.
3. Luther, commenting on Gen. 18:15 in *Lectures on Genesis*, in *LW* 3:217, where he refers to the three stations broadly as "life in the home, state and church" corresponding to the economic, political, and teaching stations.

example, the union of husband and wife for the purpose of rearing children is also a biological necessity, as seen in the procurement of food and clothing. It is important in regard to activities within this station that the laws of life are not disregarded, thereby endangering the life of one's neighbor.

The political station, too, is established by God, for God desires order in society. Service of the state includes not only governing, but also obeying. While the laws of biology (in the station of the family) are unchangeable, the laws that lie at the foundation of the political station are changeable. Here one finds an order appropriate to each era that binds people to one another. In the case of the teaching station, or churchly station, neither the laws of biology nor the laws of the state are applicable. Instead, we have here to do with specific functions, so that the teaching station has its own laws specific to itself.

Luther said, "God has prescribed a variety of stations in which one shall learn to live and to suffer—some in the marital, others in the spiritual, and still others in the station of government."[4] Yet none of these stations is higher than the others, and all have as their goal that they serve the others. To be sure, each person is placed within a specific station, but one can also change from one station over to another, for instance from the spiritual station to the political or the economic. Yet every station has its own difficulties, so none is better or easier than the others. There is also no station in which there is no sin, for there is no station in which the command of God is fully carried out.

Why did God create and establish these stations in the first place? According to Luther's explanation, the stations embody the will of God so that God might provide for order and serve the needs of

---

4. Luther, *Ein Sermon vom Sakrament der Taufe* (1519), in *WA* 43:30.13–15.

human beings through these external forms: "Without these masks [that is, stations] peace and discipline could not be preserved."[5] What is particularly important, once more to stress this point, is that none of these stations is placed above or below the others. Luther strictly rejected a higher status for the spiritual station, for there must not exist any hierarchy of stations. Each of the stations is equally necessary for human life. A station, then, is the objective range of duties connected to a particular position within society. The term *station*, however, is no way a synonym for *vocation*.

Vocation and Calling

The word *vocation,* as we have indicated, is not another way of saying *station*. Vocation, to be sure, speaks of the same reality, but from a different perspective. The stations are universally objective structures, while vocations are objective structures only when the individual is permanently connected with a particular vocation and is personally obligated to it. For instance, one is called to the pastoral office through human beings who represent God by exercising the church's right to call an individual. People are called to marriage because we are created as male or female, to rear children and establish a household. The biological perspective of the station of the family and the individual's personal decision become intertwined. Likewise, the station of a prince or that of a subject becomes a vocation inasmuch as a specific directive is given to a person to take up the tasks bound to this directive.

Vocation as Divine Service

Belonging to a particular station does not automatically guarantee that carrying out the functions of that station will be "divine service,"

5. Luther, on Gen. 41:40, *Lectures on Genesis* (1535–45), in *LW* 7:184.

that is, that it will correspond to the divine will. If a person perceives that he or she has been called by God to a certain vocation, that person will be given the necessary assurance that this is their vocation, because a Christian does nothing without divine commission—without calling. It is a gift of God that we have one who has been given to us as neighbor, that we are subject to authorities, and that we have been placed in a family, for in these points of contact with other people, we are challenged to serve and to love. In this way we do the will of God and can view our work as divine service, regardless of its outwardly secular dimension.

Helping our neighbor, being a parent, and rearing children demonstrate a commonality in our calling whereby the differences between rich and poor and between those in authority and those under authority disappear. "We should accustom ourselves to follow the order which He [God] has prescribed for us. Whatever you may be, son, servant, or maid in the meanest circumstances, stay where you are, because you are in a station where God has put you."[6]

It is an important element of Luther's concept of vocation that every genuine vocation, being derived from divine calling, demands the engagement of the whole person. Luther continually warned that the preeminence of one station over another is reprehensible because it implies a contempt for the Creator. "We should remain there [in our vocation] with a happy conscience and know that through such work more is accomplished than if one had made donations to every monastery and received every medal; even if it is the most menial housework."[7]

Thereby we are reminded of Luther's comment: "If everyone served their neighbor, then the whole world would be filled with divine service.[8]

---

6. Luther, commenting on Isa. 65:12, *Lectures on Isaiah*, in *LW* 17:384.
7. Luther, sermon on Matt. 9:1–3, *Predigten des Jahres 1529*, in *WA* 29:566.39–567.20–21.

Vocational Mobility

The question that must now be raised is whether the placement within a particular vocation or station is inescapably fixed. On the one hand, Luther held firmly to the idea of unchangeable givens that place us within particular vocations. Hence he argued, for instance, that the woman cannot become a man, the pig herder cannot become a lawyer, and the peasant is not qualified to be mayor.[9] Biological and educational differences allocate us to specific vocations. We are not only placed in a particular station but also in a particular vocation. Luther's view of stations and vocations remained within the framework of the societal structure of his time. He had to believe, therefore, that people were called into particular stations through their birth.

On the other hand, however, Luther in many ways broke through the idea that society is structured according to the stations into which people are born. He fought, for example, against the practice of barring those born out of wedlock from holding honorable vocations within the craft and trade professions. He also demanded the possibility for the advancement of children from parents of little income and schooling. But he did not, thereby, sanction the motive of increasing one's salary as justification for such advancement. Because every vocation is divine service, one cannot argue for a change in vocation on the basis of financial profit. Luther made parents vividly aware that through sufficient education, advancement to all government, educational, and ecclesiastical offices would be open to their children:

It is not God's will that only those who are born kings, princes, lords,

---

8. Luther, sermon on Matt. 22.34–36, *Predigten des Jahres 1544*, in *WA* 49:606–614.

9. Cf. Luther, in a sermon on Luke 14:1–3, *Predigten des Jahres 1544*, in *WA* 49:606–14, where he emphasizes with many examples how one shall not arrogantly seek to remove oneself from the station in which one has been placed.

and nobles should exercise rule and lordship. He wills to have his beggars among them also, lest they think it is nobility of birth rather than God alone who makes lords and rulers. . . . That is the way it will always be: your son and my son, that is, the children of the common people, will necessarily rule the world, both in the spiritual and the worldly estates.[10]

Advancement is open to all persons who have the prerequisite educational qualifications. Hence Luther impressed upon the territorial lords the great importance of the universities. He likewise wrote *To the Councilmen of All Cities in Germany That They Establish and Maintain Christian Schools*, as his writing of 1524 was titled. He demanded that basic educational opportunities be available to all people. Hence the children of poor parents were to be supported through governmental and ecclesiastical scholarships. Yet all the different possibilities of advancement are of no use if parents do not allow their children to take advantage of available educational opportunities. Parents, however, are also responsible for examining their children to determine whether they really have the necessary ability and interest to pursue higher education.

The fact that one has had a good education, however, does not automatically mean that one should demand to take up a more highly qualified vocation than what one would have had without this education. It does not, for example, do damage to a craftsperson, Luther contends, to have studied Latin just because it was an interesting subject, nor does it harm one to be well-educated, whether or not one actually takes up the kind of position normally associated with the program of studies.[11] For Luther there are no ethical distinctions between the different vocations, and a fulfilling life is possible within each of them. If someone is unable to achieve much career advancement, one should not consider oneself deprived.

10. Luther, *A Sermon on Keeping Children in School* (1530), in *LW* 46:250–51.
11. Ibid., 231–32.

One can only choose one's own vocation within certain limits, for the calling to a vocation always takes place through other people. Activity or training within a certain vocation always preceded the actual reception of a call into this vocation. Therefore, neither choosing a vocation nor the carrying out of its duties is a purely private matter. Luther frequently cautioned parents and teachers to keep in mind the well-being of the whole population when influencing a child regarding vocation. Important in regard to Luther's thoughts on vocation is a person's readiness to serve and to love:

> See to it first of all that you believe in Christ and are baptized. Afterward concern yourself with your vocation. I am called to be a pastor. Now when I preach I perform a holy work that is pleasing to God. If you are a father or mother, believe in Jesus Christ and so you will be a holy father and a holy mother. Take watch over the early years of your children, let them pray, and discipline, and spank them. Oversee the running of the household and the preparation of meals. Such things are nothing other than holy works for you have been called to do them. That means they are your holy life and are a part of God's Word and your calling.[12]

This mutual serving that we encounter in the family and in marriage, as well as in the larger community, has already been shown to us in the service of Christ. Humans are called to serve one another, just as Christ served us. Luther knew of no vocation that one could carry out without reference to the needs of the larger community. One is called when the community needs someone for a specific service and when one is qualified to meet the demands of this service. One cannot derive from this calling either an inappropriate pride in one's vocation, nor the absolute right of an individual to perform a particular vocation. A vocation is a service and can only be required when both the necessary qualifications in those who would serve in

12. Luther, sermon on Luke 5:1–3, *Predigten des Jahres 1534*, in *WA* 37:480.2–8.

this vocation and the need for it in the community are present. Under these conditions it is our duty not to forsake our vocation, even if it becomes too toilsome. If we have a genuine calling, then we dare not forsake our tasks but should stand courageously before them and accomplish them.

Luther's teaching on vocation is still able in our own day to help counter the individualistic and self-centered striving for our own advantage, and to allow us to rediscover the fact that our work is meant to serve the common good. The world has changed decisively since Luther's world of the sixteenth century. Yet many basic problems addressed by Luther remain problems relevant to our own time.

12

The Impact on Education

Philip Melanchthon was the teacher of Germany, the *praeceptor Germaniae*, on account of the numerous textbooks he wrote on a wide range of subjects from anthropology to history and geography. Yet Martin Luther laid the theological groundwork for education. We remember that the Reformation was primarily spread by the printed word. To understand that one must have been able to read. Furthermore, Luther insisted that every baptized person was a mature Christian who needed to read the Bible on his or her own. This also presupposed that one could read. Luther also never forgot that he had received a good education in school and in the university. He had a love for Latin poets, and when he entered the monastery he took with him works by the Latin poets Plautus (ca. 245–ca. 184 B.C.) and Virgil (70–19 B.C.). Moreover, he had a fondness for foreign languages and insisted that "the languages are the sheath in which this sword of the Spirit [Eph. 6:17] is contained."[1] With his translation of the Bible

---

1. Luther, *To the Councilmen of All Cities in Germany That They Establish and Maintain Christian Schools* (1524), in *LW* 45:360.

into German he had an immense influence on the development of modern German, and many phrases in that language still date back to Luther. Nevertheless, just knowing German was not sufficient in his estimate, and he cautioned, "Who must preach and exegete Scripture and does not have the support of the Latin, Greek, and Hebrew language but will only do it with the mother tongue is prone to make quite some mistakes."[2] Therefore he emphasized the necessity for pastors to have a good education, including a command of the ancient languages, something which today is still considered necessary for pastors in Germany. In order to educate pastors one needed a reform of the universities, since many things that were taught there were not beneficial.

Luther's Reforms Presupposed a Good Education

In his 1520 writing *To the Christian Nobility*, Luther asserted that many writings of Aristotle, for instance on physics, metaphysics (i.e., theology), and ethics should not be taught at the university, since they are of little use and also do not help in understanding the gospel. But Aristotle's writings on logic, rhetoric, and poetry are useful to read, as well as Cicero's (106–43 b.c.) rhetoric, without the later commentaries. The main emphasis should rest on the classical languages, including Hebrew. Canon law, including the papal decrees, can be dispensed with. The sentences of Peter Lombard (ca. 1096–1164) and others, meaning collections of quotations by famous theologians on various theological topics, should not be taught at the beginning of theological studies but be reserved for the conclusion, and there too only for future doctors of theology. Most important is the understanding of the Bible. For this, education in schools was a must. Luther wrote, "The foremost reading for everybody, both in

2. Luther, *Vom Anbeten des Sakraments des heiligen Leichnams Christi* (1523), in *WA* 11:455.30–34.

the universities and in the schools, should be Holy Scripture—and for the young boys, the Gospels. And would to God that every town had a girls' school as well, where the girls would be taught the gospel for an hour every day either in German or in Latin. Schools indeed!"[3] Luther's demand for Scripture alone and the priesthood of all believers presupposed sufficient education. But in medieval Europe illiteracy was still the norm. Just 5 to 10 percent of the population could read, and that usually only in the cities. The quest for education was therefore nonnegotiable if the Reformation should get a hold among the people.

In face of the low educational standards it was not surprising that both youth and laity had little knowledge of the gospel. This became especially evident in the visitations of the congregations in electoral Saxony during 1527–1528. As a remedy Luther composed in 1529 the *Wittenberg Hymnal* (*Wittenberger Gemeindegesangbuch*). In the same year his prayer book (*Gebetbüchlein*) was published, as well as *The Small* and *The Large Catechism*. The prayer book was not just a collection of prayers, but was intended to introduce the Christian faith. The hymnal, too, was not merely a book in which one could learn the hymns needed for the liturgy, but a comprehensive book for the songs of Christendom. The two catechisms were also not just intended to provide answers for catechetical instruction, but introduced the praxis of Christian existence. The publications contained numerous pictures, as did Luther's Bible translation. For Luther, word and picture belonged together, as well as music too, because all three were instruments to instruct into the Christian faith, or more precisely into the faith of the Reformation. Luther was an eminently practical person and he knew that one can remember

---

3. Luther, *To the Christian Nobility of the German Nation Concerning the Reform of the Christian Estate* (1520), in *LW* 44:205–6. For the reform of the universities, cf. 200–5.

pictures much more easily than texts and that a text sung can be more easily remembered than a plain text.

As aforementioned, Luther was not only interested in reforming the church. Since the call for reforms was issued largely from urban centers and from educated citizens, it was important for Luther that there existed a cooperation between church and school, not just for the educated but also for those with less schooling, so that they could understand and defend their faith. Luther accepted the traditionally stratified society. Important for him was always the idea of order, so that those standing in opposition of the Reformation could not accuse him of creating chaos. By insisting on education for everybody, however, he broke through the expectation that one was restricted to the order into which one was born, such as nobility, citizens, or peasants as we have seen in the previous chapter. Ascending to a higher level in society was possible for everybody if one had the appropriate education. Therefore Luther drove home to the territorial lords the significance of universities. Similarly, he admonished *The Councilmen of All Cities in Germany That They Establish and Maintain Schools*, as a 1524 publication is called. He demanded the possibility of education for everybody. Children of poor parents should be supported by scholarships given by cities or the church. Yet this support leads to nothing if the parents to not allow their children in due time to acquire an education. Parents must also examine their children to see whether they are really gifted and interested to attain a higher education.

Once one has obtained a good education, one should not automatically demand a position equivalent to this education. Luther interjects that it is of no disadvantage for a craftsperson that he or she has learned Latin, since it is great if a person is learned, even though the office that could be associated with this education will never be available to this person.[4] Luther does not find that a different value adheres to different vocations, since fulfillment of life can be found in every vocation. If someone does not succeed in climbing the social ladder one is not disadvantaged. According to Luther all human beings are children of God and should further the intellectual and physical gifts given to them by their Creator. These gifts should then be used to serve the others insofar as they need this service.

In 1530, Luther confessed that *A Sermon on Keeping Children in School* "has grown to the point where it has almost become a book."[5] In the preface dedicated to the town clerk of Nuremberg, Lazarus Spengler (1479–1534), Luther emphasizes that even in a city such as Nuremberg that had heavily invested in schools, there exists the danger that God's word and the schools will be neglected. For the parents it is often more important that their children earn money than to attend school. They take their son from school and pretend that he can add and subtract and read books in German. This they think is sufficient. But in a city such as Nuremberg there must be many kinds of people besides merchants.

> It must have people who can do more than simply add, subtract, and read German. German books are made primarily for the common man to read at home. But for preaching, governing, and administering justice, in both spiritual and worldly estates, all the learning and languages in the world are too little, to say nothing of German alone. This is particularly true in our day, when we have to do with more than just the neighbor next door.[6]

For the different tasks in the state, the city, and the church one needs well-educated people who on account of the international exchange know Latin, which was the common medium in which one conversed on the international level.

---

4. Luther, *A Sermon on Keeping Children in School* (1530), in *LW* 46:231.
5. Ibid., 213.
6. Ibid., 215.

From the visitations in electoral Saxony Luther had learned that there were few pastors who were actually qualified for their office both in doctrine and general knowledge. But there were also too few pastors altogether, since many had simply left their charge in the wake of the Reformation and at times, especially during the Peasants' Wars, the whole educational system had nearly collapsed. Luther was afraid that in the near future three or four cities would just have one pastor and ten villages only one chaplain if the princes would not institute boys' schools and schools of higher education, and if parents would not send their children to these schools.[7] Moreover, many pastors were almost destitute, since the people no longer supported them as they had done before with regard to monasteries, in order to obtain merits before God. According to Luther, however, the real reason why the pastoral office and the preaching skills were in such disarray was that the parents did not make their children learn. If a child is gifted and loves to learn and one nevertheless does not make this child attend school, one is guilty of neglecting the pastoral office.

But pastors are important for the worldly community. Luther explains, "For a preacher confirms, strengthens, and helps to sustain authority of every kind, and temporal peace generally. He checks the rebellious; teaches obedience, morals, discipline, and honor."[8] For Luther, however, a preacher is not a replacement of a police person, because "of all good things a pastor does these are, to be sure, the least." But Luther is mindful that preaching the law and reminding the people of the Decalogue are the tasks of a preacher. When a preacher neglects these, the moral order decays. Luther even reminds the readers that worldly peace, "the greatest of earthly goods, . . . is actually a fruit of true preaching." According to Luther, the pastoral office is an office to bring about peace. And in this way a true pastor

7. Cf. Luther, ibid., 234.
8. Ibid., 226, for this and the following quotes.

contributes to the well-being of people in body and soul. Even a king's son is not born too high to be trained for this office and work. One day God will demand an accounting from us what we have done with our children. Did we just educate them for temporal goods or did we enable them to help those who need help?

We should not surmise that for Luther schools serve only to educate pastors and teachers. He writes, "I do not mean that every man must train his child for this office, for it is not necessary that all boys become pastors, preachers, and schoolmasters."[9] Luther is also not primarily concerned about children of townsfolk or of the nobility, but about children of poor people. "Boys of such ability ought to be kept at their studies, especially sons of the poor. . . . Other boys as well ought to study, even those of lesser ability. They ought at least to read, write, and understand Latin, for we need not only highly learned doctors and masters of Holy Scripture." According to Luther, education should be available to everybody even if he primarily thought about the possible education for the pastoral office. As aforementioned, one need not pursue this vocation. One can learn Latin and still become a craftsperson. According to Luther, higher education enlarges one's horizon and one can always change to a different profession if one is needed and has the appropriate education.

Education Is for Both Pastors and Laypersons

Next to the education for the pastoral office, Luther focuses in this "sermon" in a second and larger portion on the education for the temporal authority, which maintains peace on earth, as well as law and life. For Luther "worldly government is a glorious ordinance and splendid gift of God," which God has instituted and established that

---

9. Ibid., 231, for this and the following quote.

it maintains law and peaceful order for the people.[10] Princes and even the emperor usually do not have the ability to maintain law and order because they only use "fist and weapons," meaning force. But "heads and books must do it. Men must learn and know the law and wisdom of our worldly government," writes Luther.[11] Those who maintain law in the temporal empire are the jurists and the scholars. Luther uses the term *jurists* very comprehensively and includes chancellors, clerks, judges, lawyers, notaries, and all who have to do with the legal side of government. They maintain and help to further the whole worldly government if they exercise their office properly, whether in towns, in the countryside, or at courts with the princes and with the emperor. If the parents seek their sons to be well-educated, then they also can "become such a useful person" and the money is well invested.[12] This is not a purely private decision, because God has given the people these children and the goods that they serve God with these children and therefore keep their children to the service for God. Maintaining God's order and temporal authority are divine service. For Luther, a temporal or secular task has become a divine calling in the same way as the exercise of the pastoral office.

Luther often complains about the decay of education. Educated people are needed in the cities as well as at court, and if they are not available as necessary then "kings will have to become jurists, princes chancellors, counts and lords clerks, mayors sextons."[13] Since the education to these good and useful works pleases God and the service in these works is for God's sake, they are much more valuable than if one thinks just of one's own benefit and the money that children could earn without this education. Therefore preachers and teachers need to imprint this on the minds of the boys and the parents of

10. Ibid., 237.
11. Ibid., 239.
12. Ibid., 241.
13. Ibid., 244.

these children from early on that they understand that these stations and offices are instituted by God, and that they are not to be treated with disrespect but to be kept in high honors. Ultimately they serve the peace and the unity of humans. Many people, however, do not recognize how necessary and useful these offices are in the world. One should also not forget, writes Luther, that it is much easier to learn how to use armor than how to execute properly a learned office.

In conclusion Luther admits referring to Aristotle:

> A diligent and upright schoolmaster or teacher, or anyone who faithfully trains and teaches boys, can never be adequately rewarded or repaid with any amount of money. . . . If I could leave the preaching office and my other duties, or had to do so, there is no other office I would rather have than that of schoolmaster or teacher of boys; for I know that next to that of preaching, this is the best, greatest, and most useful office there is. Indeed, I scarcely know which of the two is the better.[14]

Education in schools is extremely important for Luther. But he also remembers that before the Reformation set in, people liberally supported the churches and the schools so that one could send children to schools run by monasteries and other schools. But since the Reformation the willingness to donate money and the interest in these schools has almost vanished. The reason for this change was that before the Reformation people thought they would do good works, such as donating money or goods to monasteries and schools. This would help them earning heavenly rewards. But now they felt that since they were set right with God by grace alone they needed not be liberal with their possessions but can keep them for themselves. Giving out of thankfulness to God instead out of fear had not occurred to most of the people. Moreover, most schools run by monasteries or that were associated to cathedrals had closed their doors.

14. Ibid., 253.

Because of the new situation Luther argued that temporal authorities must establish schools and force people to send their children to schools so that temporal offices can be staffed with well-educated persons. Already in 1524 Luther wrote *The Councilmen of All Cities in Germany That They Establish and Maintain Christian Schools.* Luther recalled that prior to the Reformation, many parents send their sons and daughters into monasteries and ecclesial houses so that they no longer needed to take care of them. The learned all kinds of arts in these institutions. But with the Reformation this custom broke off, and most young people no longer had a chance to learn intellectual or menial trades. This means the decay of the monasteries and ecclesial institutions was accompanied by a similar decay of education. But this was not what Luther had in mind, since he had always put so much emphasis on education. Therefore Luther told the cities that they should become the supporters of educational institutions. He showed them that annually they spent much money on roads, dams, bridges, and other structures necessary for urban living. Then he asked whether they should not spend as much money on the poor neglected youth. As a result of the Reformation they had saved a lot of money since they no longer wasted a lot of "money and property on indulgences, masses, vigils, endowments, bequests, anniversaries, mendicant friars, brotherhoods, pilgrimages, and similar nonsense."[15] Should one then not, asks Luther, "out of gratitude to God and for his glory, contribute a part of that amount toward schools for the training of the poor children?" According to Luther, this would be an excellent investment and it would express their thanks toward God that they had been liberated from all this superstition. Therefore Luther insistently pleaded with the councilmen, for God's sake, to take care of the youth.

---

15. Luther, *To the Councilmen of All Cities in Germany That They Establish and Maintain Christian Schools* (1524), in *LW* 45:350–51, for this and the following quote.

Education for Boys and Girls

With reference to Ps. 78:5 (God "commanded our ancestors to teach to their children" [the glorious deeds of our Lord]), Luther asserted that it is the obligation of the parents to teach their children.[16] If the parents fail to do their duty, then it is the responsibility of the authorities and the city council to keep children in school. Languages and the arts help us to understand Holy Scripture and to conduct temporal government. "If through our neglect we let the languages go (which God forbid!), we shall not only lose the gospel, but the time will come when we shall be unable to speak or to write a correct Latin or German."[17] We remember that the Reformation was largely propagated by picture and writing. Therefore education in reading and writing was essential. Because of the priesthood of all believers, it was also necessary that every Christian could read and understand the Bible. For Luther education was indispensable for the spiritual estate, but also for the temporal. Since "the temporal government is a divinely ordained estate" one must "get good and capable men into it."[18] Though the Romans and the Greeks "had no idea of whether this estate were pleasing to God or not, they were so earnest and diligent in educating and training their young boys and girls to fit them for the task." Luther even concedes that if one would not need schools for the spiritual estate, it would alone be reason enough to establish everywhere

> the very best schools for both boys and girls, namely, that in order to maintain its temporal estate outwardly the world must have good and capable men and women, men able to rule well over land and people, women able to manage the household and train children and servants aright. Now such men must come from our boys, and such women from

16. Ibid., 353.
17. Ibid., 360.
18. Ibid., 367, for this and the following quote.

our girls. Therefore, it is a matter of properly educating and training our boys and girls to that end.[19]

Since common people are incapable, unwilling, or ignorant of it and since the princes and lords prefer to fool around and "are burdened with high and important functions in cellar, kitchen, and bedroom," this task of providing for the education the young rests with the councilmen alone.[20] If these young people were instructed and trained in schools or other institutions, where learned and well-trained schoolmasters and schoolmistresses were available to teach the languages, "the other arts, and history," then they would receive a comprehensive education and could "take their own place in the stream of human events."[21]

If one was afraid that children therefore would no longer be available to help at home, Luther dispersed such worries, saying,

> My idea is to have the boys attend such a school for one or two hours during the day, and spend the remainder of the time working at home, learning a trade, or doing whatever is expected of them. In this way, study and work will go hand-in-hand while the boys are young and able to do both. . . . In like manner, a girl can surely find time enough to attend school for an hour a day, and still take care of her duties at home. . . . Only one thing is lacking, the earnest desire to train the young and to benefit and serve the world with able men and women. . . . The exceptional pupils, who give promise of becoming skilled teachers, preachers, or holders of other ecclesiastical positions, should be allowed to continue in school longer, or even be dedicated for a life of study."[22]

Luther suggests here a dual track of education for the lowest level that provides skills in the crafts as well as in the intellectual faculties, while for higher education he suggests either a more intensive intellectual

19. Ibid., 367–68.
20. Ibid., 368.
21. Ibid., 369.
22. Ibid., 370–71.

education or one that is exclusively devoted to scholarship. For his time it was revolutionary to introduce education for both boys and girls irrespective of their future positions. In order to advance oneself in education Luther suggests that "no effort or expense should be spared to provide good libraries or book depositories, especially in the larger cities which can well afford it."[23] Luther refers here to the monasteries and foundations that also established libraries, though as time went on there were few good books left among them. The arts and languages declined and "there were no books available than the stupid books of the monks and the sophists."[24] Yet one should make a judicious selection. First of all, the Bible should be accessible in different languages, then the best commentaries of the Bible in the classical languages, including those of the church fathers, then books that are helpful in learning the languages, then Christian and pagan poets that one can learn the grammar. Also books in the liberal arts, and all other arts should be available. Finally, books of law and medicine and chronicles and histories in whatever language they are to be had should be acquired. We can easily notice that for Luther libraries should be of help for all ways of life.

Luther had no time for or interest in writing textbooks for students as did Melanchthon. But he provided the theological foundation for the education of a Christian. Christians must be accountable before God for faith and conduct. This presupposes a solid education in faith and life. Since they should lead responsible lives in the worldly realm, they need an education that develops both intellectual as well as manual skills. For this the knowledge of God's will in regard to ethical conduct is indispensable. Education in spiritual, intellectual, and manual matters pertains to boys and girls. For a more challenging position, a more intensive education is needed than for a less

23. Ibid., 373.
24. Ibid., 375.

demanding one. Education depends on the gifts of the individual, and the exercise of a calling depends on the demands of society. Therefore a certain education does not always guarantee that one can work in a corresponding profession. For Luther this does not cause problems, since each calling, profession, or job is of equal value and is fulfilled in service for God and therewith in thanking God for his prevenient grace. Luther's emphasis is here on the service function of a profession.

Educational Advantage of Lutherans

The education demanded and inaugurated by Martin Luther had unforeseen consequences for Lutheranism. The sociologist and economist Max Weber (1864–1920) stipulated a gap in prosperity between Roman Catholics and Protestants. The economists Sascha Becker (University of Warwick, Great Britain) and Ludger Woessmann (University of Munich, Germany) showed in a 2008 study that this gap did indeed exist in nineteenth-century Prussia.[25] It was not the work ethics that made Protestants more prosperous, as Weber had thought, but the greater proficiency in reading and writing. This was exactly the point that Luther had stressed. According to Luther, everybody should be able to read the Bible. But the income of only Protestants was higher, on account of their better education. They also generally had a higher education than Roman Catholics. The reason for this was that for a long time the idea prevailed in Roman Catholicism that higher education is primarily needed if one wanted to become a priest. For this purpose good schools were established in dioceses and in monasteries. But for intellectually gifted children of Protestants, a higher education was

25. Sascha O. Becker and Ludger Woessmann, "Luther and the Girls: Religious Denomination and the Female Education Gap in 19th Century Prussia," 3837, Institute for the Study of Labor (IZA), 2008, 1. http://ideas.repec.org/s/iza/izadps.html.

natural regardless of what kind of profession they wanted to pursue in future life. This discrepancy in education was also noticeable for a long time at my home university of Regensburg, in a predominantly Roman Catholic area. The majority of the professors was Protestant and predominantly hailed from Northern Germany, where most people adhere to the Lutheran faith.

But Luther's emphasis on education included both boys and girls, whereas with Roman Catholics it was usually boys, even if they did not want to enter the priesthood later on. This meant that many more Protestant girls went to school than Roman Catholic girls. Studying documents from 1871, Becker and Woessmann investigated the educational level of adults and came to the result that Protestant women could read and write better than Roman Catholic men at that time.[26] This fact considerably improved the advancement of Protestant women. For instance, in 1908, the year in which women were for the first time allowed to study in German universities, there were eight times more Protestant female students than Roman Catholic female students.[27] Even in the 1970s, the gender gap in regard to education was considerably smaller in Protestant states in Germany than in predominantly Roman Catholic states. Luther's emphasis on education for both boys and girls contributed to the equalization of education between Protestant men and women. Since then, however, Roman Catholics have largely closed this gap. But this does not diminish the significant influence which the Lutheran Reformation had on education.

26. Ibid., 15.
27. Ibid., 18.

13

Luther and the Economy

Martin Luther was the reformer of the church. But he was much more than that. He had become such a public figure that there was hardly any issue in the church or public life in which his opinion or advice was not sought. This held also true for economic matters, in which Luther certainly was not an expert. In contrast to his wife Katharina, who had to run the large household, he was personally indifferent to money and wealth, "other than as a means of subsistence and something to be shared with less fortunate brethren."[1] Yet with an open mind and well-versed in Scripture, Luther could distinguish between right and wrong even in these matters.

Transition from Subsistence Farming to Early Capitalism

During Luther's time, 90 percent of the population in the Germany still lived in the countryside and therefore the majority of the people were peasants. Nearly half of them did not own any property and

---

1. Translator's introduction to *Trade and Usury*, *LW* 45:234.

were dependent on the goodwill of various landlords, such as the nobility, monasteries, or prosperous citizens. Even in smaller cities such as Wittenberg, with roughly over two thousand inhabitants, many of the citizens were still active in farming, as we can see from Luther's own wife Katharina. At the same time commerce was flourishing, especially in rich merchant cities such as Augsburg and Nuremberg. The discovery of the Americas opened new dimensions for commerce from South America to India and from the Baltic Sea to Spain. Revenues for a few increased in an unprecedented way. The Fugger family in Augsburg, for instance, was so rich it could advance money not only to the archbishop Albrecht of Mainz but also to the emperor.[2] (Luther rightly wondered "how could it ever be right and according to God's will that a man in such a short time should grow so rich that he could buy out kings and emperors?"[3]) At the same time, the price of manufactured goods increased considerably, so that many craftsmen and artisans advanced to entrepreneurship while their helpers received only a tiny share of the revenues. For instance, Lucas Cranach the Elder (1472–1553) was not only a renowned painter but also owned a pharmacy and a printing press and had the monopoly of the sale on medicines in Wittenberg, and in 1531 and 1540 held the office of mayor in Wittenberg. Similarly, Albrecht Dürer (1471–1528) not only sold his paintings in his hometown of Nuremberg, but made agreements with agents to sell his copper and wood etchings from "one country to another and from one town to another" for the highest price possible.[4] With the rise of this new capitalism, the gap between the rich and the poor or the nearly poor

2. According to Martin Brecht, *Martin Luther: His Road to the Reformation, 1483–1521*, trans. James Schaaf (Philadelphia: Fortress Press, 1985), 179, the Fugger banking house made a profit of 52,286 ducats on the sum of 21,000 ducats, which it advanced to the archbishop. This was a profit or more than 200 percent!

3. Luther, *Trade and Usury* (1524), LW 45:271. Cf. also the explanatory footnote on the same page.

4. Ludwig Veit, "Albrecht Dürer und seine Familie: Dokumente," in *Albrecht Dürer 1471–1971*, 3rd ed. (Munich: Prestel, 1971), 31, quote p. 43.

opened more and more. This did not pass by unnoticed for Luther, since he also came from a family that had been on the rise in the copper mining business.

Once Luther got married in 1525, he was exposed to the daily economic problems in Wittenberg by raising his own family. His wife was astute in financing the household by having student boarders, buying a small farm near her ancestral home in Zölsdorf, and by being nearly self-sufficient in terms of food. Yet Luther noticed the high interest rates that were being charged and occasionally complained about the high food prices even if there was a good harvest.[5] It is no surprise that soon Luther addressed economic issues more specifically. Already in his 1520 publication *To the Christian Nobility* he addressed luxurious clothing, exotic spices, and buying on credit as sources of sliding into poverty.[6]

The Issue of Taking Interest

Taking interest was debated among Christians from early on, since with reference to passages such as Exod. 22:25 ("If you lend money to my people, to the poor among you, you shall not deal with them as a creditor; you shall not exact interest from them"), one inferred that Christians should not lend money for financial gain. Christian should simply help each other when they were in need. Perhaps this was too idealistic, and therefore Pope Leo the Great (ca. 400–461) prohibited both clerics and laypeople from "lay[ing] out money at interest, and wish[ing] to enrich themselves as usurers."[7] Several church councils reiterated this prohibition. Yet Thomas Aquinas (ca. 1225–1274) and

---

5. Cf. Martin Brecht, *Martin Luther: Shaping and Defining the Reformation, 1521–1532*, trans. James Schaaf (Philadelphia: Fortress Press, 1990), 145.
6. Cf. Luther, *To the Christian Nobility of the German Nation Concerning the Reform of the Christian Estate* (1520), in *LW* 44:212–13.
7. Leo the Great, *Letters* (4,3), in *Nicene and Post-Nicene Fathers of the Church*, ed. Philip Schaff, second series (Peabody, MA: Hendrickson, 1994), 12:3–4.

other scholastic theologians thought it legitimate to ask for interest if a person did not pay back the loan in time, or if the one who loaned money could not get back all or part of the loan, or if someone paid interest out of gratitude.[8] This means that taking interest was not totally illegitimate. In 1500 an imperial diet at Augsburg decided that *Zinsskauf*—literally meaning "interest purchase"—was legal.[9] In order to avoid paying interest on a loan, which was forbidden by the church as usury, the moneylender now gave a certain amount of money to a person and in return "bought" a regular *zinss* or income from this credit. This could be done in one of three ways: (1) One could borrow money and the one who advanced the money would then use a specified piece of land of the borrower's property as an exchange. It could also mean that (2) the one who gave the money would receive a fixed amount of the yield of the property. Or it could mean that (3) the whole property and not just a piece of the land could be involved in the transaction, which was termed *blind Zinsskauf*. The problem that Luther saw in the *Zinsskauf* was that the one who advanced the money had virtually no risk. The debtor had to pay a certain fixed portion either in money or in goods from the land on which the money was given, regardless whether it was a good year or a bad one. So if the yield on the land was bad the debtor still had to fulfill the stipulation of the deal. If the security for the loan was not just a certain piece of land but the whole property of the debtor, then the whole property could be lost if things went bad for the borrower. The issue of the *Zinsskauf* shows that the prohibition against charging interest had many loopholes for Christians. In case of the Jews this was even more so.

---

8. Cf. Thomas Aquinas, *Summa theologica*, II–II q 78 ("The Sin of Usury") a 2, resp.
9. According to Hans-Jürgen Prien, *Luthers Wirtschaftsethik* (Göttingen: Vandenhoeck & Ruprecht, 1992), 63.

In canon 25 of the Third Lateran Council (1179) the laws against usury were increased in severity, and Christian burial was refused to those dying in that sin. This tended to throw the business of money-lending more and more into the hands of the Jews. The reason for this was that in many countries Jews were not allowed to be involved in craftsmanship and other businesses, and in some countries they could not even own property. Therefore involvement with money was often their main enterprise. Many small businesses, however, needed more money than they had, and here it was the Jews who came to help. But in times of economic crises, they were often called usurer and even expelled from cities so that indebted persons could get rid of their debts. In the Middle Ages, then, a kind of anti-Judaism evolved and the Jews were stereotyped as rich, avaricious, and fraudulent. It is not surprising that Luther as a child of his time also lambasted them. Indeed, two editions of his *Sermon against Usury* of 1519 showed a Jew on the cover with the words "pay or give interest," while the third only depicted a teacher with four persons intently listening, two of them being Jews.[10] The same is true of three printings of his second sermon on this topic of 1520, while the other nine printings are without such caricature. Luther also admitted that he was unable also to take care of the illustrations of his publications. Since they were originally printed in Wittenberg, Luther could have avoided such caricatures if he really wanted to do so. Yet his later publications against usury do not show such caricatures, even if his attitude toward the Jews and their money-lending business reflects popular opinion among the people prevalent at that time.[11] But what did Luther actually write?

---

10. Cf. Luther, *(Kleiner) Sermon von dem Wucher* (1519), in *WA* 6:2.
11. See his publications *Trade and Usury* (1524), in *WA* 15:283ff., and *An die Pfarrherrn wider den Wucher zu predigen, Vermahnung* (1540), in *WA* 52:327–28, and for the whole issue of Luther and the Jews on economic matters, cf. Prien, *Luthers Wirtschaftsethik,* 69–71.

Luther's Sermons on Usury (1519/20)

Around the turn of sixteenth century, there was an unusual number of bad harvests, such in 1490–94, 1500–1504 and 1515–19. This caused many peasants to take out loans that they could not pay back, and they therefore were forced to lose their property. Luther then wrote a *Small Sermon on Usury* in 1519, in which he stated with reference to the Old Testament that one should willingly and with a glad heart loan money to someone who is in need without any interest (Deut. 15:7–11). Nobody should have to beg or go hungry. Pointing to Luke 6:30–35, Luther writes, "From these words it becomes evident that a Christian should freely give and loan and moreover should be nice to his enemies and neither quarrel with them or harm them."[12] If we loan out to others wine, grain, money or whatever and level on them so much interest that they must pay back more than they have borrowed, then this is "a Jewish ploy and it is an un-Christian procedure since it goes against the holy Gospel of Christ, nay even against the natural law."[13] Luther backs up this idea with reference to Luke 6:31 ("Do to others as you would have them do to you"). Nobody likes to pay interest. So why demand it from others? Luther realizes that this is not welcome advice, and therefore simply says, "If you do not do it, then you are also not a Christian and you will have received your heaven here on earth." He sums up his advice: "Christian business and benevolence with temporal goods consists of three points: give without charge, loan without interest, and let it go with love."[14]

This is different with the so-called *Zinsskauf*. Luther agreed that in this case one could charge 4, 5, or 6 percent depending how good the yield of a field was against which the interest is charged. Yet to

---

12. Luther, *(Kleiner) Sermon von dem Wucher,* in *WA* 6:4.36–5.2.
13. Ibid., 5.6–8 and 19–20 for this and the following quote.
14. Ibid., 6.12–14.

charge 7 to 10 percent is usury and robbery.[15] One should always serve the neighbor without doing the neighbor any harm. He still thought that this was somewhat questionable, since the interest was safe but one never knew how the harvest would do. So the one who advances the money can lean back, while the other party bears all the risk. Already two months later, in December 1519, Luther considerably expands his sermon in the *Large Sermon on Usury*. Evidently his publication had been met with some resistance and therefore he wanted to explain in detail his position "so that Christ's pure doctrine should not cause even more offense."[16]

For Luther, it is very important that in dealing with one another this is done without force or violence. He refers here to Matt. 5:40: "If anyone wants to sue you and take your coat, give your cloak as well."[17] While some things are not punished by the court, such as self-defense or quarreling, such is not deemed well by God. "Now for everyone to demand what is his and be unwilling to endure wrong is not the way to peace."[18] If one pushes through one's right with every means, the gain is often less than the investment in the cause. We should always attempt to settle financial matters in a peaceful manner.

Then Luther picks up his second point: "That we are to give freely and without return to anyone who needs our goods or asks for them."[19] Again he refers to a biblical precept: "Give to everyone who begs from you, and do not refuse anyone who wants to borrow from you" (Matt. 5:42). Luther distinguishes between lending and giving, saying that lending means that I will get it back sooner or later but without something in addition, meaning interest, while giving

15. Cf. ibid., 6.24–40.
16. According to the introduction of the *Large Sermon on Usury* (1520), in *WA* 6:33, introduction. This quote is not in the English translation.
17. Luther, *The Long Sermon on Usury* (1524), in *LW* 45:273.
18. Ibid., 279.
19. Ibid., 280.

means that I will not expect a return of the given item. Moreover, in Christianity nobody should need to beg or go hungry. The open hand should not only be extended to one's friends but even to one's enemies and opponents. Then Luther cautions that one should not just give to the church, especially for building St. Peter's basilica in Rome, because one thinks that this is an especially good deed. Luther does not want to "disallow the building of suitable churches and their adornment; we cannot do without them. Any public worship ought rightly to be conducted in the finest way. But there should be a limit to this, and we should take care that the appurtenances of worship be pure, rather than costly."[20] The main stream of benevolence should flow toward the poor and needy, that these deeds "would shine more brightly than all churches of wood and stone." Each town and village should build and furnish its own churches, and also make provision itself to care for its poor so that beggars no longer move from place to place.

Having summed up his main points—we should give without wanting the given item returned to us, we should lend items without asking more in return than we have lent, and we should let things go in peace if they are taken from us by force—he now turns to the novel item *Zinsskauf*. Luther cautions, "Although the *zinss* contract is now established as a proper and admissible operation, it is nevertheless an odious and hateful practice for many reasons."[21] The one who advances money is always better off than the one who receives it.[22]

In order to have the risk not just on the side of the one who receives the needed money, Luther states that the debtor should not

20. For this and the following quote see ibid., 285–86.
21. Ibid., 295–96.
22. Cf. for the following the excellent contribution by Andreas Pawlas, "Luther zu Geld und Zins. Mit einem Vorwort über Lutherische Erwägungen zu Geld und Zins," University of Uppsala, Working Paper 2013, p. 28. http://uu.diva-portal.org/smash/get/diva2:676716/FULLTEXT01.pdf.

be liable with his whole property, but just with part of it, so that the debtor does not drift into poverty by losing his whole property if he cannot pay the *zinss*. The risk should not rest with the debtor but with the one who loans the money since he does not really do anything with his money, while the debtor does. Only the debtor should be allowed to call in the advanced money, but not the one who advanced it, since this could again lead to poverty. Yet if the debtor has done wrong with the money he may be liable to the one who advanced the money for the lost profit from the deal.

Small wonder that Luther called these "loan sharks" "usurer, thieves, and robbers, for they are selling the money's luck, which is not theirs or within their power."[23] Too easily and too quickly a debtor could end in poverty without it being his or her own fault. Luther stipulates that the debtor need not pay the interest until the debtor can undertake his labor free, healthy, and without problems. This means if the debtor works on his property but without his own fault it does not yield what was expected, he does not owe anything to the person who advanced the loan. "I you want to have an interest in my profits you must also have an interest in my losses," the debtor should say to the buyer, according to Luther.[24] If there is no shared risk, there is usury, according to Luther. For him the best solution would be to follow the biblical command of tithing, which in the case of need could be lowered to the ninth, or eighth, or sixth portion.

> Then everything would be perfectly consistent, and all would depend on the grace and blessing of God. If the tithe turned out well in any year, it would bring the recipient of *zinss* a good sum; if it turned out badly, it would bring in but little. The creditor would thus have to bear both risk and good fortune as well as the debtor, and both of them would have to look for God. . . . The tithe is, therefore, the best *zinss* of all. It has been in use since the beginning of the world, and in the Old Law is praised

---

23. Luther, *The Long Sermon on Usury*, in *LW* 45:301–2.
24. Ibid., 303.

and confirmed as the fairest of all arrangements according to divine and natural law.[25]

Luther is no biblicist, but appeals both to the biblical precedent as well as to reason. He is also open to more or less than one-tenth of the yield depending on the circumstances. But he does not want a fixed amount of money to be the same every year, since that amount could quickly drive the debtor into poverty. The nobility should supervise such suggestions and an imperial diet should decide on appropriate laws so that usury would be curbed.

Trade and Usury (1524)

Just a few years later Luther was again challenged to write on this issue, when Dr. Jacob Strauss (ca. 1480–ca. 1532) arrived in Wittenberg in 1522, and then was called as a pastor at St. George in Eisenach the following year. There Strauss published a collection of articles in which he claimed that not only charging interest, but also paying it, was a sin, since with the latter one was an accomplice in usury. The debtor must be more obedient to God than to the one who loaned money, because the Bible says one should loan but not taking anything in return. As expected, some no longer paid interest, which hurt especially church institutions that depended on this kind of income. Luther then was asked to write an opinion on behalf of John Frederick the Magnanimous (1503–54), the son of the Duke John the Steadfast of Saxony (1468–1532), who was instrumental in church politics. On October 18, 1523, he wrote a memorandum to the Saxon chancellor Gregory von Brück (1484–1557). There Luther points out that the most dangerous point in the pamphlet of Dr. Strauss is his teaching

that the debtor ought not pay the interest to the usurious creditor for

25. Ibid., 309.

then he would be agreeing with the usurious creditor and would sin with him. This is not right. Because the debtor has acted correctly and is free of sin, if he tells the creditor that [the business transaction] is usury and points out its iniquity. Yet the debtor should not take revenge, but should consent to pay the unjust creditor.[26]

While Luther agrees with Strauss that lending money at interest is un-Christian, he is realistic that it can never be curbed completely and turned into a decent system, "since all the world is greedy."

Luther then elaborated the issues involved in money-lending and commerce more extensively in his writing of 1524, *Trade and Usury*, but had no illusion that his opinion would be heeded by all. But he realized that people who knew the gospel could judge by their conscience what was appropriate and what was not. Therefore he turned to those who would rather be poor with God than rich with the devil. While it is clear that buying and selling is necessary, he wonders whether all the luxury items are needed or whether they just drain money and funnel it to other countries. Luther does not approve of the idea of selling goods as expensively as possible without regard for the buyer, since thereby one sins against the neighbor. One robs and steals the neighbor's means. One should rather say, "I may sell my wares as dear as I ought, or as it is right and fair."[27] The merchant has a responsibility to God and the neighbor. There is no fixed profit, because the price depends on one's own cost, the investment, and the danger incurred in procuring the goods. This must especially be considered when the wares were from far away. The roads were not safe because they were lacking maintenance, as well as from robbers who endangered commerce. Yet "laborers deserve their food" (Matt. 10:10) is Luther's advice, and if one takes

---

26. Luther, "To Gregory Brück" (October 18, 1523), in *LW* 49:52–54 (letter no. 136) for this and the following quote. The issue was here whether social laws of the Old Testament such as Deut. 15:1–11 had to be the laws of the Christian community.
27. Luther, *Trade and Usury*, in *LW* 45:248.

too much profit, one must pray, "Forgive us our debts," since no person's life is without sin.

In a second part Luther deals with the issue of becoming surety for another. He very bluntly calls this "a foolish thing to do."[28] One should trust God alone and not humans. But by extending insurance one trusts a person and endangers one's life and property. Since this is not an option, what else should one do? Among Christians, Luther says, we should give away our property, and take it back again if it is returned to us. But if it is not returned we must do without it. We should lend freely and take our chances on getting it back or not. Christians are brothers and sisters "and one does not forsake another; neither is any of them so lazy and shameless that he would not work but depend simply on another's wealth and labor."[29] Where there are no Christians, Luther charges the secular authorities with seeking to return what has been borrowed. If they "will not help him to recover his loan, let him lose it."[30] But where the people are not Christians the authorities ought to compel them to repay what they have borrowed. Luther also stipulates that one is not obligated to make a loan except out of one's surplus and what one can spare from one's own needs. Our first and greatest obligation is to our own dependents.

He deals extensively with the emerging threat of one or a few merchants gaining a monopoly on certain items, especially if they are imported from far away. They sell them as dear as they like, or only see the neighbors' need but do not relieve it, but make the most of it and get rich at their expense. "All such fellows are manifest thieves, robbers, and usurers."[31] He calls here again on secular authorities to

28. Ibid., 253. To secure risks in commerce the idea evolved of an owner transferring the risks of his property to an insurer for a fee. Were the goods lost this could become a costly issue for the insurer.
29. Ibid., 258.
30. Ibid., 260.
31. Ibid., 262.

thwart such misuse of power. "The temporal authorities would do right if they took from such fellows everything they had, and drove them out of the country."[32] People such as these are not worthy to be called human beings and are not to be allowed to live among us. Luther then shows other examples, such as how the price of goods can be raised to exorbitant heights. It is the duty of the princes "to use their duly constituted authority in punishing the injustices of the merchants and preventing them from so shamefully skinning their subjects."[33] Yet he surmises that they are in cohorts with the merchants. He is convinced, however, that injustice will not be left unpunished by God. God "uses one rascal to flog the other."

To the Pastors to Preach Against Usury (1540)

Since usury had become rampant, Luther felt that he should take up his pen again. Abiding by that which the church had decided, Luther is very strict, saying that "if you advance money and ask or take more for it than you initially gave, it is usury and rightly condemned.[34] A charge of 5 or 6 percent interest is already usury. He is not talking about giving or selling, but loaning. According to him, we should expect that we receive back only that which we have loaned and not more. If one would object that then nobody would loan anything, Luther retorts that loaning without charge is "a good work," because nobody else does it.[35] It serves those who are in need.

Luther realizes that this is a worldly or secular issue for the resolution of which the preacher can contribute little. It is rather a case for the lawyers, who must prohibit usury, and when it occurs it should be punished. Among many other historical examples, Luther

32. Ibid., 265.
33. For this and the following quote see ibid., 270.
34. Luther, *An die Pfarrherrn wider den Wucher zu predigen, Vermahnung* (1540), in *WA* 51:332.32–33.
35. Ibid., 337.32.

refers to Aristotle who wrote that the most hated sort of getting rich is usury.

> [It] makes a gain out of money itself, and not from the natural object of it. For money was intended to be used in exchange, but not to increase at interest. And this term interest, which means the birth of money from money, is applied to the breeding of money because the offspring resembles the parent. Wherefore of any modes of getting wealth this is the most unnatural.[36]

For Luther, Aristotle was still an authority in secular matters. He followed him and argued against usury on account of natural reason. He cites with disdain that in cities such as Leipzig, one charges more than 40 percent interest so that a citizen or a peasant will be devoured within a year.[37] Lawyers and princes must join together that this thievery ceases. Then he ends this chapter by asserting once more that good works are "giving, loaning, and suffering."[38] Christians can have no part in usury.

In the next chapter Luther talks about giving, and referring to Matt. 5:42, "Give to everyone," he explains that this means we should give to everybody who is in need, both friends and foes. This does not include those, however, who do not want to work or who are not from your city. It also does not mean giving if you do not have what you yourself need, nor does it mean to give away everything, because then you could not give anything tomorrow if need arises. Freely giving should not imply that one then becomes a beggar. It also is not done so that one reaps benefits from it, or is celebrated for this deed. Luther would abhor the contemporary idea, "Do something good and speak about it." No, he says, do it with a simple mind so that

---

36. Aristotle, *Politeia* 1:10 http://classics.mit.edu/Aristotle/politics.1.one.html.
37. Cf. Luther, *An die Pfarrherrn,* in *WA* 51:365.18–19.
38. Ibid., 380.23.

you forget it "as if you had never given anything or done something charitable."[39]

Luther then talks about loaning. Again, this covers both friends and foes, and is extended to those in need. The maxim that guides us here is the Golden Rule: do as you expect to have done to you. One should not rejoice in the misery of a person, but be merciful with an open hand. "There is no greater enemy of humans—except for the devil—than a greedy person and a usurer, because such a person wants to be god over all people."[40] When Luther lashes out so much against people of that kind, it shows the rampant problems he encountered: in order to get rich as quickly as possible, one had no concern for the well-being of other people. Here Christian love was wanting. As Luther writes, worldly authority was either too weak or too unconcerned to take redeeming action. In part, this authority was an accomplice, living in splendor at the expense of its subjects. Then Luther comes to his third and final point, which he had already insisted on in his earlier writings: Christians should be willing to suffer.

Christians should not take justice into their own hands. They will find many who make people suffer among the secular authorities in the city halls, the citizens, and the nobility, since they neither give, nor loan or help. Even the pastors have their plight with these people, since they are only guests in the parsonage and once they die their widows often become beggars. Luther had learned through visitations that often the parsonages looked like dumps. Yet he does not close on a downcast note. Even if there is suffering one should not despair. "Just be a pious Christian, preacher, pastor, citizen, peasant, nobleperson, lord, and conduct your office diligently and trustworthy. . . . Just be a true Christian who suffers with a simple

39. Ibid., 387.19–20.
40. Ibid., 396.28–30.

heart for God's sake and does not give cause for suffering."[41] But Luther also ends on a note with tongue in cheek: the greedy people and the usurers should not think that he is totally against them, since there is a rich Lord who would play along with them and he would return them a hundred- and a thousandfold, namely God, the Creator of heaven and earth. "He had offered us through his dear son in the Gospel: 'Give and loan, then it shall be returned to you' not just the same but much more, namely a good measure, a measure shaken together, a measure pressed down, a measure running over."[42] Here would be the right place to exercise usury. The problem, Luther concedes, is that people will not heed this advice.

Luther's Challenge to Economic Unfairness

When one reads his four publications on usury, one realizes that over the years Luther's line of argumentation has hardly changed. At the most one could say that his tone became harsher, and that there was reason for this, since in spring of 1539 food became exorbitantly expensive in the Wittenberg area on account of little rain during the preceding summer and an artificial shortage to obtain even higher prices.[43] Many people were starving and small merchants heaped more and more debts on their possessions or were even driven out of existence. Luther interceded with the mayor of Wittenberg, Lucas Cranach the Elder, and also with the elector John Frederick. He tried to address the evil with theological arguments. In agreement with the Sermon on the Mount, Christians should not renege on paying the due interest and trust God that God will give them their daily bread. They also should give everyone without asking for a financial

41. Ibid., 412.23–25 and 30–32.
42. Ibid., 419.24–27.
43. For the following, cf. Theodor Strohm, "Luthers Wirtschafts- und Sozialethik," in *Leben und Werk Martin Luthers von 1526 bis 1546*, ed. Helmar Junghans (Göttingen: Vandenhoeck & Ruprecht, 1983), 215–17.

return. In rejecting the notion of asking for interest payments, he was in agreement with the Fifth Lateran Council of 1515, which had renewed the prohibition on charging interest, though in reality there were many exceptions. He thought it better to ask for a tithe or a certain modest percentage of the actual yield that was gained with the loan. For old people and widows and orphans he demanded loans without interest. John Calvin argued along similar lines, but otherwise approved of charging interest, as was the custom in the cities.

In his appeal to the magistrates and the nobility, Luther asked that interest rates be charged in accordance with human order, laws, and customs in an appropriate way. This meant that the interest rate should not been higher than 5 percent and should be reduced if the yield was low. Wealthy persons could be persuaded to forfeit some of the interest, while older and less wealthy persons should by all means receive their due interest. There also should be stricter laws for debts and buying on credit.

Though Luther was aware that *Zinsskauf* was a legal form of trade, it was dangerous and contradicted natural law, as well as the command of Christian love. It could easily endanger people, so that they lost their property and ended in poverty. The only justification he saw was if both the person who loaned the money and the person who received it were involved in the gain as well as in the risk. Luther was well aware that without buying and selling, and without loaning money and receiving such loans, commerce could not exist. But the command to love God and the neighbor could not be compromised. Whether this needed to imply that one cannot charge any interest on loans, as Luther preferred, must be questioned. There he based his rationale not just on the Bible, especially the Old Testament, but on Aristotle. Yet his overarching view on economic matters is still worthy of serious consideration. It is succinctly summarized in his explanation of the Seventh Commandment: "We are to fear and love God, so that we neither take our neighbors' money or property nor acquire them by using shoddy merchandise or crooked deals, but instead help them to improve and protect their property and income."[44] Caring and looking out for the neighbor's well-being without endangering our own must prevail in economic matters.

44. Luther, *The Small Catechism*, in *The Book of Concord: The Confessions of the Evangelical Lutheran Church*, ed. Robert Kolb and Timothy J. Wengert (Minneapolis: Fortress Press, 2000), 353.

14

Luther and Music

As a reformer Luther was not just a theologian, but also a person who wanted to see that his reforms worked in practical life. He had considerable didactic gifts, as we can see, for instance, in *The Small Catechism*, which is still used today. Yet his talents were wide-ranging: he was good in carpentry and also in music. In the latter field he had far-reaching influence on the churches of the Reformation, both Lutheran and Reformed. In the *Evangelischen Gesangbuch* (Protestant hymnal) of the Evangelical Church of Germany, one can find fourteen hymns in which the text, in full or in part, is credited to Martin Luther; another twelve hymns for which he composed the text (full or in part), as well as the tune; and finally, four hymns for which he composed the tune. This means in some way or other thirty hymns go back to Luther. The *Evangelical Lutheran Worship* book of the Evangelical Lutheran Church of America includes nineteen songs for which Luther either wrote the text, the melody, or both.

Altogether 36 songs have been ascribed with certainty to the Reformer.

They can be organized into poetic works based upon Latin hymns and on other traditional liturgical pieces, upon psalms or other passages in the Old and the New Testament, upon pre-Reformation German sacred and secular lieder, and upon a few examples still unknown.[1]

When one considers that Luther's hymns were only a side-effect of his work as a reformer, then one can estimate his influence on church music. It is no surprise, then, that in 1620 the Jesuit Conzenius wrote, "Luther's hymns have destroyed more souls than his writings and lectures."[2] That is to say that Luther's store of songs had a larger impact on people than his published works and sermons. It is no coincidence that Luther knew the principles of music, for music was an elemental facet of his education. But to this Luther brought talent and interest. It is to his musical training that we now turn.

Luther's Musical Education

We do not know whether music was sung and played in Luther's childhood home. But in 1497, when Luther was still thirteen years old, his father sent him to Magdeburg, since a friend of his, Hans Reinecke, was also sent there for schooling. Young Luther most likely attended the cathedral school there and lived with the Brethren of the Common Life. These Brethren were not really a monastic order, but an antimonastic reform movement with the ideal of a simple apostolic discipleship. Under Archbishop Ernst von Sachsen (1476–1513), chorale music and florid counterpoint flourished at the cathedral. One can assume that Martin Luther also regularly sung in the choir during this time.[3] Most probably he received voice training

---

1. So Friedrich Blume, *Protestant Church Music: A History*, foreword by Paul Henry Lang (New York: W. W. Norton, 1974), 41.
2. "Hymni Lutheri animas plures quam scripta et declamationes occiderunt." As found in Karl Anton, *Luther und die Musik*, 3rd ed. (Zwickau: Johannes Hermann, 1928 [1916]), 11.
3. Walter Blankenburg, "Luther, Martin," in *Die Musik in Geschichte und Gegenwart* (1960), 8:1334–36.

and, along with other young students, earned money by singing in front of homes.[4] One year later his father sent him to Eisenach, where both parents had relatives and he had several cousins. He began his studies there at the parish school of St. George, which lay on the south side of that church. There too, Luther sang with fellow schoolboys in order to earn his livelihood. The patrician Heinrich Schalbe and his family took in Luther, who also enjoyed the friendship of the priest Johannes Braun. Braun was a lighthearted man who often led spiritual and secular music in Schalbe's home, even the singing of motets. From 1501, Luther studied at the faculty of liberal arts in Erfurt. This was the largest German university at this time, with approximately 260 new students per year. As a part of his studies, Luther was required to master music theory.[5] This complemented a required lecture class on Aristotle's teachings on music. During his studies of the liberal arts, Luther also learned to play the lute and the art of musical composition.[6]

After Luther's surprising entry into the Augustinian convent in Erfurt, his theological studies, which he began immediately, brought him again into contact with, among others, Augustine, Thomas Aquinas (ca. 1224–74), and Gabriel Biel (prior to 1410–1495), and their thoughts on music. Alongside this book knowledge, Luther especially cultivated a close friendship with the cantor Johann Walter (1496–1570). When Elector Frederick the Wise died in 1525, his successor John the Steadfast wanted to abolish Walter's position, along with those of two additional cantors in Wittenberg. However, Luther vehemently protested.[7]

4. Martin Brecht, *Martin Luther: His Road to the Reformation, 1483–1521*, trans. James L. Schaaf (Philadelphia: Fortress Press, 1985), 17.

5. Ibid., 33.

6. Luther, *WA TR* 5:657.11–12 (no. 6428).

7. Luther, "Luther an Joh. Walter," *WA BR* 4:121.3–8 (no. 1041), in a letter dated September 21, 1526.

At home, Luther led songs with his baritone voice, and played the lute in his family circle. At festive occasions they liked to sing in several-part harmony. The director of the orchestra for the elector of Saxony, Konrad Rupff, and Walter stayed with Luther for three weeks in the fall of 1525 in order to assist him with the creation of the German Mass.[8] Luther was also friends with the church musician at St. Thomas in Leipzig, who later became alderman in Wittenberg, George Rhau (1488–1548). According to the historian of church music Friedrich Blume, Rhau was "the first and greatest music publisher of the Reformation."[9] Luther also praised the compositions of Josquin des Prés (c. 1450–1521), because he believed that they preached the gospel.[10] Luther enjoyed the acquaintance as well of the Munich composer and court musician Ludwig Senfl (c. 1486–1543). In 1531 Luther sent Senfl a few books as a sign of his gratitude for the few motets Senfl had given Luther.[11] Already the year before, when he left the castle at Coburg for the Diet at Augsburg, he offered to send Senfl a multivoiced composition. Although he knew that the Bavarian dukes did not view him favorably, he praised them, because they "so promoted and honored music."[12]

In this letter, he also emphasized that music drives out evil spirits and that "after theology, there is no other art to which music can be compared." Along with theology, music grants one a calm and cheerful mind. Luther consistently emphasized that music banishes sorrow and gloom. For Luther, theology and music are closely associated, which even the prophets recognized, because they

8. See the "Introduction to the German Mass and Order of Service," *LW* 53:55.

9. Blume, *Protestant Church Music*, 6

10. Martin Brecht, *Marin Luther: Shaping and Defining the Reformation, 1521–1532*, trans. James L. Schaaf (Philadelphia: Fortress Press, 1990), 376.

11. Luther, "An Hieronymus Baumgartner in Nürnberg," *WA BR* 6:1.4–7, in a letter dated January 1, 1531.

12. Luther, "An Ludwig Senfl in München," *WA BR* 5:639.8, 12–13, 21, in a letter dated October 1530, for this and the following quotes.

"preached the truth in psalms and songs." Music is therefore an instrument of preaching, as we can particularly note in Luther's songs. Music was also important to him for the upbringing of his children. For example, as he sent his son Hans to school in Torgau, he wrote to Walter, who was then church music director (*Kantor*) there. In this letter, he expressly indicated that his son "should be drilled in grammar and music."[13] This abiding interest in music demonstrates that Luther put music in the service of his reforming efforts.

Luther and Church Music

In 1523, Luther wrote to George Spalatin, the secretary of Frederick the Wise, "[Our] plan is to follow the example of the prophets and the ancient fathers of the church, and to compose psalms for the people [in the] vernacular, that is, spiritual songs, so that the Word of God may be among the people also in the form of music."[14] Therefore Luther studied the examples of the prophets (namely their psalms) and of the early church (Ambrose). The Mass had become merely a spectacle to observe, the priests holding antiphons alone with the choir. Because Luther understood every Christian to be a priest, the active role in worship was not to be left only to the ordained priest and the choir. Rather, Luther turned to the rhymed hymns of Ambrosian chant, which Luther preferred to the chants of Gregory the Great. Believing that everyone ought to sing in church, he translated the Latin hymns so that the congregation could sing them in German as chorales.

Already in 1524 a first collection of his hymns was published that contained eight hymns. The hymns had been printed individually on separate sheets. The second edition of 1525 contained eight more hymns, and a hymnal of the same year had forty hymns, including

13. Luther , "Letter to Marcus Crodel" (Aug. 26, 1542) no. 296, in *LW* 50:231.
14. Luther, "To George Spalatin," in a letter dated the end of 1523, in *LW* 49:68.

some by the Nuremberg councilman Lazarus Spengler (1479–1534) and the reformer of Eastern Prussia, Paul Speratus (1484–1551).

Particularly instructive is Luther's Wittenberg hymnbook from 1529.[15] After a preface from Luther, the book is organized in five parts. In the first portion we find twenty-eight songs written by Luther, twenty-four of which were written between 1523 and 1524. Via sheet music they were immediately spread through Erfurt and Strassburg in hymnals and liturgical books. The second section contained songs written by composers with whom Luther worked closely. In the third part one finds medieval songs that were translated in part into German. Here we find two Christmas carols, a vesper hymn, and an Easter hymn, which include "Good Christian Friends, Rejoice" (*ELW* 288) and "Christ Is Arisen" (*ELW* 372). In the fourth section other religious songs written by contemporaries are included. The fifth and final portion contains fifteen canticles, described as "Songs out of the Holy Scriptures, as the beloved patriarchs and prophets in former times created and sung them."[16] Included here is also the Magnificat, Mary's song of praise. Outside of medieval illuminated manuscripts, this Wittenberg communal songbook of 1529 is the first instance of a hymnal in which music, text, and illustrations belong together.

It is noteworthy that this hymnal appeared in 1529, for in the same year his *Betbüchlein* (prayer booklet) and the *Large* and *Small Catechisms* were published. As mentioned in chapter 12, just as the prayer booklet was not only a collection of prayers but rather an introduction into the Christian faith, so too was the hymnal not merely a book in which one could appropriate suitable hymns for

---

15. For the following, refer to Markus Jenny, "Luthers Gesangbuch," in *Leben und Werk Martin Luthers von 1526 bis 1546, Festgabe zu seinem 500. Geburtstag*, ed. Helmar Junghans (Göttingen: Vandenhoeck & Ruprecht, 1983), 1:303–21.

16. Quoted from ibid., 305.

the liturgy. Instead, it was a comprehensive book for all singing Christians. Neither catechisms was a simple recitation book for instruction, but they rather introduced one to the practice of Christian life. All of these publications are illustrated, just as is the Luther Bible. Word and picture belong together for Luther, as does music. All three train one in Christian faith, or more specifically, in the faith taught by the Reformation. Therefore, the practical theologian and expert on Luther's music, Markus Jenny, correctly perceived that Luther's

> work on the hymnal is a self-evident and integral part of [Luther's goal to develop] the congregation, the necessity of which, in the face of the catastrophic congregational visits [of 1528], became clear to Luther. It is therefore understandable that Luther did not want to delegate the work on the songbooks to any old 'specialist,' but rather wanted it to remain in his own hands.[17]

Although Luther could sing a German religious tune from his youth just as well as the Latin liturgy, he became a true composer when the Reformation was already well underway. Luther responded to needs, becoming a composer because there was not enough church music. So in 1523 he wrote,

> I also wish that we had as many songs as possible in the vernacular which the people could sing during mass, immediately after the gradual and also after the Sanctus and Agnus Dei. . . . But poets are wanting among us, or not yet known, who could compose evangelical and spiritual songs, as Paul calls them [Col. 3:16], worthy to be used in the church of God.[18]

While Luther did write church music before his intended worship reform, his musical compositions always served either "directly or indirectly to proclaim the gospel."[19] He was convinced that there

17. Ibid., 321.
18. Luther, *An Order of Mass and Communion for the Church at Wittenberg* (1523), in *LW* 53:36.

needed to be German songs so that the community could participate in and understand worship. Ever since the twelfth century, there are examples of German verses that end with the Kyrie, that is, "Lord, have mercy." They were sung during pilgrimages, processions, and other occasions, but not during Mass, the usual Sunday worship service. Some of these single-verse tunes were made into lengthier pieces before Luther's time, like the Easter song, "Christ Is Risen." In the fourteenth century, Latin hymns were translated into German, and during Luther's time, Thomas Müntzer even translated some. Important for Luther was that the joy of the gospel is conveyed by both the text and the melody. Along with this, he did not forget the didactic moment, creating a number of catechetical songs, such as "These Are the Holy Ten Commandments," a musical version of the Creed, a song about baptism, and one about the Lord's Prayer. Children's music was also important to him, as we see in the Christmas carol "From Heaven Above" (*ELW* 268).

The psalm song was a form conceived by Luther himself. Before Luther, there were not even any suggestions of psalm songs, let alone an example of one. But thanks to him, this form had "immediately a powerfully broad effect."[20] The hymn, "A Mighty Fortress Is Our God" (*ELW* 503), a musical adaptation of Psalm 46, falls under this category of music. Luther attempted to enthuse his friends about setting psalms to music, so that the Psalms could be sung in worship. Strassburg was the first place where Luther's efforts paid off, for by 1524 such psalm adaptations were already being used there regularly. Luther's idea caught on with Zwingli and the Nuremberg

---

19. Markus Jenny, "Luther als Liedschöpfer," in *Martin Luther und die Reformation in Deutschland. Ausstellung zum 500. Geburtstag Martin Luthers. Veranstaltet vom Germanischen Nationalmuseum Nürnberg in Zusammenarbeit mit dem Verein für Reformationsgeschichte*, ed. Gerhard Bott (Frankfurt am Main: Insel, 1983), 294.

20. Markus Jenny, *Luther—Zwingli—Calvin in ihren Liedern* (Zürich: Theologischer Verlag Zürich, 1983), 18.

shoemaker-poet Hans Sachs (1494–1576), who published thirteen psalms in 1526. It was in Strassburg that Calvin learned of this musical form, which later inspired him to create the widely used Geneva Psalter.

According to Jenny, "The history of Roman Catholic church music and hymnals would be impossible to understand without knowledge of Luther's initiative."[21] The first large Roman Catholic songbook of the sixteenth century, published by the apostolic administrator for Lusatia in 1567, was clearly influenced by the Leipzig hymnal of 1545. The latter was printed by Valentin Bapst, and Luther wrote the introduction for it. It is no overstatement to say that Luther is the father of Protestant church music and the creator of the Lutheran hymnal. These gave impulse not only to the Protestant worship forms and piety throughout Germany, but also to those of other confessions.

However, for Luther the songbook was not only a liturgical book, but it was intended to assist the piety and faith of Christians at home and in school, as well as in church. For this reason, it was assumed that music was a key subject in school. Luther emphasized, "We must continue to teach music in school. A schoolmaster must be able to sing, for otherwise I cannot respect him. One should also train young people in music before they are ordained as priests."[22] According to Luther, school and church belong together, for it was a basic goal of his reformation to educate both spirit and mind. Along with cloister and cathedral schools, the time of the Reformation saw also city and public schools established, as well as German writing and reading schools. In Latin grammar schools, musical instruction was a formal subject that prepared students for liturgical studies to serve

---

21. Markus Jenny, "XI. Kirchenlied, Gesangbuch und Kirchenmusik," in Bott, *Martin Luther und die Reformation in Deutschland*, 293.
22. Luther, *WA TR*, 5:557.19–21 (no. 6248).

in church. The school choir was supplemented with a few adults, thereby serving also as a church choir. That is to say that school music and church music were for all practical purposes the same.

Luther asked his friend Johann Walter to furnish songs with florid counterpoint. In 1524, the result of this work appeared in Wittenberg in the form of the first choir songbook in the history of Protestant church music. Luther's hymn, "A Mighty Fortress" appears within its pages. Walter was then the bassist for the elector's court orchestra in Torgau. When Frederick the Wise died in 1525, his successor Johann the Steadfast dissolved the orchestra. Walter was for a few years without income, until he taught at the Torgau city school. There he created the first Protestant church choir, and was thereby the first Lutheran cantor or church musician of any city.[23] In his foreword to the choir book, Luther wrote,

> And these songs were arranged in four parts to give the young—who should at any rate be trained in music and other fine arts—something to wean them away from love ballads and carnal songs and to teach them something of value in their place, thus combining the good with the pleasing, as is proper for youth. Nor am I of the opinion that the gospel should destroy and blight all the arts, as some of the pseudo-religious claim. But I would like to see all the arts, especially music, used in the service of Him who gave and made them.[24]

The choir book thereby served a didactic purpose, namely to lead young people away from questionable to decent music.

In this same foreword, Luther also emphasized that the gospel does not stand opposed to art, but rather that art, and here particularly music, is to serve God, who gave and created it. Music, and therefore Luther's compositions, should serve the honor and glory of God. However, Luther was no purist, but as has already been alluded to,

23. Markus Jenny, "Johann Walter übertrug Luthers Musikanschauung in die Praxis," in Bott, *Martin Luther und die Reformation in Deutschland*, 321.
24. Luther, "Preface to the Wittenberg Hymnal" (1524), in *LW* 53:316.

often played the lute and sang along with those gathered around his table. For Luther, music is a gift from God, a noble, wholesome, and cheerful creation of God. It makes people happy and forget their anger and worries. Therefore he announced, "Next to the Word of God, music deserves the highest praise."[25] With that, however, we have come to the relationship between theology and music, a relationship thus far only indirectly mentioned.

Theology and Music

Although Luther himself composed music, it was not his intent merely to give well-known pieces another melody, but rather to revise the text according to the gospel. According to Luther, "We are concerned with changing the text, not the music."[26] Luther did not want to be an innovator, but merely wanted to reform belief according to the gospel. Therefore he writes, "We want the beautiful art of music to be properly used to serve her dear Creator and his Christians. He is thereby praised and honored and we are made better and stronger in faith when his holy Word is impressed on our hearts by sweet music."

Music served to spread the gospel and to edify true faith. Even in his *Psalmenauslegung* (Exposition of the Psalms) (1519–21), he said, "Originally music was holy and divine. But in time, she became subservient to undue splendor and covetousness."[27] Music must move people away from self-absorption toward the service of God and the gospel.

Luther saw a relationship between music and theology, for he believed that music had both a theological and pastoral function. Music creates a cheerful mind, drives out the devil, and refreshes the

---

25. Luther, "Preface to Georg Rhau's symphoniae iucundae" (1538), in *LW* 53:323.
26. Luther, "Preface to the Burial Hymns" (1542), in *LW* 53:328 for this and the following quote.
27. Luther, *Operationes in Psalmos*, *WA* 5:98.38–40.

spirit. Luther also emphasized that "the gift of language combined with the gift of song was only given to man to let him know that he should praise God with both word and music, namely, by proclaiming [the Word of God] through music and by providing sweet melodies with words."[28] Speech is given to humanity so that it can bring melody and song together, and thereby praise God. This is what most particularly distinguishes humanity from all other creatures.

The close relationship between word and song was also important for Luther's understanding of worship. At the dedication of the castle church in Torgau in 1544, he stressed that "the purpose of this new house may be such that nothing else may ever happen in it except that our dear Lord himself may speak to us through his holy Word and we respond to him through prayer and praise."[29] "Speech alone is not the best method, for "the notes bring the text to life."[30] God also preached the gospel through music, Luther believed, and here he turned to Josquin des Prés, whose music Luther treasured and was often sung at Luther's table.[31] Although Luther did not do away with Latin music, it was important for him that people could also sing along in worship in their mother tongue. However, what was decisive for him was the word that was preached through music. So, for example, in 1542, he published funeral hymns in both Latin and German, although he reworked the Latin text.[32] Luther enjoyed medieval Gregorian chant, as is demonstrated in his comments about funeral hymns found in his preface from 1542, where he wrote,

---

28. Luther, "Preface to Georg Rhau's symphoniae iucundae," 323–24.
29. Luther, "Sermon to the Dedication of the Castle Church in Torgau" (Oct. 5, 1544), in *LW* 51:333.
30. Luther, *WA TR* 2:518. 6–7 (no. 2545).
31. Cf. Luther, Table Talks (1531), nos. 1258 and 8, in *LW* 54:130.
32. Markus Jenny, "Luther als Schöpfer des evangelischen Gesangbuches," in Bott, *Martin Luther und die Reformation in Deutschland*, 307.

This is also why we have collected the fine music and songs which under the papacy were used at vigils, masses for the dead, and burials. Some fine examples of these we have printed in this booklet and we, or whoever is more gifted than we, will select more of them in the future. But we have adapted other texts to the music so that it may adorn our article of the resurrection, instead of purgatory with its torment and satisfaction which lets their dead neither sleep nor rest. The melodies and notes are precious. It would be a pity to let them perish. But the texts and words are non–Christian and absurd. They deserve to perish.[33]

Luther praised the beauty of traditional music and songs, and wanted to adapt even more traditional tunes than were published in his little book. However, because the texts were from a medieval, and often unbiblical, perspective (as one sees in their references to purgatory, satisfaction for sins, and so on), it was not possible to integrate them with Christian burial and resurrection hope. Therefore the text had to be amended. Luther expressed it drastically when he said, "And indeed, they also possess a lot of splendid, beautiful songs and music, especially in the cathedral and parish churches. But these are used to adorn all sorts of impure and idolatrous texts."

Luther did not want to homogenize either the texts or the music so that they would be identical in all churches. He recognized that different churches have their accordingly unique melodies and customs. He acknowledged that "I myself do not like to hear the notes in a responsory or other song changed from what I was accustomed to in my youth."[34] Luther gave tradition a certain respect, and had no need to restrict its artistic freedom, as long as the bold assertion of the Reformation was not abandoned, namely that God accepts us for the sake of Christ out of undeserved grace.

Luther's hymns in the German mother tongue were "formerly tolerated, often deprecated, and very rarely promoted . . . [but]

33. Luther, "Preface to the Burial Hymns," in *LW* 53:327, for this and the following quote.
34. Ibid., 328.

became an essential and fundamental aspect of the Reformation's program."[35] They were often sung outside of worship, namely in the home and school, and were easily adaptable. Even Roman Catholic music became enriched. Decisive was the focus on the salvation historical facts, not on the sense of *imitatio*, of emulation of sympathy, or allegory, as one often finds in medieval songs. Instead, central to the musical theme was praise and thanksgiving for that which God has done for us, and encouragement in one's daily faith. Luther's efforts to create an evangelical music found repercussions in the cantatas, motets, oratorios, and passions of Johann Sebastian Bach (1685–1750) and in the oratorios of George Frederick Handel (1685–1759).

35. Martin Luther, *Die deutschen geistlichen Lieder*, ed. Gerhard Hahn (Tübingen: Max Niemeyer, 1967), xix.

Postscript

During the five hundred years that separate us from Luther's time, tremendous changes have occurred in our world. We have witnessed an enormous explosion in our knowledge, and the continuity with the past, which for Luther and his time was largely a matter of fact, has increasingly been called into question. We view as valid what we know now; what had meaning in the past seems unreliable. This break in tradition, which we can notice in all facets of life, contributes to an increasing sense of insecurity.

On the other hand, we have achieved the domestication of the world to a hitherto unknown extent. Martin Luther would only shake his head in disbelief if he were to see the technological gadgets that we use in our leisure time, at the work place, in modern medicine, and in our household chores. Because of the domination of our environment, however, the world has been robbed of its divine connection, and it has become increasingly difficult to attribute to God any meaningful activity. Yet we have less difficulty in acknowledging the work of destructive powers. Though many seemingly enlightened people no longer accept a personification of the evil one, the reality of demonic powers are readily apparent for all of us in many parts of the world. We are reminded of its reality in the holocaust in Nazi Germany, in the self-destruction of the

North African countries, in suicide bombers, and in the brutality of organized crime spawned by widespread poverty and greed. This means that the technological aspect of our world has changed our way of life in an unforeseen way. But the fact that many of us live in fear and feel threatened in our daily existence has remained unchanged.

Confronted with the mercilessness and ambiguity of our world, the question of how to obtain a gracious God is not as antiquated as we might initially think. We are simply unable to liberate ourselves from the reality of evil. But Luther was not interested in a gracious God who would, like a good fairy, take all our anxieties away from us. Luther knew far too well that such a God would be a product of our desires and fantasies and would not be the living God who in an unsurpassable way has shown God's self to us in Jesus Christ. Therefore, Luther emphasized that the God who holds the whole world in his hand must also become for us the one who is the beginning, the center, and the goal of our life if we want to overcome our insecurity and disorientation. To rediscover such a God some two thousand years after Jesus Christ had set his foot on this earth, and therefore to believe in the right way in the true God, is a rewarding challenge for us. If Luther can give us some direction in this way, then the study of his theological focus is as contemporary today as it was five hundred years ago.

Selected Bibliography

General Works on the Reformation

Bainton, Roland. *The Reformation of the Sixteenth Century*. Boston: Beacon, 1952, 1985.

Bell, Dean Phillip, and Stephen G. Burnett, eds. *Jews, Judaism, and the Reformation in Sixteenth-Century Germany*. Leiden: Brill, 2006.

Ozment, Steven. *The Age of Reform, 1250–1550: An Intellectual and Religious History of Late Medieval and Reformation Europe*. New Haven: Yale University, 1980.

———. *Protestants: The Birth of a Revolution*. New York: Doubleday, 1992.

Pelikan, Jaroslav. *The Christian Tradition: A History of the Development of Doctrine*. Vol. 4: *Reformation of Church and Dogma (1300–1700)*. Chicago: University of Chicago, 1984.

Reformation & Renaissance Review: Journal of the Society for Reformation Studies. Sheffield, UK: Sheffield Academic Press, 1999–.

Spitz, Lewis W. *The Protestant Reformation, 1517–1559*. The Rise of Modern Europe Series. New York: Harper and Row, 1985.

———. *Renaissance and Reformation*. 2 vols. St. Louis: Concordia, 1971, 1980.

Luther's Life and Theology

Althaus, Paul. *The Ethics of Martin Luther.* Translated by Robert Schultz. Philadelphia: Fortress Press, 1972.

———. *The Theology of Martin Luther.* Translated by Robert Schultz. Philadelphia: Fortress Press, 1966.

Altmann, Walter. *Luther and Liberation: A Latin American Perspective.* Translated by Mary M. Solberg. Minneapolis: Augsburg Fortress Press, 1992.

Anttila, Miikka. *Luther's Theology of Music: Spiritual Beauty and Pleasure.* Berlin: de Gruyter, 2013.

Bainton, Roland H. *Here I Stand: A Life of Martin Luther.* Nashville: Abingdon, 1950, 1978.

Barth, Hans-Martin. *The Theology of Martin Luther: A Critical Assessment.* Translated by Linda M. Maloney. Minneapolis: Fortress Press, 2013.

Bayer, Oswald. *Martin Luther's Theology: A Contemporary Interpretation.* Translated by Thomas H. Trapp. Grand Rapids: Eerdmans, 2008.

Brecht, Martin. *Martin Luther: His Road to Reformation, 1483–1521.* Translated by James L. Schaaf. Philadelphia: Fortress Press, 1985.

———. *Martin Luther: The Preservation of the Church, 1532–1546.* Translated by James L. Schaaf. Minneapolis: Augsburg Fortress Press, 1992.

———. *Martin Luther: Shaping and Defining the Reformation, 1521–1532.* Translated by James L. Schaaf. Minneapolis: Augsburg Fortress Press, 1990.

Edwards, Mark U. *Luther's Last Battles: Politics and Polemics, 1531–1546.* Ithaca, NY: Cornell University Press, 1983.

Elert, Werner. *The Structure of Lutheranism: The Theology and Philosophy of Life of Lutheranism, 16th and 17th Centuries.* Vol. 1. Translated by Walter Hansen. St. Louis: Concordia, 1962, 1974.

Evangelical Lutheran Church in America. *Evangelical Lutheran Worship.* Minneapolis: Augsburg Fortress Press, 2006.

Grane, Leif. *The Augsburg Confession: A Commentary*. Translated by John Rasmussen. Minneapolis: Augsburg, 1987.

Gritsch, Eric W. *Martin—God's Court Jester: Luther in Retrospect*. Philadelphia: Fortress Press, 1983.

———. *Martin Luther's Anti-Semitism: Against His Better Judgment*. Grand Rapids: Eerdmans, 2012.

Haile, H. G. *Luther: An Experiment in Biography*. Garden City, NY: Doubleday, 1980.

Hockenbery Dragseth, Jennifer, ed. *The Devil's Whore: Reason and Philosophy in the Lutheran Tradition*. Minneapolis: Fortress Press, 2011.

Kittelson, James M. *Luther the Reformer: The Story of the Man and His Career*. Minneapolis: Augsburg, 1987.

Kolb, Robert, and Charles P Arand. *The Genius of Luther's Theology: A Wittenberg Way of Thinking for the Contemporary Church*. Grand Rapids: Baker, 2008.

Lienhard, Marc. *Luther: Witness to Jesus Christ; Stages and Themes of the Reformer's Christology*. Translated by Edwin H. Robinson. Minneapolis: Augsburg, 1982.

Loeschen, John R. *Wrestling with Luther: An Introduction to the Study of His Thought*. St. Louis: Concordia, 1976.

Loewenich, Walther von. *Martin Luther: The Man and His Work*. Translated by Lawrence Denef. Minneapolis: Augsburg, 1986.

Lohse, Bernhard. *Martin Luther: An Introduction to His Life and Work*. Translated by Robert C. Schultz. Philadelphia: Fortress Press, 1986.

———. *Martin Luther's Theology: Its Historical and Systematic Development*. Translated by Roy A. Harrisville. Minneapolis: Fortress Press, 1999.

Luther Digest: An Annual Abridgement of Luther Studies. Ft. Wayne, IN: The Luther Academy, 1993–.

Madsen, Anna. *Theology of the Cross in Historical Perspective*. Eugene, OR: Pickwick, 2007.

McGrath, Alister E. *Luther's Theology of the Cross: Martin Luther's Theological Breakthrough*. 2nd ed. Malden, MA: Wiley-Blackwell, 2011.

Oberman, Heiko A. *Luther: Man between God and the Devil*. Translated by Eileen Walliser-Schwarzbart. New Haven: Yale University, 1986.

Olivier, Daniel. *Luther's Faith: The Cause of the Gospel in the Church*. Translated by John Tonkin. St. Louis: Concordia, 1982.

Oxford Handbook of Martin Luther's Theology. Edited by Robert Kolb, Irene Dingel, and Lubomír Batka. Oxford: Oxford University, 2014.

Pelikan, Jaroslav. *Obedient Rebels: Catholic Substance and Protestant Principle in Luther's Reformation*. New York: Harper and Row, 1964.

Sahayadoss, Santhosh J. *Martin Luther on Social and Political Issues: His Relevance for Church and Society in India*. Frankfurt/Main: Peter Lang, 2006.

Stjerna, Kirsi I. and Brooks Schramm. *Martin Luther, the Bible, and the Jewish People*. Minneapolis: Fortress Press, 2012.

Wilson, Derek. *Out of the Storm: The Life and Legacy of Martin Luther*. London: Hutchinson, 2007.

Selected Writings of Luther

The Book of Concord: The Confessions of the Evangelical Lutheran Church. Edited by Robert Kolb and Timothy J. Wengert. Minneapolis: Fortress Press, 2000.

Lull, Timothy F., ed. *Martin Luther's Basic Theological Writings*. Minneapolis: Augsburg Fortress Press, 1989.

Luther, Martin. *D. Martin Luthers Werke: Kritische Gesamtausgabe*. Weimar: Hermann Böhlaus Nachfolger, 1883–. (*WA*)

———. *Luther's Works: American Edition*. Edited by Jaroslav Pelikan (vols. 1–30) Helmut T. Lehmann (vols. 31–54), and Christopher Boyd Brown (vols. 56–). St. Louis: Concordia and Philadelphia: Fortress Press, 1955–67, St. Louis. Concordia: 1968–. (*LW*)

Maurer, Wilhelm. *Historical Commentary on the Augsburg Confession.* Translated by H. George Anderson. Philadelphia: Fortress Press, 1986.

Tappert, Theodore G. *Selected Writings of Martin Luther.* 2nd ed. 4 vols. Minneapolis: Fortress Press, 2007.

Abbreviations of Luther's Works in the Footnotes

ELW. *Evangelical Lutheran Worship.*

LW. *Luther's Works: American Edition.*

WA. *Martin Luthers Werke: Kritische Gesamtausgabe.*

WA TR. *D. Martin Luthers Werke: Kritische Gesamtausgabe: Tischreden* (table talks).

WA BR. *D. Martin Luthers Werke: Kritische Gesamtausgabe: Briefwechsel* (correspondence).

Index of Names

Index of Subjects